Red Skelton

BY THE SAME AUTHOR

ARTHUR MARX

Red Skelton

E. P. Dutton · New York

To:
Lois

This is an unauthorized biography.

My sincerest thanks to the following people for their help in the gathering of my material for this book: Harry Ackerman, Jack Bender, Pandro Berman, Seymour Berns, Ben Brady, Eddie Buzzell, Sammy Cahn, Guy Della Cioppa, Joe Cohn, Jack Cummings, Jack Douglas, Don Ferris, Benedict Freedman, Devery Freeman, Hal Goodman, Charles Isaacs, Seaman Jacobs, Jesse Kaye, Fernando Lamas, Sam Marx, John Fenton Murray, Harriet Nelson, Artie Phillips, Nat Perrin, Marty Rackin, Marty Ragaway, Joe Ross, Edna Skelton Pound, Mickey Rooney, Bob Schiller, Sherwood Schwartz, Charles Van Sickle, Ed Simmons, Harry Tugend, Rudy Vallee, Bob Weiskopf, Bob Weitman, Esther Williams, Keenan Wynn.

In a show business career that has spanned nearly fifty years and made him both a millionaire and a star of every entertainment medium from vaudeville to television, Red Skelton has run the gamut of criticism.

His admirers have labeled him one of the great clowns of our time—up there in a class with Chaplin, Keaton, Cantinflas, and Marcel Marceau.

His detractors have called him a low-down, baggy-pants burlesque comic who has succeeded as a laugh-getter only by appealing to the baser instincts of middle-class, unsophisticated America.

When it finally is evaluated, Skelton's true position in comedy's Hall of Fame will probably fall somewhere between those two poles, though leaning closer to the former than the latter.

Skelton's pantomime has never been quite so disciplined as Charlie Chaplin's, nor his monologues as smooth as Bob Hope's, nor his timing as perfect as Jack Benny's.

On the other hand, Skelton's comedy has always had two attributes that most of today's comics would trade their head writers for: his skill as a pantomimist—a tool of his trade which transcends any language barrier—and his gift of being able to evoke tears as well as laughter, which has always been the mark of a great clown.

Admittedly, the subject matter of Skelton's comedy was a little too basic, a mite too earthy to appeal to the pseudo-intellectuals of the land. His characterizations of a "mean widdle boy" first shot Skelton into national prominence when he said, "I dood it," on coast-to-coast radio back in 1941, and his hilarious impersonation of a country bumpkin with the unlikely name of Clem Kadiddlehopper, are good examples. And if one had to sum up in one word Skelton's impression of a doddering Civil War vet watching a Fourth of July parade passing by, the word would have to be "corn." But it is great corn, the kind that puts tears in the eyes of everyone in the audience and which appeals to every age group from eight to eighty.

However, it wasn't only the puerile and the senile who appreciated Red Skelton's enormous contribution to the world of comedy. Many of America's most sophisticated comedy aficionados, from the late W. C. Fields up to Steve Allen, have also found themselves in hysterics over the antics of the carrot-topped, rubber-faced Skelton.

After seeing Skelton put on a virtuoso performance in which he played six widely disparate characters without benefit of props, makeup, or costumes, Groucho Marx once labeled Red Skelton "the logical successor to Charlie Chaplin."

Jack Rose, who has written for practically every screen and television comic in the entertainment world, from Bob Hope to Lucille Ball, has stated many times that "Skelton is the great American clown, in a league all by himself. He's one guy who's funnier without a script than with one. What other comedian can make that claim?"

Harry Cohn, as hard-boiled an assayer of talent as ever lived, said when Skelton was working for Columbia Pictures, "Red is the only comic I know who you can give a love scene to without being afraid he'll get laughs. He's a clown in the old tradition. He doesn't need punch lines. He's got heart."

And W. C. Fields (who tipped his hat to no one) once told his drinking buddy, biographer Gene Fowler, "If anyone ever dares to play the story of my life, I want it to be Red Skelton." When Fowler, who at one time was practically a surrogate father to Skelton, relayed Fields' message to him, Red broke down and wept. And not crocodile tears, either. An emotional and religious man, despite a penchant for telling ribald jokes to nuns and priests, Skelton has always wept rather easily—but sincerely.

His public crying jags, however, have been relatively few, despite a life that's been plagued by one tragedy after another: the death of his only son, the suicide of a wife, and his own near emotional collapse.

In the tradition of the Pagliacci myth, Red Skelton has usually been able to put on a happy face in public, where he has worked diligently at maintaining his "clown" image, often at the expense of being accused by his critics of being tasteless and willing to do anything for a laugh. Which may not be far from the truth. Once, while dining at one of Hollywood's fanciest restaurants one night, Skelton cut up his necktie, mixed it in with his Caesar salad and actually ate it, to the amazement of the Captain, who grew so apoplectic with laughter that he actually burst his appendix.

Another time he was invited to entertain at a White House luncheon in honor of President Roosevelt's birthday in 1940. Midway through the proceedings, Red interrupted a Presidential toast by grabbing FDR's glass. "Careful what you drink, Mr. President," he warned. "I once got rolled in a joint like this." Roosevelt roared appreciatively, and until he died always insisted that Skelton emcee the annual Presidential birthday luncheons.

But the Red Skelton who eats his necktie and has the nerve

to joke irreverently with the President of the United States is nothing like the private Red Skelton who, through much of his life, was an unhappy and tormented individual, a sad and lonely man who trusted practically no one, and who was as unreachable as a distant star.

Red has always scorned the Pagliacci myth, claiming that comedy and tragedy are not very compatible bedfellows. Yet his own life belies this.

Perhaps the world has Red's mother, Ida Mae Skelton, who was no stranger to tragedy herself, to thank for turning her son into a great clown, for when Red was a little boy she repeatedly told him, "Son, don't take life too seriously. You'll never get out of it alive."

Certainly there was little else in Red Skelton's early life to account for a sense of humor that has not let up in spite of the calamities that have followed him most of his life.

As even an amateur psychiatrist could easily diagnose, the seeds of Red Skelton's strange and tormented behavior were no doubt sown in Vincennes, Indiana, the place of his birth, where he lived a childhood that was part David Copperfield, part Horatio Alger, and part Toby Tyler Goes to the Circus.

Ida Mae Skelton, a large, stout, homely woman and, according to her son, as wise as Socrates, was born in Lincoln, Nebraska, sometime in the latter part of the nineteenth century. Red's father, Joseph Skelton, came into the world at approximately the same time, in Washington, Indiana, and grew up to become a clown with the Hagenbeck & Wallace Circus.

Ida Mae and Joe met when his circus was playing a stand in Lincoln one summer: they were married in 1905 and soon after settled down in Vincennes, Indiana, a community of about 12,000 on the banks of the Wabash, whose main industries were glass making, a foundry works, a distillery, a brewery, and a paper mill.

Although Joe Skelton was away from home traveling with the circus nine months a year, he dropped into Ida Mae's bedroom often enough to beget three sons prior to Red's arrival. In the order of their arrival, they were Paul, Denny, and Christopher.

Because circus clowns didn't earn much money, the family lived in shocking poverty in a two-room shack with an attic, at what is now 111 Lyndale Avenue in Vincennes. The poverty grew worse when Joseph Skelton died of drink two months before Red was born, leaving his widow with three hungry boys to support, Red on the way, and not a penny in the bank nor a dollar's worth of life insurance.

Red, who was christened Richard Red Skelton without any quotation marks around the Red, was born at one-fifteen in the afternoon, on July 18, in the Lyndale Avenue bungalow. In later life, Red's mother recalled telling Doctor Beckus, who attended her, "Hurry, Doc, because I want my baby to be born before his brothers come home from school." According to Ida Mae's best recollection, "Red was a good boy. He arrived on time."

Red may have been a "good boy who arrived on time," but he's been no help in unraveling the mystery as to just when that time was.

The Knox County Indiana Hall of Records insists that Vincennes' most famous son made his first appearance on the planet Earth on July 18, 1913. And that is the year Skelton gives out as his birth date and which appears on all his official records, such as his Army discharge certificate, his marriage licenses, and his passport.

But those few people who have known the comedian intimately over the years suspect that he is somewhat older. They believe that 1906 is probably closer to the actual year of Red Skelton's birth. One man who is positive 1906 is Red's correct birth date is Don Ferris, musical arranger and piano accompanist on the Skelton TV show for years. "I heard Red say many times that he was born in 1906," reveals Ferris, who spent many hours shut up in a room alone with Skelton, going over musical arrangements and listening to his boss reminisce. "He never wavered. He used to tell me, 'I have one age for the newspapers and one for reality.' "

Whether 1906 or 1913, the point is Red Skelton *was* born sometime in the early part of this century and is still alive and well and living on the millions he struggled so hard for in the beginning.

However, Red's goal in the beginning was probably not millions. More than likely, he was content to keep from starving.

After being left husbandless and without a dime, Ida Mae Skelton was forced to work as a charwoman in a small-time vaudeville theater in Vincennes. Red still has visions of his mother down on her hands and knees in the theater, scrubbing floors and performing other demeaning and back-breaking chores such as polishing the brass railings and spittoons and cleaning urinals.

His earliest memories about himself are of having to sleep in an attic infested with rats and of being hungry most of the time when he was growing up—a circumstance that no doubt led to a confession he once made after he became successful: "Money is the last thing I think about before falling asleep at night."

Many people have taken that as a joke, but actually Skelton means every word of it. Millionaire or not, he has not been able to divest himself of the insecurity he knew as a child.

Another traumatic memory dates back to when Red was still a toddler and his mother once left him to spend the night with his uncle, who owned a grocery store in Vincennes. While Red was asleep in a crib in the back room, a drunken arsonist started a fire by lighting a gasoline coil drum and rolling it through the store. "Someone ran in and rescued me just before the whole place went up in flames," recalls Red.

That narrow escape from a flaming death manifests itself in a number of ways. When anyone lights a match around Red today he instinctively backs away. And he never lights his cigar; he just chews on it.

There were other things for the young Red to contend with besides poverty and fire.

While Ida Mae was on her hands and knees scrubbing floors in order to keep food in the house and a leaky roof overhead, she often had to leave Red in the care of his older siblings. With three roughneck older brothers for baby-sitters, the young Red Skelton had no need for an enemy.

According to Skelton, his brothers resented him deeply. Twice they played such egregious pranks on him that he almost didn't live to tell about it.

Once Paul and Chris tied him up and dragged him through the streets of Vincennes tied to a long rope attached to a motorcycle. A policeman stopped the mayhem before Red sustained damage any more serious than a couple of skinned knees and a badly bruised psyche.

Another time Paul and Chris threw Red into a gravel pit half-filled with rain water and tried to drown him by not letting him climb out. Luckily, a workman came along, became suspicious of what the bullies were trying to accomplish, and chased them off.

That Skelton survived these mischievous pranks without serious physical damage shows that he came from the kind of timber of which born clowns are made. In future years no pratfall or sight gag was ever too dangerous for him to attempt on stage. He was hospitalized on several occasions for injuries sustained while trying to wring a laugh from an audience. But he worked so hard at his trade that he probably needed the enforced rest anyway.

There was no time for rest when Skelton was starting out. He was, in fact, one of the busiest pre-teenagers in the town of Vincennes. When he was only seven, he sold newspapers on a Vincennes street corner for a penny apiece before and after school. "My family was hungry," he recalls, "and I had to make money somehow."

When he was a little older he took on a variety of other part-time jobs as well: washing dishes at a diner, ushering at a theater for fifty cents a night, and racking up balls at Kramer's Pool Hall for two cents a rack. In between pool setups, he would collect all the used playing cards left on the poker tables by the poker customers and sell them afterwards to people on the streets of Vincennes for whatever he could get for them. When local employment was scarce, Red would sometimes hitchhike to neighboring towns where he'd perform on street corners, doing a song and dance act for pennies.

Seymour Berns, who produced the *Red Skelton Show* during the sixties, says that Skelton once confessed to him about having also served a brief stint as a towel boy in an Indiana whorehouse. But Berns isn't sure whether that's apocryphal or not. "With Red you never knew whether he was telling the truth or just trying to shock you to be funny. But with his background, anything's possible," believes Berns.

One of Skelton's fondest memories of his Indiana youth took place on a Vincennes street corner around six in the evening when he was trying to unload his last dozen newspapers. A stranger in town—a dark-haired man with twinkling eyes and a springy gait—came out of the town's leading hotel and approached the red-haired youngster to purchase a paper. During the transaction, the stranger asked the boy if there was anything fun to do in town. Red pointed across the street to the Pantheon Theater, where comedian Ed Wynn's name was up in lights as the headliner of that week's vaudeville show.

"Have you seen the show?" asked the stranger.

Red shook his head, wistfully adding that he'd like to but didn't have the price of admission.

"Here," said the stranger, handing Red a dollar for the balance of his papers. "Meet me in front of the theater at seven and I'll give you a ticket."

Skelton raced home, gobbled down some dinner, took a bath, changed into what passed for his best clothes, and dashed back to the theater.

When a somewhat breathless Red showed up under the marquee, the stranger was waiting. He pressed a front row ticket into Red's hand, then smilingly disappeared around a corner of the theater toward the stage door. When the headliner finally appeared on the other side of the footlights, it was his benevolent benefactor.

As Wynn's impish clowning wrung laugh after laugh from the audience, something inside the young Red Skelton told him he was capable of doing the same thing. Rushing backstage immediately after the performance, he thanked Wynn profusely and got him to autograph the back of his sweatshirt. When Wynn asked Red how he liked the show, the boy confessed he liked it so much that he wanted to be a comedian himself.

"That's fine," said Wynn. "But stick to comedy. Don't spread yourself too thin."

Ironically, Ed Wynn didn't take his own advice.

Four decades later, after Ed Wynn's career had peaked and then went into a steep decline, his agent got him a part as a serious actor in Rod Serling's *Requiem for a Heavyweight* on *Playhouse 90* over the CBS network. When the network demanded a current big name to bolster the cast list and insure a good rating, Skelton signed on to play a bit part, and without salary, just to repay Wynn for his earlier generosity.

The night before the show the aging comic suddenly began to doubt his ability to play a serious role and took to the bottle. By dress rehearsal the following afternoon, Wynn was too drunk to go on. The producer wanted to fire him but Skelton intervened. He promised to sober Wynn up by show time, or he'd play the role himself just so Wynn could keep his salary. The producer agreed and Red spent two hours pouring black coffee down the elderly comic's throat and walking him around the CBS parking lot.

As it happened, it wasn't necessary for Red to substitute for Ed Wynn. The black coffee and moral support got Wynn on his feet in time to do the show. His performance drew raves from the nation's critics, and started a whole new career for Wynn as a straight actor.

The young Red Skelton, however, never aspired to be a serious actor. After seeing Wynn's artistry on the vaudeville stage, Red's only ambition was to be able to go through life getting paid to make people laugh.

He got this opportunity the summer of his twelfth year, with the arrival in Vincennes of Doc Lewis's Patent Medicine Show.

Beguiled by the slick patter of Doc Lewis, as slippery a pitchman and charlatan as ever mesmerized an audience of Clem Kadiddlehopper's with rhapsodies about snake oil, Skelton approached the boss after the first show and asked him for a job.

"What can you do?" snapped Doc Lewis suspiciously, surveying the carrot-topped youth.

"Sing and dance," answered Red.

"Let's see ya do your stuff."

Red went immediately into the song and dance act that wowed them on street corners in neighboring hamlets. But Doc Lewis had no ear for music—at least not the kind Red was making. He rejected Red as an entertainer, but seeing the disappointment written all over the boy's face, he sent him out into the crowd to try his hand at hustling bottles of his elixir.

Red fared better at that. A-bubble with youthful enthusiasm, Red sold out the first batch in a matter of minutes and galloped back to the platform for a new supply. In his hurry he tripped on the steps and nose-dived off the stage into Doc Lewis's supply of patent medicine bottles.

When the audience howled, Doc Lewis was impressed.

"Okay, boy, you're hired," he said.

"To sing?" asked the delighted Red.

"Course not," cracked Doc Lewis. "To fall off the stage."

Though he was only twelve, Red ran away from home for the first time that night to hit the road with the medicine show, touring the green and gullible hinterlands of Indiana, Arkansas, Illinois, and Missouri for the rest of the summer.

Although Red's major responsibility was to keep falling off the stage at perfectly timed intervals, Doc Lewis eventually grew to depend on the boy to perform other duties as well. Red acted as general flunky for the Doc, he sang songs in blackface and in between towns, he'd sit in the back of the truck and fill bottles with Doc Lewis's allegedly health-giving elixir.

"That stuff was nothing but Epsom salts, water, and brown sugar," Skelton recalls, "and the Doc was getting a buck a bottle for it. One bottle of that junk in your stomach and you either called in the undertaker or you had a constitution that could take arsenic."

As a result, Doc Lewis's medicine show was never welcome in the same town twice, and if Red had to return home for anything, it had to be under the cover of darkness.

Red stayed with Doc Lewis's Medicine Show until it was time to return to school in the fall. It was a reluctant return, to be sure, for although Techumseh Grammar School was one of the best in the city and could boast of a brand new building with the latest academic and playground equipment, Red was anything but a born scholar.

And after getting a taste of show business the past summer, his mind was no longer on the "three R's" at all. He couldn't even concentrate on one R, so fascinated was he with the glitter of spangles and footlights.

Red went through the perfunctory motions of learning, but reading, writing, and arithmetic seemed completely beyond his ken. His best class was ditching. Whenever a circus or carnival came to town, Red would take the day off. While his peers were studying he'd be at the site of the circus watching the men unload the animals and put up the tents. Sometimes he helped carry water to the elephants for a nickel a bucket and a seat in the bleachers.

For the next two years Red put up a valiant struggle at Tecumseh Grammar School. But summer vacation and Doc Lewis occupied most of his thoughts. By the time Red was fourteen he was nearly six feet tall and he had filled out in both flesh and worldly experience. But he was still struggling to escape the fifth grade.

Deciding he was too mature to be sitting in the same classroom with a bunch of ten-year-old smart-alecs whose main goal in life, it seemed, was to ridicule him, Red decided to throw in the scholastic towel and go after a career in show business.

Opportunity in the theater did not come knocking on Skelton's door immediately, however. It took several months.

During the interim he worked as a shipping clerk for J. C. Penney's department store. But his knowledge of geography, acquired by getting straight A's in truancy, proved his undoing in that job. Asked to address an important shipment to Springfield, Red addressed the package to Springfield, Massachusetts, instead of the one in Illinois. The package got permanently lost. So did Red's job as a shipping clerk.

Fortunately, the end of his career with J. C. Penney's coincided with the arrival in Vincennes of the John Lawrence Stock Company—a roving repertory troupe which was edifying rural America by presenting "serious drama" under a tent. After seeing the stock company's initial performance in Vincennes, Red was impressed. He sought out the entrepreneur who was running the show and applied for a job as a "serious actor."

Although Red was only fourteen at the time, he looked older and had a good line of chatter. Lawrence probably did not believe Red's story that he was an experienced actor, but evidently he was impressed enough with the tall, good-looking, redhead to make him a member of his cast.

Red memorized several serious roles, but audiences laughed

firmly and long whenever he tried to act. He had the kind of face that just called for guffaws. The management wasn't interested in getting laughs, however, and cut his sufferings short by firing him after he was with the stock company only a week. As a result, Red was left broke and stranded in a flea-bag of a hotel on the banks of the Missouri River.

Red was in desperate financial straits. Just when the hunger pains in his stomach had about convinced him that he ought to start considering other, steadier forms of employment, like pan-handling, a steamboat came chugging round the bend, thereby living up to its legendary image.

The large stern-wheeler was a showboat called *The Cotton Blossom*, which was owned and operated by Captain Hittner. And true to the scenario of most rags-to-riches show business stories, Captain Hittner's *Cotton Blossom* just happened to be in need of an all-round entertainer to take the place of an actor who'd just been shot dead over a dispute with a riverboat gambler in a card game.

Red auditioned for Captain Hittner by singing a song in blackface while he accompanied himself on a ukelele. To insure the job, he also took several spectacular pratfalls that included landing on his head. Onlookers wondered just how long the young comedian could last without spilling the rest of his marbles—if he had any to begin with.

Concluding that the young man's sanity was Red's own affair, Captain Hittner hired him on the spot and Red spent the next several seasons afloat on the Mississippi and Ohio rivers, performing blackface skits and songs and telling jokes and monologues.

Ironically, his lack of education proved a boon to his development as a pantomimist. Because he was none too facile with the English language, it became essential for him to get his laughs mainly through sight routines—slapstick and pantomime. When a joke wouldn't work he could always insure instant hilarity by falling off the stage into the orchestra pit and climbing back with a drum draped around his neck. Audiences ate up that kind of fare, causing him to rely more and more on sight comedy and less and less on verbal wit.

Skelton probably would have remained aboard *The Cotton Blossom* until showboats went out of style if he hadn't suddenly become aware of sex and the Captain's daughter at about the same time.

It was love at first sight between Red and Samantha Hittner, who, having completed her schooling at a boarding school one spring, joined her father aboard *The Cotton Blossom* for a cruise down the Mississippi.

Halfway between St. Louis and the City of Jazz, Captain Hittner wandered out onto the fantail one night and caught his daughter in the arms of what had been his favorite redheaded, blackface comedian.

In those days about the lowest thing you could be on the social totem pole was an actor and to hand your daughter over to one, no matter how honorable his intentions, was tantamount to selling her into White Slavery. And Red's intentions weren't that honorable; he was light years away from being able to afford a wife.

Despite Red's protests that he was only tutoring Samantha in how to play a love scene, Captain Hittner fired him and dropped him off at the next landing. He also dropped all of Skelton's belongings into the river, leaving him with only the clothes on his back and a large welt on his rear end where the Captain had taken his foot to him.

Natchez, Mississippi, had the dubious pleasure of playing host to the penniless, girlless, and clothesless clown. To make an honest living in Natchez you either had to grow cotton or pick it. To make a dishonest living you could either be a bouncer in a whorehouse or make moonshine.

While Red was sitting forlornly on a bale of cotton down by the waterfront mulling over this wealth of opportunity, a long-sideburned, dapperly-dressed man strolled up to him and introduced himself as Jeremiah Higgins, the manager of a "Tom Show" that was currently playing a series of one-night stands through the South. A "Tom Show" was a repertory company of actors who toured the country playing *Uncle Tom's Cabin*, which had been the theatrical rage in the sticks ever since the Civil War.

Higgins told Red that he had once caught his act on *The Cot-*

ton Blossom and had been very impressed. He said he had also seen Red chased off the showboat. From that he assumed Red was looking for work, and he invited him to be a member of his company. He said the play had several parts in which Red would get paid for being chased.

Red jumped at the first offer, which was fifteen dollars a week and traveling expenses and he spent the next year touring the South and Midwest, playing every part in *Uncle Tom's Cabin* except Little Eva and the bloodhounds that chased Eliza across the ice.

Playing a variety of roles and working with real hounds on stage proved invaluable training for a man who was to develop into a master of the sight gag—the kind of comedy that depends on tricky props not misfiring.

One night, while playing one of the fleeing slaves, Red could not get the bloodhounds to chase him. It was a fiasco. Determined not to be made a fool of by four-footed actors at the next performance, Red filled his pockets with raw beef liver before taking off with Eliza across the ice.

This time the bloodhounds performed a little too realistically. They ripped Red's clothes to shreds trying to get the liver. To this day he still has fang marks on his thighs.

After months of Uncle Tomming it, Red found himself one week in the same town where the Hagenbeck-Wallace Circus had just pitched its big top. This was the circus in which his father had performed. Drawn to it for sentimental reasons, Red auditioned for a job and landed one—as a "walk-around clown." Working as a clown in the same circus where his father had performed was the kind of thrill most boys of Red's tender years only got to read about in story books. But Red was actually going to live it.

As he prepared for his first circus parade, a veteran clown helped him get into his clown trappings and showed him how to slap on his makeup. Red was impressed with the camaraderie of the other circus performers and felt sure this was how he wanted to earn his living for the rest of his life. By the end of the parade, when he suddenly found himself in deep hock to the management, he had a few reservations about circus life.

The whole problem revolved around, of all things, a suitcase. Having lost a fairly serviceable one into the Mississippi, Red had acquired a secondhand suitcase which was so beat up it looked as if it had been through the Johnstown flood, if not the Battle of Gettysburg. He had felt envious when he joined the circus the first day and had to compare his battered suitcase with the fine luggage and wardrobe trunks the other circus performers sported.

Caught up in the excitement of preparing for his first circus parade, Red temporarily dismissed his suitcase envy from his mind in order to concentrate on the job at hand. That job, as it was explained to him, was to sit on the band wagon and beat a big brass drum as the parade wound through the streets of Madison, Missouri.

By an unfortunate coincidence, the parade went down a street on which there were an inordinate number of luggage shops. And since Red's drum-beating job wasn't very demanding, he kept glancing over his shoulder at the beautiful trunks in the windows at every opportunity. How was he to know that he was defying one of the sternest superstitions in circus lore? To look over your shoulder during a circus parade is regarded in big top circles as more foolhardy than attempting the "triple" with a drunken catcher and no net below.

To discourage that kind of thing, a stiff fine was slapped on anyone in the circus who turned around in a parade *each* time he turned around.

By the end of the parade, Red was so heavily in debt to the circus management that he would have to work an entire year before he'd collect a pay check.

Realizing this, the neophyte clown sat down on a wagon step and wept unashamedly. Luckily, his performance of the legendary grief-stricken clown did not go unnoticed by his fellow workers.

The next day, when Red slunk into his corner of the dressing room tent to get into his clown's uniform, he discovered that his shabby suitcase had disappeared. In its place was the most beautiful object Red had ever laid eyes on—a brand new wardrobe trunk, and it even was marked with the initials "R. S."

The circus troupe, notoriously sentimental and softhearted, had taken up a collection in order to help soften the blow of working *sans* salary for the coming year.

If Skelton hadn't been a suitcase freak prior to then, he turned into one immediately after taking possession of his gift. Being a born clown but not a born trunk-handler, Red had never been particularly concerned about luggage. Now anyone who dared come near his trunk would have to face wrath comparable to that of a jealous lover. To avoid dents, scratches, and bruises, Red insisted on loading the trunk on and off baggage wagons himself. Before long he came to regard all baggage attendants as sadists whose chief aim in life was to draw blood from his trunk.

After playing the role of clown long enough to get back in the black with the circus management, Red started to entertain loftier ambitions. He felt he'd like to be a lion tamer like Clyde Beatty, who worked in the ring with the big cats. Red loved animals—all kinds—and felt he had sufficient rapport with them to justify his getting an apprenticeship.

To that end he struck up an acquaintanceship with Beatty, who, one afternoon when there wasn't a matinee, decided to let Red in on a little secret of his profession. According to Beatty, the prescribed way to get a lion or tiger to respond to your orders when you stepped into the cage was to exude an odor similar to one of them. You did this by anointing your body with lion or tiger urine before stepping into the cage.

Somewhat discouraged, Red asked Beatty how one went about procuring the aromatic fluid.

"Easy," said Beatty. And he handed Red a large specimen bottle and pointed him toward the cageful of ferocious-looking man-eaters.

Red turned white, suddenly remembered he "had" to go practice his tumbling act, and said he'd have to put the chore off to another day when he wasn't quite so busy.

Red spent several days avoiding Beatty and reassessing his career ambitions. Finally he worked up the nerve to ask Beatty if there wasn't a safer way to obtain the lion urine. For example, couldn't he just slip the bottle in the cage through the bars and leave the rest up to the lion?

When Beatty threw back his head and started to laugh, along with a group of other circus performers including three midgets and a bearded lady, Red realized that he had been the victim of a practical joke. Not that the urine anointing wasn't one of the ways of cozying up to a lion or tiger; one just didn't get the liquid in the manner Beatty had suggested.

A week later Red was still vacillating about a lion tamer's career when he saw Beatty severely mauled in the ring by a tiger. After Beatty was carted off to the hospital, Red wisely decided, "I'd better stick to the less hazardous occupation of being a clown."

3

Yet it was not Red Skelton's destiny to remain a clown forever. At any rate, not a circus clown, for circuses were about through.

As the Roaring Twenties roared toward their appointment with the stock market crash and subsequent Depression, new entertainment forms came along to steal a large part of the circus audience. Talking pictures were suddenly all the rage, and about the same time films took the country by storm, RCA's enterprising General Sarnoff decided that Marconi's wireless could be used for something more profitable than sending distress signals at sea. He proved it in 1921 by beaming the Jack Dempsey–George Carpentier heavyweight title fight directly into American homes. From then on, people no longer had to leave their rocking chairs to be entertained. They could stay in their living rooms and thrill to Rudy Vallee's nasal tones warbling "The Whiffenpoof Song" or laugh at Amos and Andy and the Kingfish making jokes about the black race that probably wouldn't get much of an audience in the socially conscious America of today.

With the encroachment of talkies and radio, circus attendance fell off sharply, causing many of the big tops either to fold permanently or lay off circus personnel in order to economize.

After the crash, only the giant names of the big tops survived to pitch their tents in the coming decade—Barnum and Bailey, for example, and Ringling Brothers. But eventually even they had to consolidate in order to get by on decreasing revenues.

Hagenbeck-Wallace was not among the circuses that were prospering. Red Skelton did not wait to be let go. He packed his prized trunk and struck out for greener sawdust rings.

After leaving Hagenbeck-Wallace, Red led the nomadic, but by no means atypical, existence of the unsuccessful performer of that era. For a time he drifted aimlessly along the sleazy pike of big tops and third-rate carnivals. When he ran out of them it was back to more showboat cruises on the Mississippi, small parts in a stock company playing one-nighters in all kinds of crummy tank towns, a few months as a barker for a side show, and a season as a "Mammy" singer with Clarence Stout's Minstrels.

Although Red never for a moment wished he were back home in Indiana, the years following his circus apprenticeship were grim ones of poverty and hunger; to this day they remain in his mind a bleak montage of living in moldy boardinghouses and traveling over thousands of miles in creeky buses or sitting up nights on train coaches. His traveling and living companions often included con men, chronic drunks, petty thieves, and ladies of doubtful or no virtue.

"Most of the time we never got paid," recalls Skelton. "The managers paid our fare in and out of town and got us a deal with a restaurant. If you got laughs, you were okay. If not, you got fired in a hurry."

Unrewarding as those years were financially, the places they took Skelton, the things they forced him to do to make a living, and the people they introduced him to along the way provided the inspiration for many of the characterizations he later improvised. Not only that, he was able to file away in his mind the gags and routines of every comic and clown he ever saw and admired as a youth, and thus forever afterward had a vast reservoir of basic comedy material on which he could make variations at will, or steal, depending on how you look at it.

Unlike many of today's younger comics, Red Skelton by the age of seventeen was already a well-rounded performer. He could sing, tell a joke, perform pantomime, play a straight role, take a dangerous pratfall without killing himself, and even tap dance.

Thus he was well prepared when he finally was given the opportunity around 1930 to get out of tents and off showboats and into a legitimate theater—that is, one with a stationary roof.

The name of the place was the Gaiety Burlesque Theater in Kansas City, and Red just happened to be hanging around the stage door one Saturday, ogling the girls, when he got wind of the fact that the "third banana" in the show had suddenly been stricken with an acute attack of appendicitis. Red applied for the job, introducing himself to the manager of the Gaiety as one of the world's most gifted comedians. When the manager looked skeptical, Red put on an impromptu audition, which encompassed all his various talents from cracking ribald jokes, of which he had a traveling-salesman's-sized collection, to taking a bellyflop into a bass drum. "Okay, young fellah, you got the job," snapped the manager. "You start Monday night. Just be sure you're as funny in front of an audience."

Red's starting salary in burlesque was seventy-five dollars a week. This was not to be sneezed at, considering there was a depression on and millions were out of work. And most of them, it seemed, were in the audience at the Gaiety. If they weren't unemployed, they certainly ought to have been, judging by how disreputable the gang patronizing the Gaiety looked to Red.

Moreover, what they came to see at the Gaiety was not Ibsen or Euripides or even George Kaufman. Contrary to myth, however, the burlesque into which Red Skelton was inducted was not a particularly dirty medium, either. In fact, the burlesque of the late twenties was quite innocent compared with the topless and bottomless and "live sex" shows in any of America's metropolitan centers today. The shows featured comely girls, some scantily clad, but they never completely divested themselves of their raiments. The jokes were suggestive, but the four-letter words so loosely bandied about by today's entertainers would have brought the cops running if anyone had dared try them on the stage around 1930.

According to Skelton, the burlesque he played "was as clean as a whistle. It was burlesque in the literal sense of the word. We burlesqued Broadway shows."

For a finish to his act, Red usually fell into the orchestra pit and came up with a drum ring around his neck.

While Red was performing at the Gaiety, the manager of the theater introduced him to a girl who was to change his whole life. She was an usherette at the Gaiety and her name was Edna Marie Stillwell.

At fifteen, Edna was two years younger than Red, with dark brown hair, vivacious blue eyes, a trim body, a driving personality, and the mind of a businessman.

Edna was the daughter of a Kansas City couple who had separated when she was six months old. She had been raised by her mother and had an older brother who lived with her father. She'd only seen her father once in her brief lifetime and hadn't the faintest idea what he did for a living. But whatever it was, it evidently wasn't very profitable for he rarely sent any support money home to his former wife. Mrs. Stillwell had to scratch out a bare existence for herself and her daughter, taking whatever odd jobs an untrained housewife could get in a depression: sewing, washing, and sometimes clerking in a store.

The only person of means in Edna's family was an uncle, who was an undertaker. Because he didn't like to see his sister starve, he would sometimes slip her a few bucks. As for his niece, he promised Edna a job in his undertaking establishment after she got her high school diploma. Not overjoyed at the prospect, Edna had said she'd think about it. Meanwhile, Edna helped her mother out by working part-time as an usherette at the Gaiety.

Red was attracted to Edna the moment he laid eyes on her and after making a few suggestive remarks to her (he considered himself quite a ladies' man), he invited her out for a drink after the show. An ice cream soda, that is. In those days ice cream sodas were his only vice. But Edna Stillwell wasn't interested in what beverage Red was serving. She told him he was too "fresh" and refused to go out with him. Not only was she turned off by his crude sense of humor but she thought his act so deplorably bad that she complained to the management that he ought to be fired.

"Even back then Edna had good sense," recalls Red.

But Red stayed on. "I don't have to fire him," argued the manager. "He'll probably kill himself falling into the orchestra pit."

Red still had made no progress with Edna by the time he had to leave Kansas City to play the other towns on the burlesque circuit—St. Louis, Indianapolis, Buffalo, and Wilkes-Barre, Pennsylvania.

After a year of seasoning on the road, Red was back again at the Gaiety in Kansas City falling into the orchestra pit. By now he had worked himself up to being a Top Banana at $125 a week, and, still in his teens, was featured on the marquee as "the youngest Top Banana in burlesque."

His future seemed assured.

But then burlesque changed radically.

Legitimate theater business was generally off because of the Depression and producers had to come up with a new gimmick to lure customers to the box office. What they came up with was the "strip-tease"—a form of terpsichore in which a beautiful young lady would come out on the stage fully clothed, and to the accompaniment of appropriate music, artfully tease the audience by removing her clothing, one item at a time. When finally the last item had been removed, she would disappear quickly behind a curtain, leaving the mostly all-male audience panting and with only a fleeting vision of what she looked like nude—except for pasties and a G-string.

In some burlesque theaters unstarred ladies of the chorus also performed with nothing on but G-strings and pasties.

With the innovation of nudity, burlesque suddenly lost its innocence. The all-male customers ate up the strip numbers, cheering and hollering enthusiastically for the strippers to "take it off—take it ALL off," as they glided around the stage to sexy music. But police departments and other watchdogs of the public morals took a dim view of the new trend in entertainment. As far as they were concerned, burlesque was the start of another Sodom and Gomorrah.

The Gaiety was raided a number of times and its strippers and management hauled off to the Kansas City jail, and not released until they came up with the money to pay costly fines. The Gaiety finally was forced to close its doors for good. The theater was going broke bailing performers out of jail night after night. So, through no fault of his own, the youngest Top Banana in the land was once again without an orchestra pit to fall into.

But not for long. He was saved by the Walkathon, a bizarre new entertainment phenomenon that had arisen out of the despair of the Great Depression and which was sweeping the country as nothing had since the introduction of the Charleston.

The Walkathon, or Dance Marathon, was actually an endurance contest in which fifty to one hundred couples dragged themselves around a dance floor for days, and sometimes weeks at a time, until they collapsed, one by one, much to the amusement of an audience that had about as much class and compassion as the ones who enjoyed watching the lions eating the Christians.

The last couple to remain on its feet was, naturally, declared the winner of this daffy event and allowed to walk off (or more than likely be carried off) with a purse ranging anywhere from $100 to $500, depending on the size of the town holding the Walkathon and the generosity of the promoter.

If the Walkathon had to be compared to any other event it was probably closest to the six-day bike races, only less humane, for its contestants weren't permitted the luxury of wheels.

Contestants ate, slept, shaved, and digested while in a state of vertical mobility. As a concession to human physiology, each contestant was allowed off the floor for ten minutes every hour to attend to his or her toilet needs. The rest periods were carefully clocked and when the ten minutes were up, a siren sounded, the weary dancer was rounded up, dragged back to the arena, propped up against his or her partner, and the agony would begin all over.

If a contestant collapsed, he or she was expected to do it in front of the paying customers and not off the dance floor. Collapsing was what the so-called ladies and gentlemen of the audience had paid to see. Some crusaders among the American populace felt that Walkathons were so inhumane that they ought to be outlawed, along with capital punishment. Just as many people, however, defended Walkathons on the grounds that the Walkathonees actually got better food, shelter, and medical care than the average non-millionaire citizen during the Depression. Nurses attended the contestants day and night. There were chiropodists on call to attend to their corns and blisters and, if necessary, massage their aching arches. And every contestant was entitled to seven meals a day, eaten on his feet, of course, but expertly prepared by professional nutritionists. (At least that was the claim: usually the fare consisted of hot dogs, hamburgers, Cokes, and potato chips.)

Around the country there were even well-publicized instances of Walkathon contestants actually *gaining* weight. So, in reality there was about as much chance of ending the Walkathon craze before it ran out of steam on its own as there was of getting rid of cock fights in Tijuana.

Which turned out to be a fortunate thing for a certain unemployed Top Banana named Richard Red Skelton who, while killing time in his rooming house in Kansas City one day, was tipped off by a friend that the promoter of the local Walkathons was looking for a clown to replace the one who had just deserted him.

Red wasted little time in applying for the job. In fact, he was out of breath and perspiring profusely from his sprint down Kansas City's sidewalks to the Civic Auditorium by the time he presented himself and his credentials, to the promoter of the dance contest, Max McCaffrey.

Until that moment Red had no idea what the duties of a Walkathon clown were or even why one was necessary. Being a gullible type, he'd always assumed that it was the contestants who provided the entertainment.

McCaffrey quickly set him straight.

Walkathon customers, he told Red, were not only sadistic, they were becoming jaded. Between collapses they demanded other entertainment, and that was where the comic fit in. All he had to do was keep the customers amused.

The hours the comic had to keep were not as onerous as the ones the contestants danced and collapsed to, but they were long enough: ten hours a day, seven days a week, until the marathon ground to its inevitable conclusion. If he couldn't keep the audience constantly in stitches, or if the people walked out on him or fell asleep, the comic was automatically fired.

Red assured McCaffrey that he could handle the assignment and begged to be given a shot at keeping his customers awake.

McCaffrey seemed dubious, but since he was apparently in desperate need of someone, he said he'd give Red a chance at the Walkathon starting that night.

"If they like you, you've got the job. If they don't, you're out."

They not only "liked him," they loved him.

The tall, skinny, rubber-faced, be-dimpled, completely engaging carrot-top was an instant hit with Walkathon audiences, and soon had a reputation as the best of the Walkathon clowns. Not only because his diamond-in-the-rough talent stuck out like a giant redwood in a forest of saplings, but because he literally knocked himself silly in order to please audiences. What's more, he accomplished this without a stage, without a mike, without a set, without a curtain or spotlight or stooge or orchestra, without a script or a prompter or sound effects. All he had to fall back on were his enormous energy, a retentive memory that kept every joke or gag or routine he'd ever heard or seen before neatly catalogued in his brain, and a genius for comic inventiveness. The last was a definite requirement for that kind of work.

For ten hours out of every twenty-four—starting at 5 P.M. and not quitting until 3 A.M.—Red kept up a running patter of jokes, sang songs, made faces, did imitations, took pratfalls, kissed ladies, crawled under seats, climbed chandeliers, sat on laps, ate neckties, broke plates, undressed, doused himself with soft drinks yanked from customers' hands, walked on all fours, imitated drunks and rubes and "mean widdle boys," recited poetry, performed card tricks, rode a tricycle around the edge of the balcony. Once he even stole a mounted policeman's horse from the street and galloped around the auditorium on him, with the gendarme in hot pursuit.

At the start of Red's second Walkathon, he became cognizant, while the contestants were being briefed as to the rules and regulations of the contest, of a familiar face. Closer scrutiny proved that the face belonged to none other than the former Gaiety Theater usherette who had brushed him off: dark-haired, feisty Edna Marie Stillwell.

Edna had been hired to be cashier at that particular Walkathon. But on a dare from a friend, she entered the contest instead. Edna figured that if she could win the $500-pot at the end of the terpsichorean rainbow, that she could avoid becoming a mortician at her uncle's mortuary.

After seeing Edna shuffle around the floor in the arms of another man, Red was more determined than ever to make an impression on her. But there was little opportunity for romance or even small talk during a Walkathon contest, except between the members of each couple. Red's only chance for contact was to intercept Edna on her way to and from the Ladies' Room, and understandably her mind was not on romance at moments like these. Red settled for working doubly hard in his act, so that possibly Edna would notice him and be impressed.

After thirty-four days, Red's persistence and clowning paid off. Edna actually smiled at Red on her way back to the dance arena and promised him a date after the contest was over.

From her bedraggled, worn-out appearance Red was confident this would be any moment—for her, anyway.

But the diminutive Edna, with a fighting heart, outlasted all the other contestants.

She danced for two and a half consecutive months, or 1,872 hours, wore out five full-grown male partners (substitutes were permitted as long as one member of the original duo remained), and won the championship and the $500-prize.

While the prize was being handed out, the newspaper photographers wanted pictures of the winner with the master of ceremonies. After a few mundane poses, one of the photographers said, "Now let's have one kissing."

For Red, the kiss did it. He was knocked completely off his feet. He couldn't sleep, he couldn't think.

Although Edna liked the kiss, too, she did not have the same trouble sleeping after being on her feet for 1,872 hours. As soon as she pocketed the check, she disappeared into a dressing room, flopped down on a cot, and fell into a coma-like sleep. Red's after-the-Walkathon date with her had to be postponed until she awakened.

When she finally did open her eyes three days later, the $500-prize money was gone, along with Edna's dreams of being financially independent. Apparently there were sharpies who made a living by hanging around Walkathons, waiting to steal the bounty from winning contestants who had dropped from exhaustion.

After reassuring Edna that he wasn't the culprit, Red took her to a restaurant and bought her the first sitting-down meal she had had in two and a half months—a Kansas City corn-fed steak dinner that set him back sixty-five cents. It was the most expensive item on the menu, but he was willing to spring for it in the interest of furthering the relationship.

In return for the steak, Edna apologized for trying to get him fired from the Gaiety, and even admitted that as a comedian Red wasn't half bad.

"I know the rest of that joke," he quipped. "I'm *all* bad."

"No, you're pretty good," she said. "In fact, you have the makings of a great comedian if you handle yourself right."

That cemented the relationship. He escorted her home on the streetcar and three months later he proposed to Edna Stillwell.

Edna accepted, but on the condition that she didn't have to be saddled with children right away.

Her mother was in favor of the union, too, so in June of 1931—four days after the bride's sixteenth birthday—Red married Edna in Kansas City, much against the advice of several of his friends, who, upon learning of her uncle, warned him never to get in a fight with her. They said she might slit him open while he slept and pump him full of embalming fluid.

Red wasn't frightened off, but after he became successful he did get considerable comedy mileage out of Edna's background. "To this day," he used to say, "I sometimes wake up in the middle of the night in a sweat—and I have to go out of the room when she slices bread."

However, there wasn't much bread to slice in the early days of their marriage. Despite his recognized talent as a Walkathon clown, Red was so broke when he married Edna that he had to borrow two dollars for the license.

There were several reasons for his lack of cash. In addition to running a close second to the legendary Diamond Jim when it came to heavy spending in restaurants, Red was also the world's softest touch for any panhandler, unemployed vaudevillian, or circus artist who hit him for a loan. "He'd give anybody, whether he knew them or not, his last buck if the person needed it and he had it," recalls Edna. "One thing about Red. He was never afraid of work and he was never afraid of being broke."

Further, the country was still in the depths of the greatest Depression it had ever known, and Walkathon promoters—a shifty lot at best—had a tendency to leave town with the gate receipts, under cover of darkness, conveniently forgetting to pay not only their employees but also the winners of the contests.

Having been the victim of several such hidden salary plays, Red found himself so strapped financially two months after their marriage that he was unable to give a firm commitment to the promoter of a Walkathon in Atlantic City, New Jersey, who wanted him desperately—but not desperately enough to pay his and Edna's bus fare East. Red and Edna didn't have the money, and the most logical person they could turn to for help—Edna's uncle, the undertaker—was suddenly pleading poverty.

It wasn't that the undertaking business had fallen off. People were still dying during the Depression. But surviving relatives weren't springing for big, expensive funerals anymore. They were packing their loved ones away as economically as possible, a practice which cut down considerably on Edna's uncle's profits. As a result, he was not investing his money in such a poor risk venture as a trip to a Walkathon half a continent away.

Fortunately, Mrs. Stillwell was of a more generous nature. The only impediment to her generosity was that she had even less money than Red and Edna. She was determined to raise it, however, and had some fillings extracted from her teeth and sold the gold.

In Atlantic City, Edna immediately demonstrated her forceful personality and business acumen by waiting until Red was a huge hit at the Walkathon opening night, and then confronting the promoter with two conditions of employment she felt it necessary to insist on before she would allow her husband to continue his services the second night.

Number one, she wanted Red's salary raised to $100 a week—they'd only offered fifty. And number two, Edna would be hired as head cashier and posted in the ticket booth. That way she would get her hands on Red's salary before anyone could run off with it.

The promoter had no alternative but to agree to her terms, and the arrangement worked out so satisfactorily in Atlantic City for the Skeltons that Edna insisted on getting the same deal everywhere they played. The success of this fool-proof salary payment plan eventually led Edna to assume all of her husband's business affairs, leaving his time completely free to concentrate on developing new routines.

This he seemed to be doing most of his waking hours—even when he was eating and supposed to be sleeping.

Since he couldn't afford writers, Red, with suggestions from Edna, was forced to devise most of his routines himself. His inspiration generally came from diligently observing the movements, facial expressions, and other physical characteristics of those with whom he was thrown in daily contact. He was particularly fascinated by locomotion—the way drunks, babies, and ballet dancers got around. But his routines weren't always inspired by the obvious. For example, his classic drunk imitation was born while he was sitting in a railroad station one day, watching the unbalanced movements of a baby trying to walk. The similarity to a drunk was uncanny. The child staggered forward, then staggered back, caught himself, regained his equilibrium, then moved forward again unsteadily.

In a way, it was a little bit like Red's career at the time: two steps forward and one, possibly three steps back.

When Red worked, and with Edna managing him, the two remained reasonably solvent. "For two, possibly three years," recalls Edna, she and Red worked the Walkathon circuit, drifting from Atlantic City to St. Louis, Columbus, Minneapolis, Cincinnati, Louisville, and Atlanta.

During that period, Red established a reputation as being the King of the Walkathon clowns and became something of a legend in that sleazy universe. Even so, following the Walkathons wasn't a very secure existence—mainly because there wasn't one of these events every week of the year. Sometimes the in-between weeks stretched into months.

Red is one performer who doesn't look back on his youth—at least that part—as "the good old days." As far as he is concerned, he and Edna led an absolutely wretched existence during their Walkathon period.

"We were so hungry in those days," he remembers, "that I'd lie in bed and cry. Edna would reach over and put the blanket around my shoulder and pet my cheek and keep saying, 'Go to sleep, honey. You got to get your rest. Go to sleep.' "

They didn't always have a blanket that she could put around him. They were thrown out of one hotel because they owed the huge sum of nine dollars. They might have raised the nine dollars by hocking Red's prized trunk, but the management had already impounded it, and was holding it for ransom.

A small business loan from Edna's mother helped the Skeltons get their luggage back and move on to the next Walkathon site. But soon they were in arrears with the rent at another hotel.

With no possibility of receiving more money from home, it suddenly became imperative for them to devise a way of sneaking their belongings past the front desk. It was imperative because Edna had just landed Red a job at a Walkathon several hundred miles away, but he needed his costumes and props in order to be able to play the engagement.

The scheme they came up with was right out of a Marx Brothers film. To distract the desk clerk, Edna pretended to be romantically interested in him. While she was making her phony advances to him in an alcove out of sight of the lobby area, Red sneaked past the front desk wearing more than the customary number of coats, vests, and trousers, plus all the socks, underdrawers, and neckties he could stuff into his pockets.

The extra padding caused him to look more like Oliver Hardy than Red Skelton. But corpulence had its advantages, too. It enabled him to conceal Edna's suitcase behind his back as he sidled out the front entrance.

Poverty led Red into exercising his ingenuity for other purposes as well.

To raise eating money in one Iowa town, he first invested his and Edna's few remaining silver coins in several bars of soap and some Christmas foil paper acquired at the local Woolworth's. He then cut each soap bar into five pieces, wrapped them individually in the foil, and labeled them "Skelton De-Foggers."

Following that he set up shop at a busy intersection and went into a pitchman's *spiel* that would have made old Doc Lewis proud.

"Step right up, folks, and get your Skelton Automatic De-Fogger—the latest marvel of automotive science. Just rub a little of this on your windshield, and never again will you be troubled by trying to see through a fogged-up windshield in a rainstorm or blizzard. Hurry ... hurry ... hurry and get yours before they're all gone. The supply is limited because of the rarity of the ingredients.... Only one to a customer.... Absolutely guaranteed to prevent fogging."

So convincing was Skelton's sales pitch that before the afternoon was half over he had to return to his and Edna's hotel room and make up a new batch of "Skelton De-Foggers"—which he also managed to unload.

By the time Red's customers caught onto the fact that his product was absolutely worthless, he and Edna were on their way to the next town, but with full stomachs and confidence in the future born of the knowledge that if Red couldn't make it as a comedian, he could always become an inventor.

In some towns, however, especially during the drought season, it wasn't always easy to move the Skelton anti-fogging compound. In that case, Red would have to invent another product.

Once, after Edna read in a local newspaper that someone's prize-winning collie had died of rat poisoning, Red invented a brand new product for getting rid of the vermin—"one that was absolutely guaranteed to be harmless to pets and children." Red's new product was as marketable as his anti-fogging formula. It lived up to its inventor's promise, too—it was absolutely harmless to pets and children. It also was harmless to rats.

Being basically an honest type, and raised in a Catholic household where he was taught to obey the Ten Commandments, Red did not care to go on bilking the public permanently for a living. It was just an expedient to keep his and Edna's bellies full. Whenever there was a Walkathon to play, he eagerly put his pitchman act back in mothballs and returned to making people laugh—his only real love outside of Edna.

As the Depression deepened, however, it was becoming more and more difficult to make people laugh. Red found himself going to greater and greater extremes in his sight gags in order to bring down the house. Sometimes this included risking his life.

At a Walkathon in Elizabeth, New Jersey, where there was a particularly dour audience who hadn't cracked a smile in about an hour and twenty minutes, Red grew panicky that he might be fired. Desperate for a laugh, he commandeered a little boy's tricycle and tried to ride it around the parapet of the balcony.

Believing it was part of his act, the audience roared with delight when Red and the bike fell to the floor, about fifteen feet below.

It wasn't funny to Edna or Red, however. Red fractured an arm and a couple of ribs in the accident, and Edna had to spend three weeks and the last of their money in a hotel room nursing him back to health.

It was during Red's captive convalescence that Edna wisely decided that her beloved redhead was far too talented as a comedian to spend the rest of his professional life falling off balconies. He was ready for something bigger than that—big-time vaudeville. Red had always dreamed of graduating to big-time vaudeville himself, so Edna got no argument out of him. The only question was: did big-time vaudeville want Red Skelton?

Unfortunately, none of the major vaudeville booking agents were interested in giving Walkathon's Top Banana a job. Red and Edna couldn't even get past their receptionists.

"I've got to break into the newspapers," he told Edna when they were packing for Atlantic City, where he was due to emcee another Walkathon. "That's the only way to get people in show business to notice me."

"How do we do that?" asked Edna. "We can't afford food, much less a press agent."

Red thought he had the answer to that, too. During the ride to Atlantic City he dreamed up a series of screwball stunts that he was sure would capture the fancy of the crowds at the seashore resort.

He promenaded down the Atlantic City boardwalk in his suit jacket, vest, shirt, tie, and shoes—but no trousers—just his undershorts. He walked off the end of the Steel Pier fully clothed and plummeted into the ocean. He lay down in gutters on rainy days so women could cross over him without getting their feet wet. And he threw temper tantrums in department stores.

One stunt that never failed to attract a large crowd would be staged in a department store during the start of a long awaited sale. Edna, holding Red by the hand, would enter, pulling her charge toward the clothing department as if he were a small child. On the way there they would pass through the toy department, where Red would suddenly see a child's plaything he just couldn't live without.

"Mommy, will you buy me that fire engine?" he'd ask.

"No," Edna would reply adamantly. "Wait till Christmas. Maybe Santa will bring it."

"But your widdle boy wants it now," Red would cry out.

"Mommy can't afford a fire engine now, dear."

"Then I want a hobby horse," he would scream.

With each denial, Red would become increasingly hysterical, and the two would continue the act until they had pulled most of the customers away from the sale. When the crowd was large enough, Red would fling himself to the floor and throw a tearful temper tantrum, kicking away anyone foolhardy enough to try to come near him. Finally, the management would have enough and donate the fire engine to this incorrigible, overgrown, redheaded monster in the interest of getting the customers' minds back on the sale.

None of these stunts accomplished Red's goal of getting into big-time vaudeville, or even breaking into the newspapers. Atlantic City reporters could easily spot the difference between a publicity seeker and a genuine news event, and they ignored his antics completely.

It was the Easter Sunday Caper, however, that motivated Red to start hunting for other methods to accelerate his career up the show business ladder.

On Easter Sunday, with a capacity crowd parading up and down the boardwalk in their Easter Sunday best, Red invited Edna to take a stroll along the beach with him and an accomplice, whom he had just introduced to her as a friend from his circus days.

Edna, also clad in her very best clothing—a wool knit dress she had gone into hock to buy—accepted Red's invitation, and the two men linked their arms in hers, and they set off along the sand.

But after a few steps, Red abruptly changed direction and he and his friend started walking Edna toward the surf. Being no dummy, and having been married to Red for a couple of years by now, it didn't take Edna long to figure out what he was up to, and she struggled to get free before the baptism could actually take place. But one helpless female was no match for Red and a former strong man from a carnival.

Struggle mightily though she did, she could not prevent them from walking her into the surf all the way up to her neck.

By the time the dunking was over and the trio was once again back on the boardwalk, the hem of Edna's wool knit had shrunk up to her navel, and she was the proud owner of the first mini-dress.

Understandably, Edna was furious with Red, which precipitated one of their first marital crises. After she had simmered down slightly in their hotel room, Edna reached a decision.

"Honey," she said, "I think the time has come when you better decide whether you want to be a great comedian or a buffoon."

After making Edna define what a "buffoon" was, Red took umbrage at her remark. This caused another stormy quarrel, at the end of which he stalked out of the room and headed for the boardwalk.

On his way to the lobby, Red's sense of humor overpowered his anger. He thought of a way of getting back at Edna for being so unreasonable—short of divorce, that is.

Stopping at the front desk, he said to the room clerk, "I'm worried about Edna's nerves."

"Edna, sir?"

"My wife. That's the reason I brought her here, you know. The doctors. They said she needed a long rest. Has to be watched."

"Watched?" Now the clerk was turning pale.

Red shook his head solemnly. "She could be dangerous. Unfortunately, I can't be with her every minute."

Then, whistling cheerfully, Red exited, and took a long promenade down the boardwalk.

When he returned several hours later, Red found that the management had barricaded the door to his and Edna's room and that a screaming Edna was trying to crawl out through the transom. She was unable to escape, however, for two chambermaids were beating her back with mops and brooms.

"I can handle this now, ladies," said Red, giving each of the maids a small tip, and pushing the furniture aside. "Thanks a lot."

Although it took the better part of Easter Sunday afternoon, Red somehow managed to get Edna to listen to what he euphemistically called "reason." But being a born prankster, Red couldn't leave well enough alone. No sooner had he reconciled her to a life enriched with Skeltonian whimsy than he had an irrepressible urge to spring an encore on her.

"I've got a great new undertaker gag to use in my Walkathon monologue tomorrow night. It's a sure-fire recognition joke. But first I have to know the name of the best undertaker in town."

Snapping at the bait, Edna immediately picked up the phone and asked the hotel clerk for the name of the best undertaker in town.

Ten minutes later, the police arrived.

As Red had anticipated, the nervous hotel clerk had jumped to the conclusion that Mrs. Skelton had just finished slaying her husband.

No doubt about it, life with Red Skelton was a laugh a minute. But who could laugh the way his career was going? Or rather, not going.

By 1933, Red was still playing the Walkathon circuit, and for peanuts.

It was a lonely life for Edna, who sometimes, when she didn't land the cashier's job, had to spend as many as ten hours alone while Red was off in some smoke-filled, drafty auditorium. She knew those routines backward, forward, and inside out, and it would take at least a platoon of Hitler's storm troopers to force her to watch them again when she didn't have to.

Edna still didn't want children. And, realistically, the Skeltons couldn't afford any, even if she would change her mind. Nevertheless, being a woman, she needed someone to mother.

To fill that void Edna bought a Boston bulldog.

Since it was often very late when Red returned to their hotel room after entertaining at the Walkathon, and Edna would be asleep, the chore of walking the bulldog usually fell on him.

Being a lover of animals, Red didn't mind these outings, except during the winter. Despite the cold weather, Red would often be dripping with perspiration by the time he finished up at the Walkathon and made the long trek back to the hotel—usually by foot. Since he didn't own an overcoat, the walk in the cold night air was an open invitation to pneumonia. He'd be shivering when he arrived at their hotel room. Then to have to turn right around and go out again with the bulldog on a leash was just one more hardship the redhead didn't need. Red thought of a solution one week when the Skeltons were staying at the Whitman Hotel in Camden, New Jersey, where he was playing another Walkathon.

Unbeknownst to Edna, Red had a harness made for the bulldog at a local saddle maker's, and bought a fifty-foot length of manila rope at the hardware emporium.

Then, instead of accompanying the dog on his nightly round of tree trunks and fire hydrants, Red would lower him out of the third-story window. The bulldog would roam up and down the sidewalk at one end of the rope, while Skelton, at the other end, reclined like a king on the bed.

Things might have continued that way indefinitely if it had not been for the repeal of the Eighteenth Amendment—the Prohibition law—in December of 1933.

In February 1934, Red and Edna were back staying at the Whitman Hotel. By then a saloon had opened on the ground floor of the Whitman, under their hotel room.

Business was booming at the saloon, too—until some of its steadier customers began staying away, claiming the proprietor was serving rot gut.

"Rot gut?!" exclaimed the exasperated proprietor, upon learning of their complaints.

"Yeah, rot gut. Drink it, and you start seeing flying bulldogs!"

Later that night, the proprietor positioned himself on the sidewalk outside his saloon to investigate this canine phenomenon for himself. And, sure enough, just a little past midnight, he saw the flying creature his customers had been raving about. The bulldog floated out of a third-floor hotel window, right to the sidewalk, where it walked back and forth, did its duty on a lamp post, and after a little while, ascended.

Since the proprietor had deliberately not touched a drop of his own hooch all that evening, the bulldog was clearly not the result of anything he was serving in his establishment.

Obviously the flying canine had something to do with the tenants in that hotel room. So the barkeeper complained to the

Whitman's manager, who promised to speak to Skelton about it the next time he saw him. But when confronted with the accusation, Red denied any knowledge of the caper, and the following night he was back at the window lowering the bulldog to the sidewalk again.

This time the saloon keeper was prepared to handle the matter himself. With the help of a small piece of sirloin, he struck up a friendship with the pooch as soon as its paws touched the pavement. After that it was just a question of cutting him free of the rope and taking him home, where he held him hostage overnight.

Red, of course, was panic-stricken when he discovered that Edna's beloved bulldog had somehow gotten off its tether. And when he had to confess to Edna exactly how their bulldog happened to be walking around down below by himself, he almost lost his wife as well.

The saloon keeper saved the marriage by showing up at their door the following afternoon with the bulldog in his arms. But he refused to return the pooch to the Skeltons until Red agreed to desist from performing the rope trick in the future.

Red's next appearance before the public was at the W. E. Tebbets Walkathon in Atlanta, Georgia. From every indication this would be just another routine engagement. But once Red arrived there he found that the management was planning a different kind of entertainment to keep the customers awake. Tebbets was more ambitious than other Walkathon producers: he planned to produce a nightly musical review called *As Thousands Hear,* a spoof of the Broadway musical hit, *As Thousands Cheer.* Red was to emcee the review and act in the sketches. This gave him an unexpected chance to prove he was more than just a baggy-pants clown, because in it he was given an opportunity to sing, dance, and act, in addition to performing his usual routines.

This one appearance did more for getting Red into vaudeville than the entire previous year's array of wild stunts. While Red was performing in Atlanta, his clowning caught the attention of a man who was to have the most important influence on his and Edna's lives until then. This man was Jim Harkins, a veteran of vaudeville and a minor star of half a dozen New York shows such as the *Ziegfeld Follies* and George White's *Scandals.*

Harkins had only one criticism of Red's act—he didn't like the rubber cigar Red used as a prop, and which he'd worked with ever since his burlesque days.

"Use a real cigar," Harkins advised him. "You don't need that rubber thing flapping all over your face. It looks too hokey."

So Red went out and bought a real cigar, and has been using one ever since—only he doesn't light it.

Aside from the complaint about the cigar, Jim Harkins thought Red a major talent. He also liked Red and Edna personally, and after getting to know them, wanted to help them succeed—even to the point of "loaning us a buck or two or ten, if he had it," recalls Edna today. "And of course, when Red found out he had been in vaudeville and knew all those people who could help him, Red loved him, too."

Harkins, or "Uncle Jim," as the Skeltons referred to him after their friendship ripened, believed that Red was wasting his time performing in Walkathons, and that he ought to get into big-time vaudeville.

Red and Edna concurred with his opinion, but said that so far they hadn't been able to interest any of the major vaudeville houses or even any important Broadway agents.

Uncle Jim said he knew of an agent who could help them— Tom Kennedy. "Just look me up the next time you kids come to the big city, and I'll get you together with him," promised their latest benefactor, before leaving Atlanta for another engagement.

Little did Uncle Jim realize that someday their positions would be reversed, and that Red would be rich enough to help him over his financial rough spots by putting him on the Skelton payroll whenever Harkins was between acting jobs.

5

By early 1934 the Walkathon fad was beginning to die out, threatening to cut off the Skeltons' future income from that source. As a result, Red and Edna decided to take Uncle Jim's advice, return to New York City, and put their careers in the hands of the agent Tom Kennedy. It was a long shot that Kennedy could do anything, but they hoped he had the necessary clout to get them at least a chance in vaudeville.

The Skeltons' home base, when they were in the Manhattan area, was a boardinghouse around the corner from the old Madison Square Garden. It was a dingy place, full of other starving actors, but the Skeltons were lucky to be able to afford that. And at least it was within walking distance of where all the threatrical action was.

Red and Edna's fortunes took an immediate turn for the better after renewing their contact with Uncle Jim. Uncle Jim treated them to a sumptuous meal at Nedick's hot dog stand, then escorted them to Tom Kennedy's office in the Brill Building just off Times Square.

"This is one of the funniest men you'll ever meet," said Uncle Jim, introducing Red to the paunchy, gray-haired agent, and then going off to look for work himself.

Kennedy won Red's immediate love by telling him that his comedy needed no introduction. He had seen Skelton's work at several Walkathons in New Jersey, and felt he had a great future as a comedian if he were handled by someone with the right contacts. That "someone," Kennedy felt, was himself. In short, he wanted to sign Red to a combination agent-management contract for 25 percent of Red's income. Red's immediate impulse was to ask for a pen and the contract, inasmuch as no other agent had ever shown an interest in him before.

Edna, however, thought 25 percent too high, and before she would allow Red to sign, she first demanded to know what specifically Kennedy was going to do for her husband. She'd heard of agents signing actors to "exclusive" contracts, then sitting back and doing nothing but collecting unfair percentages of their salaries while the actors actually got the jobs for themselves. "We want to get into vaudeville," said Edna. "We're tired of Walkathons."

Kennedy told them that he was pretty sure he could get Red a shot at vaudeville; he also spoke vaguely, but interestingly, of a movie career for Red.

This intrigued the Skeltons, and they signed a management contract with Tom Kennedy, giving him 25 percent of Red's take.

Kennedy proved that his talk about getting Red into the movies wasn't just so much agent's malarky. A few days after Red signed with Kennedy, he took him out to RKO Studios in Astoria, Long Island, where he had made arrangements for a screen test. Kennedy's only mistake was in not specifying that

Red's forte was comedy. As a result, the director tested Red as a straight romantic lead.

Red Skelton as a leading man was not as outrageous a notion as one might think. Now in his early twenties, Red could almost be considered handsome. He was tall and lean, his flaming red hair was abundant enough to give him a Robert Taylorish widow's peak, and his features were regular and not the slightest bit rubbery, except when he was deliberately contorting them into funny postures for the sake of a cheap laugh.

So it wasn't Red's looks that destroyed his chances. His problem was simply that he couldn't handle a dramatic line with any more assurance now than he could when he was touring with the stock company through the South. The moment he opened his mouth on the screen, the studio executives, viewing the test in their cigar-filled projection room, became limp with laughter. Unfortunately, hysterics were not the emotion the scene was intended to evoke, so Red's film career was, for the moment at least, derailed.

Taking heart from all those laughs, and using the screen test as palpable proof of another studio's interest in his client, Tom Kennedy was soon pitching Red to the people running Vitaphone Studios in Brooklyn. But this time as a comedian.

Vitaphone Studios was about to embark on a series of comedy two-reelers, and because they couldn't afford any of the name comics of that era, they were looking for fresh new faces who would be willing to work for "short money."

What more logical choice than Red Skelton? Not only did he have experience before the cameras, but he'd work for shorter money than anybody.

That apparently sold them, and the next day Kennedy delivered his client, in the flesh, to Vitaphone Studios, where he again undertook to conquer the movies.

"The shorts were one-day things," remembers Edna, "and they didn't amount to very much—about seventy-five bucks a short. It amounted to something for us, however. It was money—eating money."

One of the shorts had a dude ranch background, and in it, Red did a comedy musical number called "Never Be Rude to a

Dude." The song was written by Sammy Cahn and Sol Chaplin, who would be composing some of America's biggest pop tune hits of the forties and fifties. But at the time, they, too, were complete unknowns, trying to get a break in the movie business, just like Red.

"It was a lousy song," recollects Sammy Cahn today, with a sheepish grin, "but Red's never forgotten the lyrics. Every time I run into him at some Hollywood affair, he always stops me and sings it for me. Personally, I can't remember the words at all, but he knows them by heart."

The shorts were poorly produced and distributed, so very few movie-goers actually got a chance to see them, or view Red Skelton, either. Before long, the two-reelers were back in Vitaphone's film vault, and Red was back in his Ninth Avenue boardinghouse, contemplating more dreary years as a Walkathon clown.

It was at this nadir of Red's theatrical life that Tom Kennedy was able to get him his first crack at a vaudeville engagement.

The place was the Majestic Theater in Paterson, New Jersey, and Kennedy was able to sell the theater operator his client by resorting to telling a small fib. Correction: a *large* fib. The gist of it was that Red Skelton had just completed smashing all kinds of box office records while playing a vaudeville house in Manhattan, and the only reason he would consider appearing in Paterson at all was because it was a small town and the atmosphere was more relaxing and he would be able to rest there.

For some reason the manager of the Majestic bought Kennedy's story. This alone made Red nervous, and after he and Edna checked into their hotel in Paterson, he began to panic about his ability to do a "one-man" show. As a result, he persuaded Edna to go out and hire a supporting cast to back him up. Edna obediently combed the boondocks for acceptable talent, and finally came up with a tap dancer, a juggler, and two pugilistic stumblebums who promised to put on a boxing exhibition every bit as thrilling as the Dempsey–Tunney "long count" fight.

Edna also appeared in the act with Red for the first time opening night in Paterson and she remained with him as his straight man until he was important enough to get along without one.

"I was the no-talent part of Red's act," recalls Edna, "but we couldn't afford to hire another girl. And Red had to have someone to bounce his routines off. So I stooged for him. But I didn't have to take falls or pies in the face."

In Red's estimation, the first performance in Paterson was a hit. At least no one threw chairs or hissed or gave him the hook.

After the curtain came down on the final act, Jack Williams, manager of the Majestic, appeared backstage to dispense money to the performers—an old vaudeville custom on opening night. Performers who needed it were allowed to draw money against their weekly salaries right after the first show.

When it was his turn, Skelton, in order to fortify the lie about his smash-hit New York engagement, grandly pretended to be above the need for immediate cash.

"You don't have to pay me now, Mr. Williams. You can wait till I'm through," said Red.

Williams nodded agreeably and snapped, "You are through!"

After being fired from an engagement that ran one night, one would think that even a comedian as accustomed to hard knocks as Red Skelton was would recognize that the time had probably come to sit down, reevaluate his career, and perhaps give some serious thought to entering a profession for which he was better suited. If any thought of retirement ever entered Red's mind at this juncture, it certainly hadn't occurred to Tom Kennedy.

While the Skeltons were packing their bags and retreating across the Hudson to Manhattan, Kennedy was busy making arrangements for Red to appear on the great stage of the Roxy Theater that afternoon—not to entertain an audience but to audition for Eve Ross and Jesse Kay, who were booking acts for the Fanchon & Marco circuit.

Fanchon & Marco were in the business of supplying complete entertainment units, usually consisting of a singer, an adagio team, a novelty act of some sort, and a line-up of beautiful dancers known as the Gay Foster Girls, to various nightclubs and vaudeville houses in the United States and Canada.

Eve Ross was in charge of the dance numbers and the staging of the shows at their various locations, while it was Jesse Kay's job to select the acts that would be sent along.

Twice monthly they held afternoon auditions in the Roxy Theater for the purpose of viewing fresh flesh and putting shows together, and it was to one of these that Kennedy dragged Red and Edna. The audition on this particular afternoon was for the purpose of selecting some suitable acts to send up to the Lido, a nightclub in Montreal, Canada.

When Kennedy brought Red over to meet Eve Ross and Jesse Kay, the cavernous theater was empty except for about a dozen acts who were either in the process of auditioning or were just standing around waiting to do their stuff.

Eying Skelton, Jesse Kay said to Tom Kennedy, "Who's the tall skinny kid? What's he do?"

"He's a comedian," said Kennedy.

"Well, I don't want to audition comedians," said Kay.

"Why not? Red's funny as hell."

"Because it's not fair to audition a comedian without an audience," said Kay rather adamantly. "I want to audition dancers, singers, novelty acts. But how the hell can I audition a comedian without an audience? Now get him out of here."

Suddenly Red pulled some papers that resembled script pages from his pocket, and said, completely dead-pan, to Kay and Ross, "Whose act do you want me to do—Milton Berle's?" He then did Milton Berle better than Berle did.

"After that," remembers Kay, "Red reeled off two or three other current names of comics and did great imitations of them, too. Also some very funny bits of his own. Well, inside of three or four minutes he had us all in stitches. So I turned to Eve and said, 'I'm going to take a chance. Let's send him up to the Lido.' "

Eve Ross also sensed that the tall, skinny redhead had a gift for comedy that was greater than most, so she went along with Kay and they booked him into the Lido Club, for two weeks, at $150 a week, with an option for a third.

Neither of the two bits that made Red famous—the doughnut dunking routine, or "Guzzler's Gin"—were in his repertoire yet. His act mainly consisted of about twenty minutes of stand-up jokes, a few imitations, a blackface Mammy number, and some back-and-forth patter with Edna.

The opening night audience at the Lido was less than enthralled with what Red had to offer.

Red had barely finished the first joke of his monologue—some crack about the fact that he thought he was opening in Canada and instead he must have got on a train going to France by mistake—before he was interrupted by a loud raspberry. This was followed by a raucous shout, "Hey, carrot-top, where'd you get that hair dye job—from Sinclair Paint?"

No one had bothered to warn Red, but the Lido Club was frequented nightly by a rowdy clique of hecklers, who felt it their right to cut in on a performer's lines, to guffaw in the wrong places, to utter many novel and impolite sounds, and to otherwise show acute critical distaste.

Even Red wasn't used to quite so much hostility from an audience. He was frightened, hurt, and upset as he struggled through his act. In addition to the humiliation of being razzed so relentlessly, his timing was being thrown off, so that even his funny material wasn't getting over. He desperately wanted to answer his tormentors with some choice, and extremely earthy language of his own. But Edna, every inch a lady, refused to let her husband sink to their level. Every time he opened his mouth to strike back, she quieted him with an angry look.

Somehow Red managed to survive the nightmare and get back to his dressing room where he and Edna could at least cry without being heckled.

But Puggy Dettner, the manager of the Lido, was absolutely livid with rage that Jesse Kay had stuck him with such a bomb act. The moment the show was over—about one o'clock in the morning—Dettner had Kay on the phone in New York, and was telling him, in extremely picturesque language, that he wanted Skelton "the hell out of Canada tonight, or I'll have the Mounties after him for 'impersonating an entertainer.' "

"What happened?" asked Kay.

"He's just no good," screamed Puggy. "You gotta take him back and get me someone else."

Kay couldn't understand it and he asked Dettner to put Eve Ross, who was standing beside him, on the phone.

"What happened?" asked Kay. "He seemed funny to me."

"He's not doing well at all," said Eve. "He's just dying."

"How long was he on?" asked Kay.

"About twenty minutes."

"Twenty minutes! That's a long time," said Kay. "Were any of his jokes funny?"

"A few were funny."

"Let's hear 'em."

According to Kay, he and Eve Ross then went over Skelton's entire act, joke by joke, with him advising her which jokes Red should retain and which to cut. When they were finished, Eve said, "Well, if he cuts all that, his act'll only run about six or seven minutes."

"Fine. At least it'll be funny. Now put Dettner back on."

After Eve turned the phone over to Dettner, Kay said, "Puggy, you can't close a guy like this . . . he's a young fellah . . . he looks like he's got talent. If you close him now, he's gotta go back to soda jerking . . . just don't do that . . . he'll never get over it . . . so don't do it . . . it's not human."

But being human wasn't Puggy Dettner's primary aim in life. He wanted another comedian. "Who you got?"

"At the moment, nobody," replied Kay. "I'm not sitting here with a comedian in my bed. It'll take a few days to find you someone and get him up there." At the time, there were no airline flights between New York and Montreal. "So you gotta stick with the kid until then."

"I'll go along with you on that, Jesse, I'll give Red two more days. After that, you better have somebody else here." Puggy Dettner was all heart.

Before returning to slumberland, Kay spoke to Eve Ross one more time and asked her to phone him with a report after the next night's show.

Meanwhile, Eve Ross spent the following day with Red, helping him trim the deadwood out of his act. She also gave him a bit of advice on how to treat nightclub hecklers. "Don't stand there and take it, kid. You've got to fight fire with fire. That's how Berle and Frank Faye handle tough customers."

"But Edna said—"

"Forget what Edna said. Do as I say. I know what I'm talking about."

Between dinner and performance time, Red worked on developing some heckler squelches. When he returned to the spotlight it was with a whole new attitude about his audience.

The first time a drunk cut into his monologue, Red silenced him with, "You know, sir, you show possibilities of developing into a total stranger."

The line brought down the house, and is, in fact, still being quoted as an example of a classic heckler deflater.

Another time a heckler greeted one of Red's jokes with, "You must be stupid if you think anyone would laugh at that."

"Not as stupid as you are," retorted Red. "You spent your money to hear it."

Another huge laugh.

Later that night the phone in Kay's bedroom in Manhattan rang, and it was Eve Ross delivering her nightly report. "The kid's doing a little better," she said. "The audience seemed to like him."

"So I had her put Dettner back on the phone," relates Kay, "and after he got on, I said, 'Puggy . . . do me a personal favor. Let the poor guy stay till the end of the week . . . be a *mensh*. . . . Don't let him go . . . don't kill him.' There was a long pause, and finally he said, 'Okay, he can stay till the end of the week.' "

At the end of the week, Puggy Dettner phoned Jesse Kay and said, "He's doing a lot better now. I'll let him play out his two weeks."

Toward the end of the second week, Dettner phoned Jesse Kay again. "I want to keep him a third week," he said.

"Now you got me on a spot," said Kay. "I've got another act I'm about to send up there."

"Well, get out of it," shouted Puggy. "I want Red a third week."

By the end of the third week, Red was a big smash. Lido audiences liked the way he talked back to them, and came to hear his heckler squelches as much as his set routines. When he finished his act every night, it was usually to a standing ovation. Which pleased him and Edna, but Puggy Dettner even more.

On Saturday night of the third week, Dettner phoned Kay and said, "The kid's great. I want to hold this guy over indefinitely."

Kay said that was impossible. He already had another comedian booked into the Lido to replace Red. "Send him somewhere else," screamed Dettner.

"Okay," agreed Kay, playing hard to get, "but then you have to raise Red's salary to $200 a week."

Puggy Dettner wasn't anxious to pay him that much, but in the end, he agreed, and Red stayed on for three more weeks. For this stand, however, Dettner made Red emcee of the entire show instead of being just one of the acts.

As loved as Red was by the Lido Club patrons, he still had problems during his run there. Because he was the youngest— also the greenest—of any of the masters of ceremonies who'd ever worked at the Lido, Red had to contend with a lot of resentment from some of the older, more experienced vaudevillians who were sent up from the States. They felt he was much too young to be featured entertainer, with a large photograph of himself on a sandwich board on the sidewalk in front of the club.

The old-timers manifested their resentment in various ways, all aimed at destroying the young man's self-confidence. They ignored him, patronized him, upstaged him, made noises during his stints at the microphone, and made insulting remarks about his material.

Their strategy was to get Red fired so that one of them could take over as the club's emcee, a job which naturally carried with it considerable prestige.

To restore his self-confidence, Red dreamed up his own stratagem. It worked miracles.

Each Monday morning, before opening a new show, Red would gather the new performers up from the States on the stage of the Lido and give them an enthusiastic welcoming speech.

"It's wonderful, your coming up here to Montreal," he'd say, with the utmost sincerity. "You'll knock 'em dead. These audiences go crazy over anyone who speaks French."

"French?!" a startled vaudevillian would exclaim, his face turning ashen. "What do you mean, French?"

Keeping a completely straight face, Red would reply innocently, "Why, you give your act in French, don't you? These people are all French Canadians, you know. They don't understand a word of English."

To bolster his statement, Red would go out front that night, and as his rivals watched uneasily from the wings, he would open the show in flawless "French." This was actually doubletalk flavored with Gallic intonations and a few words and phrases Red had picked up since moving to French Canada.

The audience, familiar with Skelton's act after eight weeks of exposure to it, would yell with delight. But his rivals for his emceeing job, not knowing a word of French, would again turn gray with fright.

"By the time I'd get done with my monologue," chuckles Red, "some of those fellows'd be so scared they'd be speechless."

Not just speechless, but so upset that they would put on shaky performances, and Puggy Dettner would have to fire them before their two weeks were over. Some of the more cowardly would be too frightened to open at all, and would retreat across the Border, mumbling imprecations against their agents for failing to warn them.

Toward the end of Red's sixth week at the Lido, Jesse Kay was on the phone with Eve Ross and Puggy Dettner talking to them about another matter, when the club manager happened to mention that he'd like a replacement for Red Skelton.

"Why? Isn't he doing well?" asked Kay, surprised. No one had ever lasted at the Lido for six weeks.

"He's doing great," said Dettner.

"Oh, he's doing very well," agreed Eve Ross. "He's handling the whole show now ... he's the emcee ... he's very much at home up there ... he's working with the girls ... he's doing everything."

"Then why get rid of him?" asked Kay.

"Audiences might get tired of him," said Dettner. "Better to bring him back in a few weeks."

"Once they go, they don't usually come back—if they're any good," pointed out Kay.

"He's not that good," said Puggy Dettner, irritably.

"We'll see," said Kay, who turned out to be the better prophet of the two.

On the following Monday, Red and Edna were packing to leave for New York, when a man named Harry Anger called them and offered Red the job as master of ceremonies at Montreal's Princess Theater, which he managed. He'd pay Red $350 a week, and the reason he was willing to go that high was because "by then," according to Jesse Kay, "Red was already a half-ass name in Montreal and a pretty good draw."

After two weeks at Loew's Princess, Red was such a hit and the word of mouth was so good that he was invited to display his comedy wares next at Shea's Theater in Toronto, which was also part of the Loew's Canadian chain, and which Anger also managed.

Red was a solid hit at Shea's, too, and as a result of that engagement he wound up playing Montreal and Toronto, alternate weeks, for a solid year.

Sweet as it was to be a regular fixture at both Shea's and The Princess, there were built-in problems to playing to the same "old friends" week after week.

"You'd better get yourself some new material," Harry Anger advised him one night after the show. "I think my audiences are getting tired of your act, Red."

"They're still laughing, aren't they?"

"But not as hard."

As any performer would, Red resented being told that his material was getting old. And he was still smarting from Anger's criticism when he and Edna went across the street a few minutes later to have a midnight snack at a coffee shop.

But in looking back on the incident, Red is extremely grateful to Harry Anger for shaking him out of his complacency. Without Anger's friendly words of advice, Red might never have been on the lookout for new material when he sat down at a table in the coffee shop that night and noticed a man at the counter clumsily dunking doughnuts in a cup of coffee.

Not every artist can pinpoint the exact moment when he quit being just another entertainer and crossed over to the ranks of the superstars.

But as far as Red is concerned, that was the moment it happened to him.

As he watched the fumblings of that unknown but by now immortalized doughnut dunker, Red became so fascinated he couldn't take his eyes off the fellow. This in turn inspired Red to work out a hilarious pantomime involving the various kinds of doughnut dunkers: the careful dunker; the sloppy dunker; the fancy dunker; the one who allows the doughnut to dissolve in his coffee and disappear altogether; and finally, the cowardly dunker. He's too timid to flaunt one of Emily Post's most hallowed "No-Nos" in public, so he waits until he thinks nobody is watching before sliding his doughnut into his coffee.

It took Red several sleepless nights and a couple of performances to perfect all the nuances of doughnut dunking, but by the time he finished working out the many variations on the theme he had a brand new half-hour act that absolutely kept the Canadian audiences in a continuous state of convulsions.

As word of this bit of nonsense reached the populace, Red became an even bigger name in Canada. His waistline got bigger, too.

In order to give the doughnut dunking routine reality, Red had to eat twelve doughnuts in different ways for each of the three daily shows. The result was a gain in weight of thirty-five pounds after three weeks of doing his new act.

As the world's foremost doughnut dunker, Red was now so popular north of the Border that the Canadians were beginning to regard him as one of their own. Theaters were sold out in advance everywhere he played and he now commanded a weekly salary of $750 for the act—the most money he and Edna had ever earned. They were still broke most of the time, because the $750 wasn't clear profit. In fact, very little of it was profit. Between the 25 percent commission Tom Kennedy took off the top and another 15 percent for bookers' fees, they hardly had anything left to live on, because they also had to pay their own hotel and traveling expenses between Montreal and Toronto.

The train fare was the most burdensome—until Red, resorting to the same kind of ingenuity that enabled him to sell de-fogging devices in Iowa, figured out a way to eliminate one of the railroad fares, thus cutting their traveling expenses in half.

Edna would buy the railroad ticket and board the train first. Red would be at her heels, but moving toward the railroad car with such a wobbly gait and glazed expression that it seemed as if nothing short of a miracle would stop him from throwing up all over the train steps and possibly the conductor. One look at this intoxicated redhead, and the conductor would wave him aboard, without asking to see his ticket, and point to the men's lounge. No conductor, no matter how much of a stickler for railroad rules, would take the chance of having some drunk throw up all over his clean uniform.

Every weekend for over a year Red made the 338-mile run between Montreal and Toronto for free, by doing the same drunk act. The only thing that ever varied was the audience. If the trainmen looked too familiar, Red would judiciously wait for the next train, one whose personnel weren't likely to recognize him or his act.

This triumph of talent over economics not only enabled Red to polish his drunk act for theater audiences, but it allowed him and Edna to salt away a few bucks in the bank for the first time in their marital lives.

Toward the end of Red's Canadian run, he was making up in his dressing room one night when a man with a slightly familiar face, which Red couldn't quite place, barged in without knocking.

Introducing himself as a big fan of Red's, the stranger said he was anxious to see that night's show.

Red told the stranger that he'd have to buy a ticket—just like everyone else.

"I'd like to, Mr. Skelton, but the house is all sold out. I thought maybe you'd let me watch the show backstage from the wings."

Red said he'd like to help him out, but that it was against the policy of the theater to let anyone in for nothing.

The man sighed and exclaimed unhappily, "Gee, Mr. Skelton, I don't think it's asking so much of you. After all, you've been riding free on the Canadian-Pacific for over a year."

As Red stared at him in amazement, the stranger explained that he was a railroad conductor, and that he'd been onto the ruse from the first day Red pulled his drunk act.

"Now do I see the show, or are you going to pay me the $374 in back fares you owe the railroad?"

The conductor saw the show.

By early 1937 Red's fame had reached as far south as Washington, D.C. When the manager of the Capital Theater, Joe Ford, got wind of how a certain redhead north of the Canadian border was killing audiences night after night, he invited Red to play his theater.

Ford billed Red as the "Canadian Comic," but despite this handicap, Red won the hearts of the Washingtonians and was held over for a number of weeks. By the time Red finished that engagement Harry Anger had defected from the Princess Theater in Montreal to manage the Warner Brothers' Theater in Washington, D.C. Hearing of Red's availability, he booked him into the

Warner house, where Red also stayed for a record breaking engagement.

After a successful stand there, Red proved, and beyond a reasonable doubt, that he was capable of making American audiences laugh, too. As a result, Tom Kennedy had no trouble booking him into the prestigious Loew's State in New York City, as its emcee, the following June.

This was to be Red's first appearance on Broadway and, understandably, he and Edna were nervous. They knew that New York audiences were the most sophisticated in the world and that Red's routines were not. As a result, they overcompensated for this imagined shortcoming by hiring a couple of bright New York writers to supply them with "sophisticated" special material.

Can you imagine Red Skelton doing sophisticated comedy?

Well, the audience couldn't either.

Red's function at Loew's State was to act as emcee for the entire vaudeville bill, as well as do his own bits along the way.

When Red opened the show with a monologue liberally sprinkled with the "bright" new material, the audience started out by sitting on its hands and ended up by competing with each other to see who could be quiet the longest. They were even too well-mannered to heckle Red, a response he would have gladly welcomed, for at least it would have given him the chance to retaliate with some sure-fire squelches.

When he retreated to the wings after introducing the opening act, Red was quietly raging over such complete indifference and was tempted not to return to the stage at all for his next stint at the mike. He did, however—only this time he reverted to the kind of slapstick that had been fracturing audiences in the Canadian provinces and the American Midwest for years, including, of course, his doughnut dunking bit.

Suddenly the theater exploded with laughter and applause. Laugh segued into laugh until the cavernous Loew's State was filled with what seemed one nonstop thunderous roar so loud it drowned out the noise of the Seventh Avenue subway below. That was the end of the sophisticated material.

Skelton finished to a standing ovation and the next day there were lines at the box office extending clear around the block to Eighth Avenue.

What happened to the sophisticated audience theory?

"All the comics were changing their material when they got to New York," explains Red. "They thought their stuff wouldn't go over on Broadway. So New Yorkers never got a look at the material that was bowling them over in the sticks and the Middle West. With me, they saw it. And they like to tore the place down!"

Variety—the week of June 16, 1937—was less effusive than Red, but by no means displeased with what it saw:

Red Skelton, so-called because his hair is the color they don't like on ledgers, is a young comic whose chances appear exceptionally strong. He has an easy, affable manner of working, quickly ingratiates himself, and is pretty well-equipped with material.

His first portion consists of five minutes of talk, during which an unbilled girl [Edna] plays straight. He is a little Joe Penner-ish at times with hands, cigar, and gestures, but it doesn't spoil his work.

A little scene showing the various ways of dunking, accompanied by bright chatter, comes later, while farther down Skelton gives 'em an idea of the different kinds of walking that can be found. The drunk features of the walking exhibition are very funny, especially of the girl stew. Both these little scenes are admirably sold. He offers no singing, nor does he dance.

He's not going to have any trouble at all getting along in this or any other town, either on stage dates of this character, in picture houses, or on nitery floors.

Someone else who saw Red on the stage at Loew's State and was impressed with his work was Pandro Berman, RKO producer of the Astaire and Rogers film musicals, in addition to a number of other hits. Berman was in New York to finalize arrangements to secure the rights to cinematize Arthur Kober's hit Broadway comedy, *Having Wonderful Time,* a story about the love entanglements of a group of Jewish stenographers, CPA's, and other New York stereotypes who were off on a two-week holiday at a resort in the Berkshires called Camp Kare-Free.

What made the Broadway version funny and appealing—and also a hit—was how accurately it reflected the humorous side of life in a Jewish summer resort that boasted a Milton Berle-type social director to keep the tumult going.

For the movie version, however, there had to be a slight change in the ethnic ingredients of Camp Kare-Free, the reason being that in pre-World War II Hollywood, studio heads deemed Jews unfit subject matter for successful motion pictures. The film moguls didn't feel the American public, which was 90 percent gentile, was interested in seeing a film about a camp that catered only to Jewish people.

But rather than "pass" on the vehicle altogether, RKO decided it could have the best of both worlds. With a wave of its magic wand, RKO transformed Camp Kare-Free into the kind of place that served chicken salad on white toast rather than corned beef on rye, and gave the love interest to Ginger Rogers and Douglas Fairbanks, Jr. Milton Berle, of course, would have been ideal for the camp's social director, but since Camp Kare-Free had turned gentile, he would never do, so Pan Berman decided, after seeing Red Skelton at Loew's State, to go after him for the part.

After finding out who Red's agent was, Berman made a deal with the world's most famous doughnut dunker, for $2,500 a week for six weeks, and Red was soon on his way to Hollywood.

Red's agent, incidentally, was no longer Tom Kennedy. After several years of trying to keep their financial heads above water as Kennedy's clients, Red and Edna realized that 25 percent was too much to be paying for management, "so after we were in a position where we could afford it," recalls Edna, "we went before the actor's union and got permission to sue Kennedy to break the contract. Which we did, and we won. After that, we went with the William Morris Agency."

The Morris Agency handled the Skeltons until they settled down in Hollywood for good, which, unfortunately, did not happen due to *Having Wonderful Time* (1938). The charm and humor of the Kober play was lost in the translation. Most of the nation's critics were unanimous in that, but Bosley Crowther of the *New York Times* summed it up for all, when he wrote on July 8, 1938:

There is nothing genteel about Arthur Kober's *Having Wonderful Time*, and bless its folksy heart, there was nothing gentile either. But RKO's film version, which came into the Music Hall yesterday, is both. Mr. Kober's hillbillies from the Bronx are *alle goyim* now.

He had a number of reservations about the picture but wrote: "Lee Bowman is faultless as the camp cad; and so, we might as well admit, are Richard 'Red' Skelton as Itchy, the irrepressible master of ceremonies; and Lucille Ball as Miriam, one of the harpies."

Red was actually the hit of the picture, doing his famous doughnut scene. And that was gratifying to Red and Edna.

But as so often happens with a bad picture, even the blameless in it get blamed for the totality of its failure. As a result, Red couldn't get another job in Hollywood after he checked off the RKO lot, even though it was a year before *Having Wonderful Time* was actually released. What followed was a long lay-off.

The Skeltons were not anxious to retreat to vaudeville, however. That, they felt, would have been a step backward in Red's career. Instead, they decided to become impresarios, and in the weeks they were out of work they put together a lavish musical review called *Paris in Swing*, which they took on a tour of one-night stands through the United States.

In addition to appearing in it, Red and Edna wrote, directed, and produced the review, which featured, along with the Skeltons, a fading John Boles, Zasu Pitts, and a line-up of Gay Foster Girls.

According to Red's recollections, *Paris in Swing* broke a number of box office records as it wended its way around the country, but it wound up losing money because of excessive production costs. It was $5,000 in the red when it closed at the end of a ten-week run.

After the scenery from *Paris in Swing* was consigned to Shubert's warehouse, Red and Edna made a reluctant return to vaudeville, where they could still make a comfortable living as long as vaudeville lasted.

While the Skeltons were playing the RKO Theater in Baltimore, they received a phone call from a man in Chicago who identified himself as Freeman Keyes, President of the Russell M. Seeds Advertising Company, a small ad agency in the windy city that handled many of the country's burgeoning radio accounts.

Keyes said he'd caught Red's act at the Chicago Theater when he was playing there several months before, was impressed with his comedy, and had been trying to track him down ever since. He'd heard through the manager of the Chicago Theater that Red was handled by the William Morris Agency, but when Keyes contacted them, nobody there seemed to know he was a client. Keyes insisted Red was a client of theirs, however, and demanded they track him down, so they sent word out to their various offices around the country. Finally, an office boy in their New York branch remembered that they handled an unimportant comic named Red Skelton, and located him.

Keyes thought Red extremely funny and wanted to know if he'd be interested in going on radio.

Red said he would, and Keyes invited him to come to Chicago and audition.

"At first we said 'no,' " recalls Edna. "In those days we had made so many auditions that didn't come through that we just couldn't afford to take on any more. However, we told him we would go if he would pay Red for an appearance as well as our expenses there. So that's what he did. He sent for us and paid us for a night's work to do the audition."

In Chicago, Red cut an audition record at the National Broadcasting Company, and he and Edna met Freeman Keyes in person for the first time. Keyes was a sandy-haired, stockily built Midwesterner in his mid-forties and as fine an assayer of potential radio talent as any in the business.

After Red cut his audition record, giving NBC an option to do a show with him, he and Edna returned to Baltimore, but not before Freeman Keyes signed the redhead to a contract which gave his agency the right to handle Red exclusively for radio—and also television, if that medium ever fulfilled its inventor's prophecies.

In those days, it was the ad agencies that packaged the radio shows and peddled them to the networks. The more talent an agency had under exclusive contract the more advertising accounts it attracted, and the more clout it had in dictating to the networks what shows the public would get. At the time that they signed Richard "Red" Skelton, the Russell M. Seeds Company also had under contract Bing Crosby, Tommy Dorsey, and Red Foley, a country-Western singer who was a graduate of Nashville's "Grand Ole Opry," and who was extremely popular in both the Corn Belt and Chittlin Country in the mid-thirties.

Keyes was confident he could sell Red to a network, and told the Skeltons so before shipping them back to Baltimore. But Red and Edna had heard many unfulfilled promises before and really didn't expect anything to happen with this one either. They were content just to pick up $400 for a few hours' work. But they didn't know Freeman Keyes—as determined and aggressive a man who ever sharpened his claws in the jungles of the ad agency business.

Signing with Freeman Keyes turned out to be one of the wisest decisions the Skeltons ever made. Not only was he a shrewd advertising man, but he gave Red such good advice on all aspects of his career that eventually the comedian would let his other agents go and enter into a partnership arrangement with Keyes that lasted well into the early 1950s.

"On New Year's Eve, 1937, I think it was," recalls Edna, "Freeman sent word that the network had picked up Red's option and wanted him to start on radio the following week."

Red made his radio debut in January of 1938, on "The Red Foley Show," which was broadcast locally over station WLW, in Cincinnati, Ohio. It was a weekly half-hour of country-Western music, with Foley twanging the guitar and singing, and Red supplying the comedy relief.

Although Red was not at his very best in a medium where he couldn't be seen, his folksy comedy and mugging at the mike caught the fancy of the country-Western music fans. His big forte—pantomime—was of no help to him at all on radio, but because the Foley fans dug bucolic humor, Red took advantage of the opportunity to develop many of his country bumpkin characterizations.

"Red went over very big on 'The Red Foley Show,' " remembers Edna, "so after a couple of months in Cincinnati, Freeman Keyes wanted him and Foley to move to Chicago and do a straight variety show on NBC. They would have more station outlets and a bigger audience from there. But Red Foley, who had a beautiful voice and was a heck of a nice guy, didn't want to move to Chicago. He wanted to move to some small community called Remco Valley, with his own show and his own outlet.

"So the Boss—that's what we called Freeman—moved us to Chicago anyway, and made plans to star Red and Tommy Dorsey in a variety show, with the two of them getting equal billing. But Dorsey told the Boss, 'No way am I going to split the billing with some hillbilly comic out of the Middle West!' So Dorsey refused to do it with Red, and Freeman found another band that wasn't such a name, and Red did several seasons out of Chicago, from the NBC station there doing his own show, with Raleigh Cigarettes for a sponsor."

While "The Red Skelton Show," out of NBC in Chicago, reached more people than he played to on WLW in Cincinnati, Red was still not on a coast-to-coast hook-up. Most of his audience was still in the Midwest and South.

Red's first opportunity to be heard in all sectors of the U.S. at once came on August 12, 1938, when Freeman Keyes got him a guest shot on "The Fleischmann Hour," a coast-to-coast network program emanating from NBC in New York. Starring the nasal-noted Rudy Vallee at the peak of his career, "The Fleischmann Hour" was one of the top rated radio shows in the country.

On it, Red did one of his sure-fire routines from vaudeville, and was paid $400, which he and Edna considered a lot of money for a few minutes' work.

From all accounts of that night's happenings, Rudy Vallee wished Red's appearance had been even briefer.

Because Red was obviously more comfortable relying on pantomime than reading bright quips off a script, he frequently strayed from the lines written for him and did plenty of mugging for the studio audience as well.

To the staid Mr. Vallee's chagrin, the studio audience ate up Red's clowning, which only encouraged him to stray further from the written word. When Vallee, at one juncture, accidentally dropped his script, Red cracked, while the crooner was retrieving his pages, "Rudy's ad libs are scattered all over that floor."

While it did not please Vallee to see Red Skelton making a shambles of his well-ordered musical variety show, he could not object to that night's Hooper ratings, which more than made up for whatever indignities he might have suffered. As a result, Red was invited back to the "Fleischmann" stronghold for another appearance two weeks later. When Red again wowed Rudy's radio fans, Keyes got him a third booking on the show in November.

By then it was obvious that Red was someone to be reckoned with on radio in spite of the fact that he was basically a "sight comic."

After three successive smash appearances on "The Fleischmann Hour," Red was becoming a nationally known comic. This exposure helped to catapult his own show out of Chicago to the top of the ratings locally.

Being a hit on radio was extremely gratifying to the Skeltons, for it meant they could settle down in one town for a while and not have to be constantly on the move as they were in vaudeville. What was even more of a pleasure, they could now afford to stay in better hotels, such as the Palmer House and the Ambassador East.

There was a problem to doing a weekly radio show, however, that Red had not yet conquered, and which had been the undoing of many of the vaudeville comics who tried to convert to radio. This was the problem of having to come up with new material every week—something that many years later nearly knocked Red out of the box when he tried to conquer television.

As Red was discovering, weekly radio devoured material a lot faster than Red and Edna could dream it up. In vaudeville you could do the same act for a whole year because only one city saw it at a time. In radio, the entire country heard your routines simultaneously. Something brand new had to be dished up to them the following week.

One of the earliest to recognize Red was going to have a material problem was comedy writer Jack Douglas. Today Douglas is noted as the author of humorous books, such as *My Brother*

Was an Only Child, and as a wise-cracking humorist on the nightly talk shows. But in the summer of 1939, Douglas was an underpaid staff joke writer for Bob Hope, who had just shot up into the firmament as a radio star. In 1939, Hope's "Pepsodent Show" was fourth in the ratings, right behind Jack Benny, Fred Allen, and Edgar Bergen, and was closing in on the others fast.

Jack Douglas was working in Chicago during the summer of 1939. He had just finished the Hope show for the season, and was meeting his summer expenses by writing "The Ransom Sherman Show," another local program out of Chicago.

Douglas heard "The Red Skelton Show" one night while sitting in his hotel room, and was so appalled by his material that he sent him the following wire:

DEAR RED,
    I HEARD YOUR SHOW LAST NIGHT.
    YOU NEED ME.
                  JACK DOUGLAS

"It was pretty fresh of me to send it," recalls Douglas, "but, by golly, Edna got in touch with me and I started writing for Red on the side."

With Jack Douglas writing spots for Red, the Skelton show maintained a fairly high degree of quality. When it went off the air at the end of the summer, Freeman Keyes landed Red the top comedy spot on "Avalon Time," a program starting in the fall. In between radio stints Red continued his vaudeville career with Edna, playing all the top picture houses in New York, Washington, Chicago, Milwaukee, Buffalo, and anywhere else that was willing to meet his new asking price of $2,500 a week.

During this period, Red was talked into taking a brief sabbatical from radio and vaudeville to accept the role of the "comedy love interest" in *Gentlemen Unafraid,* a new Jerome Kern operetta that was slated to open on Broadway after a six-week shakedown tour of the Midwest. Red seemed a "natural" for musical comedy, and with the prestige of even being cast in a Jerome Kern show to his credit, was looking forward to a possible career ahead of him in the legitimate theater.

However, in its first try-out week in St. Louis, *Gentlemen Unafraid* took an unmerciful beating from the local critics, in spite of the fact that they had some nice things to say about Red's gift for light comedy, and the presence in the score of some "pleasing to the ear" Jerome Kern melodies. Business was so poor that the producer of *Gentlemen Unafraid* was very much afraid to take it anywhere else, and closed the show on Saturday night. Despite future successes in every other medium, Red never again attempted to do a legitimate show on Broadway.

Thanks to all that national radio exposure, however, Red was soon able to command up to $3,000 a week in vaudeville, and most theater owners were happy to pay it, because suddenly he was breaking box office records everywhere. Skelton's name on the marquee insured long lines at vaudeville houses—no matter what movie was playing or who the "big band" leader was on the bill with him the same week.

That was the era of big bands and often Red appeared on the same bill with the likes of Harry James, Glen Miller, Artie Shaw, Glen Gray, Benny Goodman, or one of the Dorsey Brothers.

One vaudeville engagement that stands out vividly in Skelton's memory was Shea's Buffalo, the week of New Year's Eve in 1939. The movie was *Balaleika*. Skelton was the star of the vaudeville bill. His supporting cast consisted of Burt Lancaster doing an acrobatic act and a little-known singer named Frank Sinatra vocalizing for Harry James and his orchestra.

By the beginning of 1940, Red's act was so sought after that his salary at vaudeville houses was up to $4,300 a week. Sideline personal appearances at nightclubs and county fairs raised his weekly gross to around $7,000, making him suddenly one of the highest paid entertainers in show business.

The inclusion in his act of a brand new piece of material was causing Red to be a sensation. This new routine later became immortalized under the title of "Guzzler's Gin."

For the edification of those unfortunates who've never seen it, "Guzzler's Gin" was a take-off of a radio announcer doing a commercial—for a gin company, with a glass and a bottle of his sponsor's product in hand.

Skelton, dressed neatly in a Brooks Brothers suit complete

with button-down collar, comes on to pitch his product, "Guzzler's Gin." He's full of zest, false heartiness, and sincerity as he sets out to charm his audience. "Guzzler's Gin, folks. A nice, smooth drink." He proves the sincerity of his words by taking a large swallow of the alcoholic beverage he is plugging. "No bad aftertaste, no upsetting of the nerves. Just a nice, smooth drink." He takes a second drink, renders another sales pitch and then introduces the entertainment part of the show—a seedy poet played by himself.

The poet does his thing by reciting his latest poem:

> I bought my girl some garters
> Bought at the 5 and 10;
> She gave them to her mother;
> That's the last I'll see of them.

After the poet does his bit and exits, the announcer returns to deliver another commercial:

"Try Guzzler's, folks," he beseeches his audience with utmost sincerity. He imbibes more of the potent liquid. "Just a nice, smooth—" Suddenly his head jerks to one side as if someone had just massaged it with the heavy end of a Louisville Slugger. Obviously, the gin is taking effect. He clears his head with a brisk shake, then segues into more commercial. He pours more gin from the bottle, winces perceptively, shuts both his eyes and starts to drink, but with such trepidation one would think his throat were lined with broken glass. Now his body starts to tremble, and his eyes take on a glassy look. His complexion turns apple green and bilious. From this moment on, it's just a matter of how long the announcer can last before his job does him in. The more he announces, the more liquor goes down the hatch, and the more inebriated the pitchman becomes. In desperation, he continues to repeat, "a nice smooth drink." As a result, the "smooth" gets smoother and smoother until it is a nice "smooooooooooth drink. . . ."

Suddenly he's a changed man. He not only likes gin, he *loves* it. He can hardly wait for another drink. With shaky hand, he pours gin into a glass. His aim is bad. He misses the glass and pours gin on the table and a lot more on his trousers. With his hand, he desperately sweeps what's left of the gin into his glass. "A nice, smooooooth drink, folks." He gulps it down. From his ecstatic expression, it's evident he wouldn't trade jobs with the President.

Now he's as playful as a baby seal. He squirts gin through his teeth. He fills his mouth again. He gargles with the gin. He loves the taste and he's wild about "Guzzler's Gin." His rubbery expression of joy tells his audience all that. There seems to be no end to his inventiveness in the art of gin drinking. He tips the bottle to his ear and the liquid comes out of his mouth. He stops the flow with his hand and the stream sprays into his nostrils. More gin douses his hand, and his hand suddenly disappears up his coat sleeve. Shocked, he gazes at the empty sleeve. How's he going to get by with only one hand? A lugubrious expression darkens his face. As he stands feeling sorry for himself, tears well up in his eyes, then start running down his face. Miraculously, his hand emerges again as suddenly as it had disappeared. He is overcome with joy. Now there's much to be celebrated. And what better way than by taking another, much larger swig of "Guzzler's Gin" than before. Zow! Now he is thick-tongued. As a result, his booze-sodden sales pitch takes on the tones of a hunter's moose call: "A nice, smooooooooooooooooth drink."

The gin continues its destructive work. Now this gray-flannel-suit, button-down-collar-boy, with the great future in broadcasting, is staggering around the microphone in alcoholic euphoria. On his face is a sublimely idiotic grin as he reels around the stage, swaying, giggling, even starting to hum. His humming begins to sound like a hummingbird's. His face suddenly seems at peace with the world, an expression somewhere between punch-drunk and death. Suddenly he sinks to the floor, sideways, in a magnificent pratfall.

The "Guzzler's" bit became so renowned that when Red was doing it at the Capital Theater in Washington, D.C. early in January of 1940, reports of how funny the red-haired Canadian from Indiana was reached all the way to the man in the White House. With America heading toward war, Roosevelt was in need of a good laugh and he invited Red to perform at his birthday luncheon on January 29—an event that kicked off the annual Infantile Paralysis fund-raising campaign. It was at this luncheon that Red stole the show by taking Roosevelt's glass out of his hand, with the admonition, "Careful what you drink, Mr. President. I once got rolled in a joint like this."

Several weeks later, while Red was wowing audiences with his "Guzzler's" act at the Brooklyn Paramount, the William Morris Agency was trying to sell him for a guest spot on "The Kate Smith Hour," one of the top rated radio shows in the country in 1940. Ted Mack, who booked the talent for Kate Smith, was delighted with the idea of having Red on the show.

His recommendation alone, however, wasn't enough. Before anyone could appear with Kate she would first invite him up to her offices on Forty-second Street and ask him to do his bit for her personally. Since it was supposed to be an honor to appear on "The Kate Smith Hour"—not to mention great national exposure—nobody ever turned Kate down.

But Red's agent at William Morris didn't tell him he was supposed to *audition* for Kate Smith. He thought he'd been invited to her office just to meet her and talk over what he would do on the show.

When Red arrived there, Smith's office was empty except for the lady herself, who was seated regally behind an oversized desk.

After they'd shaken hands and exchanged small talk, Kate Smith regarded Red skeptically and said, "Okay, Mr. Skelton, perform!"

"Perform?"

"Yes. I want to see what you do."

"For one person?" exclaimed Red. "Impossible! I can't do my act for one person."

"If I don't see your act, how'll I know if you're any good?" asked Kate bluntly.

"Go to the theater, like everybody else," shouted Red. And with that he picked up his hat, strode out of the door, and never spoke to Kate Smith again.

A few weeks later, Red was booked into New York's Paramount Theater for two weeks. Sharing the spotlight with him that time were Tommy Dorsey and his orchestra and Lupe Velez.

The program called for them to do fifty-five minutes of stage entertainment before the feature film went on. But there was such a "laugh spread" that the stage show lengthened to sixty minutes by the second day. This was mainly due to the inclusion in Red's act of the "Guzzler's Gin" bit, which New York audiences hadn't seen before.

By the end of the week the stage show was lasting ninety minutes and the projectionist was screaming to Bob Weitman, who managed the New York Paramount at the time, that he didn't have time to complete the motion picture bill which consisted, in addition to the feature, of several short subjects and a newsreel.

Weitman cautioned Red to shorten his act, but whenever Red cut something, audiences complained that that was the bit that they had especially come to see. So Weitman would be forced to let Red put it back in. He made up the time by withdrawing the short subjects and cutting the newsreel in half.

By the second week, Red and his gang weren't satisfied to be doing ninety minutes. After the house darkened and the feature flashed on the screen, the three would skip out on the stage and heckle the movie actors.

Audiences loved it, loved him, loved Lupe Velez, even loved Edna. As a result, they were held over for six record breaking weeks.

One of the things audiences loved about the show was how much fun the actors seemed to be having up there on the stage. Once, for example, one of Tommy Dorsey's musicians put live goldfish in the bottle of water Red was using for his "Guzzler's Gin" act. The people in the first few rows noticed it and started to snicker in anticipation, but Red wasn't aware of the gag until he took a man-sized mouthful and felt two of the little finned monsters starting to slip down his esophagus. He gagged to keep from swallowing them as the audience and the entire Dorsey band went into hysterics. Then he, too, doubled over with laughter.

Red also had fun between shows, but of another kind.

In show business circles, Lupe Velez's reputation for being a nymphomaniac was one of the worst-kept secrets of the century. There was hardly a leading man with whom the "Mexican spitfire" had ever worked that she didn't eventually succeed in luring into her bed, including Mr. Diffidence himself—Gary Cooper, whose child, it's been rumored, she was pregnant with at the time of her suicide years later.

Probably the only one naïve enough not to have heard of Lupe's man-eating reputation was Red. From Edna he had been taught to respect women—also to stay away from them. But how could you stay away from Lupe?

According to Bob Weitman, "Red always used to wear long underwear, the kind with the open window in the back. Frequently that's all he'd have on when he wasn't in costume, backstage between shows. Now invariably, Lupe would see him that way and chase Red—who was kind of proper with the ladies—around with a long stick or a twig, trying to unflap the flap in the back. It was really funny to see Red trying to run away from her," recalls Weitman.

Evidently, Red didn't run fast enough, however, because according to what he later confessed to a friend, one of the highlights of that Paramount engagement was that Lupe and he would bed down together in her dressing room "between shows." They were doing three shows a day at the time.

The affair did have one worthwhile consequence, from which even Edna benefited.

During their successful run at the Paramount, Lupe phoned an old friend in Hollywood, film director Frank Borzage, who was under contract to MGM at the time, and told him that he ought to give Red Skelton a screen test before some other studio grabbed him. "He ees a very funneeee *caballero!*" she pointed out.

Meanwhile, in Louis B. Mayer's office on the West Coast, a young talent scout named Mickey Rooney, who had seen Skelton perform at President Roosevelt's birthday luncheon the previous January, was trying to sell the red-haired comedian to his boss. "You've got to sign him, Uncle Louie," urged Rooney. And with that he related the story of how Red had stolen the show at the birthday luncheon. The gag didn't exactly knock Mayer out of his seat, because jokes at the expense of an authority figure—even one for whom he didn't vote—made him nervous. Being something of an authority figure himself, he identified with the victim.

But when Frank Borzage, a man for whom he had nothing but respect, came to him the following week with raves about the audacious redhead that were even more enthusiastic than Rooney's, Mayer had to pay attention.

"Okay, test him," he grunted.

Not many weeks later Red Skelton was back on a movie set, this time in Culver City, putting on a one-man show for Frank Borzage, the cameramen, and the usual army of grips, lighting men, and electricians, all of whom had seen the best comedians in the world come and go.

Red was not anxious to go. He also was not quite sure what was expected of him, so he threw everything he had ever done before into the test, including two certain show-stoppers—"Guzzler's Gin" and his impression of the soda jerk who is allergic to ice cream.

When his performance fractured the camera crew, and even brought a smile to the hard-boiled Frank Borzage's puss, Red and Edna figured they were in. But between camera setups, Borzage, who was only the instrument—not the final judge—through which Skelton would become a screen star, had some qualms about what the front office brass would think. He suspected that the executives, a hypercritical and bad tempered lot—particularly Louis B. Mayer—might regard Skelton's comedy as too corny for motion picture audiences.

Borzage's criticism didn't make a lot of sense, of course, since Red had made his reputation in vaudeville playing mainly in motion picture houses.

Edna pointed this out, but Borzage was still worried and wondered if perhaps the Skeltons had some "fresher material."

The Skeltons didn't, but faced with flunking out of Hollywood a second time they resorted to a stratagem of stalling, which they reserved for just such emergencies.

Racking her brains, Edna would pull an old idea out of the air and present it to Red as being part of their extensive repertoire. If it didn't strike a chord with Red, he'd shake his head and say, "Naw, I don't feel like doing that number."

Edna would try again, and again, and again, if necessary,

until finally she'd come up with a notion that Red felt he could take off on, ad libbing as he went along. But because most of Red's ad libs were simply new twists on old themes, most of which Borzage was already familiar with, he kept nixing each bit Edna suggested.

Finally, out of desperation, Edna, looking at Red hopefully, gulped, "Maybe Mr. Borzage would like your Dying Heroes routine."

Red looked at Edna blankly. "Do you think he'd like it?" he asked after what seemed like a year's pause.

"I think he'd like it fine," said Edna.

"Well, I don't know."

"Why don't you just try it?"

"It's been so long—" He was fishing for some clue as to what she was talking about.

"Oh, it'll come back to you."

"But I'm not sure if I remember exactly how it starts—"

"Oh, sure you do. You know, you take off on different movie heroes, showing how each one dies. Errol Flynn, Jimmy Cagney, Lionel Barrymore, George Raft flipping a nickel in the air even after he's been machine-gunned down."

"Well, if you think Mr. Borzage would like that kind of thing." As Edna nodded for him to *do something* before they blew it, Red suddenly launched into a completely ad lib Dying Heroes routine that was so side-splittingly funny that it not only clinched the movie deal but was responsible for causing his screen test to become more celebrated than any screen test in the history of the movie business.

So renowned did this bit of film become in the year immediately following that it was written up in a feature article in the *New York Times*—a distinction no screen test before had ever achieved.

Of all the screen tests on file in the Hollywood vaults, Red Skelton's has undoubtedly had the most intensive workout during the past couple of months. Whenever an executive wants to forget his troubles, he has the Skelton test run off. Whenever the publicity department wants to entertain a visiting fireman, out comes the Skelton test. It's infallible. . . .

To have ad libbed a brand new routine on a moment's notice, while standing quaking before a camera and a battery of klieg lights in an unresponsive motion picture sound stage, is a paean to Red's genius as a clown. It also says quite a bit about the smooth teamwork that existed between him and Edna in those days.

Soon after the test, Red was offered a one-picture deal and a chance to play a supporting role in Frank Borzage's next film—*Flight Command,* a service picture starring Robert Taylor, Walter Pidgeon, and Ruth Hussey.

Red played the role of Lieutenant "Mugger" Martin in a picture that most of the nation's critics considered a forgettable one. The *New York Times* labeled it, "A routine adventure film that might appeal to kids," and said, "it is plotted mainly out of clichés."

No mention was made of Richard Red Skelton's contribution. Nevertheless, MGM thought he had a bright future as a film actor and offered him a long-term contract beginning at $1,500 a week, with annual increases if his option were picked up.

The only wrinkle in the deal arose when Red refused to sign his MGM contract until a clause was included permitting him to star in television as well as radio.

This was an unusual request for an unfledged movie star, and not one the Metro brass ordinarily would have granted. But inasmuch as television in 1940 was still in an experimental stage and nobody—particularly movie executives—took it seriously, and certainly not as a threat to films, MGM acceded.

As Skelton later recalled the incident, "L. B. Mayer and the other executives laughed at this request and gave it to me without an argument. However, seven years later they argued themselves blue when I informed them that I was going to make a TV appearance. I reminded them of the clause that they had considered so inconsequential that they laughed at it. Then I laughed."

Although his job as head of MGM brought Mayer into daily contact with some pretty zany characters he had never, before signing Red, run up against anyone with quite so many foibles and eccentricities as Red Skelton. Red couldn't sit still in any kind of a conference for over five seconds. He'd take a shower with a cigar in his mouth. And he refused to talk on the telephone if there was any way of avoiding it. He claimed it confused and frightened him not to be able to see the person on the other end with whom he was talking. "People used to call up and keep asking me to do things and I'd agree," Red once admitted while attempting to explain his unusual ailment, Telephonophobia. "I got into the darndest trouble, promising people things. Some people are just out to take advantage of you. It was terrible."

After this happened a few times, Edna persuaded Red to allow her to take all his phone calls. This arrangement suited Red fine, but it drove Louis B. Mayer right up the wall the first time he had to deal with it.

Soon after Red signed with MGM, the telephone rang in his and Edna's suite at the Hollywood Roosevelt Hotel. Edna, of course, answered it.

The caller turned out to be Red's new boss, Louis B. Mayer. "Mrs. Skelton, let me talk to Red," he snapped officiously.

"Red doesn't talk on the phone, Mr. Mayer," explained Edna. "But he's right here. I'll relay the message."

Mayer made a sound of frustration at the other end. "Do you mean to tell me that Skelton is standing there next to you and knows I'm on the phone and still he won't talk to me?"

"Yes, sir. But that's nothing to do with you. It's because—"

"Tell him to come right over to the studio," demanded Mayer. "And you come along, too."

When Red and Edna arrived in Mayer's office twenty minutes later, the executive was fuming.

"Now you two listen to me," he raged. "It's too soon for you to start going Hollywood on us. Who do you think you are, pulling a gag like that, about not talking on telephones?"

Edna explained that it wasn't a gag—that her husband had an almost psychotic fear of Alexander Graham Bell's device, so she did all his telephone talking for him.

"Do you expect me to believe that?" Mayer asked, turning to Red.

Red just nodded miserably.

Louis B. started to sputter like a steam engine running out of fuel. "Well—but—God dammit—if you don't answer the phone how do you get any business done?"

"That's what Edna's for," explained Red.

Fixing his rat-like eyes on Red, Mayer regarded the comic with the sinister sneer of a calculating D.A. who knows he's about to trap his victim with his next question. "Young man, just let me ask you one more question," he snapped. *"Who answered the telephone before you met Edna?"*

Red gulped uncomfortably, and said, "Before I met Edna, no one ever called me."

7

Edna modestly claims today, "I didn't give Red anything. He was born with it. And he worked hard for what he has." But most people who knew the Skeltons in their struggling years feel that Red wouldn't have made it into the big-time without her and that he was in deadly earnest when he told Mayer nobody ever called him before he married Edna.

Up until the time the Skeltons hit Hollywood, few people in the entertainment world had ever seen a marital arrangement quite so extraordinary—and seemingly successful—as the one they showed to the public.

Edna was not just Red's wife; she was also his mother, pal,

confidante, writer, personal business manager, valet, nurse, press agent, bookkeeper, guardian, straight man, phone answering service, and, yes, even his tutor. During their last years in vaudeville, Edna, recognizing that it might be advantageous for even a comedian to be reasonably literate, took on the additional task of educating Red.

This she did by sending away for a mail order course she had seen advertised in a pulp magazine. She also hired a professional tutor for Red whenever he played one town long enough to make the hiring of one practical. But wherever they were—in a train coach, railroad station, or in a hotel room—when Red had some free time on his hands, she would sit him down and try to drum into him the elementals of reading, writing, grammar, and arithmetic.

Educating him hadn't been easy because Red was completely undisciplined. Moreover, his sense of humor frequently interfered with any serious tutoring; if he didn't know a correct answer, or just didn't feel like applying himself, he would respond with a wisecrack or some physical bit of hi-jinks such as pouring a glass of water over his teacher's head.

Edna, however, was too clever and forceful a personality to be sidetracked by his diversionary tactics for very long. Eventually her doggedness took, and in 1938 Red qualified for a high school diploma.

So, no matter how he had struggled against it, even this thin veneer of an education turned out to be a blessing for Red after he and Edna stopped mingling with the little people of burlesque, circuses, and nightclubs and began to be accepted by Broadway and Hollywood sophisticates.

If these people thought the Skeltons' relationship unusual, they had another surprise in store for them the first time they heard Edna call Red "Junior," and this six-foot-two hulk of a man call his wife "Mummy."

Yet these were their pet nicknames for each other and neither felt the slightest bit of self-consciousness about using them in public.

There have always been two schools of thought as to

whether Red's appellation for Edna had Freudian undertones. On the pro side is the evidence that Mummy sounds a great deal like "Mommy." However, speaking for the non-Freudian camp, Red always claimed that the nickname simply evolved from the fact that Edna used to become so angry with him at times that she would stand before him, completely immobilized, in silent disapproval. Eventually the silent treatment would lead Red to attempt to break the ice with, "Well, say something. Don't just stand there like a mummy!"

First thing Red knew, "Mummy" had become his favorite nickname for Edna and pretty soon even people outside the family were calling her that.

But Mommy or Mummy, Freudian or mere affection, Edna continued to act as Red's right arm—and also his surrogate brain—even after he became a budding star at Metro-Goldwyn-Mayer.

The only change in their relationship after they settled down in Southern California was that Edna quit acting after Red signed with Metro. Of course, she had very little choice in the matter because MGM had no interest in signing Edna to a film contract. First of all, though she certainly wasn't unattractive for a woman approaching thirty, her angular build and Modiglianish nose clearly indicated she was no candidate for being a pin-up girl, either. Added to that, she wasn't much of an acting talent. Even she admitted that. So in a way she was only too happy to use Red's movie career as an excuse to announce her retirement from the stage. Even relieved of her acting chores, Edna still had her hands full as Red's wife and general overseer to his career.

One of the first things Edna had to do after Red signed his seven-year contract was to put him on a diet. To Red's bosses it was an absolute "must" that Red take off the thirty-five pounds he had put on doing his doughnut dunking act three times daily for the past three years. His eating habits off the stage were not conducive to the trim waistline of a movie star, either. From years of traveling, Red had grown fond of good old-fashioned American stick-to-your ribs food like Southern fried chicken with mashed potatoes and thick country gravy, macaroni and cheese, and peanut butter and jelly sandwiches. He even could knock off a dinner-sized portion of pork chops and fried potatoes with his eggs at the breakfast table. In addition, he was no longer a teetotaler, which was also adding to his daily caloric intake.

The exact moment when Red switched from cokes and ice cream sodas to beer, bourbon, and vodka has never been put on record. But there is strong evidence, supplied by the late Marty Rackin—a publicist friend of Red's from his vaudeville days who rose to become production chief of Paramount Studios—that the conversion happened as a result of a practical joke.

"The city slickers always took advantage of this childlike country boy, and that's how he first got on the booze," maintained Rackin. "When Red and I were kids together in vaudeville, he drank nothing but ice cream sodas. Then one night some wiseguy in the Glen Gray orchestra substituted some gin for the water in a glass Red was using for his guzzler routine he did on stage. The tragedy is that he decided he liked the gin better than water—and that's what set him off."

Whether that was the start, or just one of those legends that gets invented and becomes written into history because it makes good telling, the fact is that by the time he and Edna reached Hollywood, Red was a confirmed "social drinker" with more than an average thirst for drinks of high alcoholic content. Moreover, he had the kind of body chemistry that converted alcohol into unbecoming fat rather quickly.

But as a dieter, Red was a wash-out. Instead of cutting down on his food and drink intake he invested in an oversized suit to fool the Metro executives. Whenever Mayer asked him how he was coming along with his diet, Red would say, "Just fine, sir," and pull out the top of his trousers to show him the contrast between them and his old waistline.

He got by with this for a few weeks but when Mayer discovered the ruse he absolutely insisted that Red take his diet dictum seriously. "We hired Red Skelton—not Oliver Hardy!" ranted Mayer. And with that he sent Red off for daily workouts in the MGM gymnasium.

Between the gym workouts and Edna's supervising of his diet, Red dropped enough poundage to mollify the brass. As a reward they gave him a role in a second picture, *The People Versus Dr. Kildare.*

After getting Red trimmed down to performing weight, Edna's next assignment was to go house hunting.

Now that she and Red were through with the vagabond life as vaudevillians and were about to become permanent citizens of the film colony, they were anxious to have their own house with a backyard adorned with fruit trees and flowers, and possibly even a swimming pool, just like the other movie stars.

Like most transplanted Easterners, the Skeltons were attracted to the San Fernando Valley, which was full of small ranches and farms, orange and walnut groves. The Valley also abounded with Hollywood royalty—Clark Gable, Carole Lombard, Barbara Stanwyck, Bob Hope, Robert Taylor, and Fred MacMurray were among the many movie and radio stars who had established roots there.

Houses were cheaper in the Valley, too, which was another consideration.

After considerable hunting, Edna found their "dream ranch," a sprawling bungalow of orange stucco, with lots of tiny rooms, on an acre of sun-baked ground in a section of the Valley named Tarzana—in honor of its first settler and leading citizen, Edgar Rice Burroughs. The place was on Clark Street—not a very posh neighborhood, being surrounded by tract-type homes. But the price was right—about $18,500.

Like most homes in the Valley, the Skelton spread had little to justify the label "ranch" except that it was in the Valley, had a few scraggly citrus trees, some flies from a neighbor's stable, and was fifteen miles away from the glamour oases of Beverly Hills and Hollywood and about twenty miles, over a winding, two-lane road through the Santa Monica Mountains, from MGM. Not an ideal location, one would imagine, for two people who'd never owned an automobile and didn't know how to drive. In their vaudeville days there'd been no necessity for a car—cabs, buses, and subways served them just fine. In Los Angeles, however, it was difficult to survive without an automobile. So not long after they took possession of their new home, the Skeltons bought a car and learned how to drive.

The next pressing thing on the Skeltons' agenda was to put a swimming pool in their backyard.

A swimming pool might seem like an unnecessary expenditure for a man who not only couldn't swim, but still had a deep-rooted fear of water dating back to when he nearly was drowned in a Vincennes gravel pit.

Nevertheless, there were two reasons a pool was of vital importance to Red. First of all, no self-respecting MGM star could rightfully consider himself a movie star without his own swimming pool to pose by when the studio sent a photographer and a bevy of beautiful girls over to take publicity shots. Second, a pool was not actually a luxury but a necessity if you lived in the Valley in pre-air-conditioning days. Valley temperatures often climbed as high as 115 degrees in the summer.

Not wanting to be out of the social swim, Red contacted the Paddock Company and signed a contract for a pool that eventually wound up costing him $20,000. In those days, the best pool in the world didn't run more than $5,000. But Red, despite the poverty of his childhood, has never been one to economize when it comes to luxuries. He was from the school of spending that believes that if you could get a nice pool for $5,000, then you'd get one four times as good for $20,000. So if he had it he spent it, which meant he didn't always have it for long. Which in turn meant he sometimes had to skimp on other things—at least before he became one of America's superstars.

Illustrative of that is an incident recalled by Jack Douglas, who dropped in on Skelton one day in his new home to bring him a housewarming present and, not incidentally, discuss the possibility of writing for him again if Red ever got another radio program. After two years with the Hope Show without a raise, Douglas was becoming fed up.

When Douglas arrived at Skelton's home he found a swimming pool "that seemed to be in the wrong neighborhood, it was so huge and over-decorated with expensive tile work." In the pool, floating around on an inflated rubber mat, with a bottle of bourbon in his hand, was comedian Rags Ragland, a pal of Red's from his burlesque days, who had just signed with MGM for three pictures.

Skelton, however, had no time that day for socializing with Ragland—at least not while Jack Douglas was around. Instead, he was deeply involved in a do-it-yourself home improvement project. Glistening with sweat, Red stood in a suit and tie over by the front of the house, covering its stucco exterior with bricks. Not real bricks—but the kind you paste on in sheets.

"Are you nuts?!" exclaimed Douglas, grinning at Skelton's handiwork. "The house didn't look bad enough before. Now you're pasting on phony bricks. What kind of way is that for a movie star to act?"

Red laughed sheepishly and replied, "I spent so much money on the pool I can't afford real bricks."

Although Red didn't know it at the time, the way his career was about to take off he'd soon be able to afford not only real bricks but the whole brickyard as well.

Red's second film for MGM, *The People Versus Dr. Kildare,* which was released in May of 1941, didn't seem to augur much optimism. The *Kildare* series, though popular, were really just B-picture fillers on the average double bill, and Red's part was so small he wasn't even mentioned in most reviews.

Nevertheless, Red came off so well as a light comedian in the *Kildare* picture that the Metro executives suddenly were convinced they had another Bob Hope on their hands. And even an ersatz Hope wasn't to be sneezed at.

In addition to having the Number One show in radio in 1941, Hope had suddenly blossomed as a movie star. His seventh film for Paramount, *The Cat and the Canary,* in which he co-starred with Paulette Goddard, was proving to be a tremendous money-maker.

Because MGM couldn't have Hope, they figured they had the next best thing in Red Skelton. Red was developing into a very competent, smooth actor. And like Hope, he was becoming tremendously popular with servicemen at the various Army and Navy camps he played around the country. Especially with his "Guzzler's Gin" routine, which was knocking 'em dead everywhere he went.

Since the comedy mystery genre had served Hope so well in

The Cat and the Canary, MGM figured they would serve up Red Skelton in the same kind of broth.

The vehicle they bought for Red was *Whistling in the Dark,* a hit Broadway play about the star of a radio detective series known as The Fox, who is called upon to solve a real murder mystery.

Red played The Fox—but only after Edna gave her approval, another one of her wifely functions.

Ordinarily Louis B. and the other Metro brass pretty much dictated the vehicles for their stars. But to Mayer's annoyance, Red never said "Yes" to any movie script unless Edna read it first, gave it her seal of approval, and then read it aloud to him. Edna recognized a good comedy vehicle when she saw one and except for a few minor suggestions quickly okayed *Whistling in the Dark.*

Although there were moments when Louis B. Mayer often found it annoying, inconvenient, time-consuming and also extremely frustrating to have to deal with Red through Edna, there were some occasions when her influence was cause for rejoicing. These were the times around the studio when Red himself became so contentious or stubborn that nobody but Edna could come up with a solution.

Esther Williams recalls witnessing such an incident during the filming of one of her earliest motion pictures, *Bathing Beauty,* in which Red played the comedy love interest opposite her.

According to Miss Williams, there was a swimming scene shot at poolside that called for Red to appear only in bathing trunks. But when Red strode out on the set in this costume the director, George Sidney, considered the thick carpet of red hair on Skelton's chest too unsightly to photograph.

"That'll have to come off," said Sidney, pointing to Red's hairy chest.

"What will?"

"All that red hair on your chest, Red. You'll have to shave it off. It'll look lousy on the screen."

Red shook his head and said absolutely not. It had taken him thirty years and plenty of applications of Vigoro to acquire such a luxurious growth. Sidney said he had to—it would ruin the picture. Red said he didn't care. Sidney said he was the director—Red had to do what the director ordered. Red said he'd take it to a higher court. Sidney said there was no one higher than the director—he was the last court of appeal. Red said then he'd take it to a lower court. Sidney said he'd report him to Mayer, who'd put him on suspension. Red still resisted; no one was going to make him shave off his hirsute symbol of manliness. He sat down in the director's chair and pretended to be reading the script.

Finally an assistant director had the inspiration to phone Edna. Perhaps she could get him to listen to reason.

"Just offer Red $200," was Edna's advice. "He'll shave it off."

The offer was made forthwith and accepted, the cash exchanged hands, and five minutes later Red was blithely posing before the cameras with an absolutely naked chest as if he didn't have a care in the world.

Ordinarily, Red wasn't difficult, according to most people who knew him and worked with him on the MGM lot. He was mild-mannered and polite. He was usually the first one on the set in the morning. He always knew his part. And, unlike a lot of stars, he didn't have to learn his lines through the torturesome process of blowing one take after another until the dialogue finally sank in.

If a piece of physical business was needed to fill an awkward gap in the script, Red could usually invent it on the spot, and more often than not it would turn out to be the most delightful thing in the finished film.

Joseph J. Cohn, one of a triumvirate—Louis B. Mayer, Eddie Mannix, and himself—which made most of Metro's important decisions in those days, remembers seeing many examples of Red's inventiveness. "When he was making, I believe it was the first *Whistling* picture," remembers Cohn, "there was a sequence that called for Red to be chased by the heavies, in the course of which one of them was shot and killed. The death was necessary to the plot, but it seemed awfully serious for a light comedy.

"Then Red thought of just the right touch to lighten it up and at the same time accomplish what the script called for. As the heavy keeled over and expired, Red stopped running, took his hat off his head and solemnly held it over his heart for a moment in memoriam to the man who'd just tried to kill him. Not to be outdone, the two remaining heavies stopped the chase long enough to place *their* hats over *their* hearts. As they did, Red sprinted off and the chase continued. Only Red would have thought of that, and it got us a nice laugh just where we needed it."

Besides being inventive, Red kept the cast and crew constantly entertained between takes with his incessant clowning and joke-telling. No gag was too outrageous for him to pull. One rainy day, for example, he stepped out of the sound stage onto the studio street just as a group of rubbernecks on a tour of the studio came by. The fans recognized Red and looked at him hopefully, as if imploring him to "do something funny."

Red obliged by taking a forward pratfall into a mud puddle—and completely ruining a $300-Marianni & Davies custommade suit he was wearing for the first time.

One of the little white lies that Red has always tried to foster throughout his career is that he never had to rely on ribald language or dirty jokes to get a laugh. "Not even when I was playing burlesque," he once told a magazine biographer. "You can always get a big laugh with a dirty joke, but often the people are laughing out of embarrassment."

Red may have been against vulgarity in theory, but evidence indicates he rarely practiced what he preached about ribaldry. Red hadn't been a member of the Metro Stock Company very long before he had acquired an almost Rabelaisian reputation for his extensive vocabulary of four-letter words and a penchant for entertaining the cast between takes with the filthiest dirty jokes imaginable.

"I think I learned every four-letter word I've ever heard from Red," recalls Esther Williams, who was a young, and presumably virginal, girl of twenty when she made *Bathing Beauty* with him. "He used the filthiest language on the set imaginable. He'd shock me so I'd go back to my dressing room and cry."

Like many performers, Red used ribald language not so much for its shock value as to ease the tension that he felt building up within himself as the time to film a scene approached. Despite his clowning around on the set and his outwardly easygoing appearance, Red has always been a bundle of nerves when he's about to put his performing to the ultimate test before a movie camera or a television audience.

Red's lack of confidence should have been laid to rest once and for all with the release of *Whistling in the Dark*, which opened at Loew's Criterion in New York City on August 28, 1941, and became the surprise hit of the year. And while many of the nation's critics found enormous similarities between Skelton's style of comedy and Bob Hope's, this didn't seem to stop any of them from rushing to their typewriters and pounding out rave reviews about the picture, which in addition to Skelton's portrayal of "The Fox," featured Ann Rutherford in the romantic lead opposite him, and a supporting cast of Conrad Veidt, Virginia Grey, Eve Arden, and Rags Ragland.

The nation's most influential reviewer, Bosley Crowther of the *New York Times*, while not bowled over by the plot of *Whistling in the Dark*, was ebullient in his praise of Red's comedy skills. He began his review with:

> To the cheerfully swelling list of bright new film comedians you may add the rosy name of Richard (Red) Skelton. For Metro has really turned up an impressive young Bob Hopeful in the person of this jaunty chap with wavy blond hair and wild expressions.

And he ended by writing:

> To Mr. Skelton it is a pleasure to extend a warm welcome. And it is comforting to have him on hand. The screen needs smooth comics like this one. While there is Hope, there's Skelton, too.

Time magazine's review, the week of September 8, while allowing that *Whistling in the Dark* was not the "funniest picture to come out of Hollywood," singled out Red Skelton as being the best of the up-and-coming young comics.

As proof that Red had finally made it, *Time* also devoted two full columns to an account of his rise from circus clown to his present position of eminence as a Metro-Goldwyn-Mayer star, crediting a large assist to his wife Edna.

With *Whistling in the Dark* such a rousing success, and with so many of the nation's movie critics putting Red on the same comedic plateau as Bob Hope, it was inevitable that Freeman Keyes would soon be able to provide him with a coast-to-coast radio show of his own.

The sponsor that put in its bid first was Raleigh Cigarettes, another of Freeman Keyes' advertising accounts. A relatively new product, Raleigh Cigarettes was badly in need of national exposure if it expected to make a dent in the highly competitive tobacco market, which at the time was virtually monopolized by Camel, Lucky Strike, and Chesterfield.

And what better way to sell a new product than with a fresh face named Red Skelton fronting for it. Of course, Red never touched cigarettes and when he did sully his mouth with tobacco, it was only to chew on an unlighted cigar, a prop with which he was fast becoming identified.

Raleigh bought the Skelton show, officially announced as "The Red Skelton Scrapbook of Satire," for $15,000 per week for a firm thirty-nine weeks. That figure included Red's salary of $2,-500 a week, plus the emoluments of Ozzie Nelson, the orchestra leader; his wife and vocalist, Harriet Hilliard; and the writers, who at the show's inception consisted of Edna; Jack Douglas, who finally managed to get away from Bob Hope; and Benedict Freedman, who at nineteen, was considered the youngest gag man in the business.

Fifteen years later Ben Freedman would quit writing gags for Skelton to become a novelist with his wife, Nancy. Together they wrote the best-selling novel, *Mrs. Mike,* and another one called *Lootville,* which just happened to be about a red-haired television comedian.

"But when I went to work for Red in 1941, I was really sort of a junior writer," recalls Freedman. "Jack Douglas had been hired to be 'head writer,' but Edna actually functioned as head writer, because she took over completely, even though she couldn't write.

"There was another writer, too, when I first joined the show. But I can't remember who he was, it's so long ago. He wasn't anyone who ever became a name, I don't think. Another reason I can't remember any other writers except Douglas is that after our first script conference, Edna wouldn't let any of the writers see each other. She resented Douglas trying to assert himself and dominate Red with his ideas. . . . I guess because she had been the one who guided Skelton to where he was, and she was the one who helped mold his characters in the beginning, and she was jealous of anyone else influencing him.

"So the first script conference was actually the last script conference where the writers and Edna and Red all got together and made suggestions."

From then on, the mechanics of preparing the show would go something like this, according to Freedman.

The format of the show was the same every week. It would open with Red's monologue, usually consisting of topical jokes about political things or other items in the news. That would be followed by a band number and song, along with some cute banter between Red and Ozzie and Harriet. And for the final spot Red would rely on his various characterizations—Junior, the "mean widdle boy," whose favorite phrase was "I dood it"; Clem Kadiddlehopper; San Fernando Red, the politician; Cauliflower McPugg, the punchdrunk prize fighter; and any other new characters the writers might come up with.

Before any writing was done, however, Edna would assemble a rough draft—actually a dummy script—of what she believed the finished script ought to be, inserting old jokes and routines to indicate where she wanted certain things. "And it would really be rough," recalls Freedman. "There'd be blank pages with perhaps one joke on them. Then she'd hand out her version to the writers, and it would be up to us to fill in the blank pages and replace the old jokes with new ones, while sticking to her basic format. Sometimes, if there was a particular old joke that was a favorite of Red's that he wanted to do that week, we'd have to write up to it or around it.

"Each writer would then do an entire script by himself. When they had finished, their material would be funnelled back to Edna, who, with some input from Red, would select what she considered the best material from everybody's script and paste it all together in one master script."

"The scripts would be in terrible shape by the time they went to mimeo," recalls Jack Douglas. "And no wonder! Christ,

I'd go over there to deliver a routine or something, and I'd see Skelton on the floor, cutting and pasting things. And he cut so quickly with the scissors you knew damn well he was probably cutting off the most important lines in the whole routine. As you've probably heard, he wasn't much of a reader anyway. When I'd go over to the house and he and I and Edna would be sitting around his great big dining room table he'd want me to read the stuff aloud because he couldn't read it. Not couldn't, but it would take him a lifetime to read four pages. And he'd laugh at everything. Even the stuff he hated."

The rejected material would be stored for future use in his and Edna's joke files. "They had files like nobody's ever had," continues Douglas. "Every joke and routine was filed and cross-filed under its correct category: doctors, lawyers, plumbers, marriage, children, politics, etc. I never saw the inside of their files, but I remember they had those big steel filing cabinets all over the joint."

"The rejected material wasn't necessarily bad or faulty," explains Freedman. "It was simply that Red was suspicious of anything new, didn't always understand the humor of it right away. He might have to mull it over for a couple of weeks or perhaps months. Later he'd pull it out of the joke file and offer it as something he'd just originated and put it in the script and then say, 'Now why can't you guys come up with something like that?' If any of us dared say we already had, he'd blow his stack."

After all the material was compiled and put into one overly-long master script, there'd be a preview performance in front of a live audience a couple of hours before the actual broadcast. A preview show was routine on most radio shows during the days of live broadcasting because it was really the only way to pre-test the material and insure against going coast-to-coast with a bomb show. The jokes that got laughs remained in; those that didn't were cut and perhaps new ones substituted between the preview and broadcast time.

"If something we'd written happened to get an extra big laugh," recalls Douglas, "Red would generally ad lib, 'Glad I thought of that one.' If something didn't get a laugh, the writer who had thought of it might not be around long."

According to Douglas, one of the things that made it hard to assess the material beforehand was that at a first reading "Red would laugh at anything, which really gave you nothing to go on. So we could never tell whether he liked the stuff or didn't like it. Also, he was very stubborn about material sometimes. I used to say before a preview, 'Try it, for God sakes, and see what happens.' Then he'd take a joke and go out there and dog it deliberately and nothing would happen. Then he'd come back after the preview and say 'See, I told you it wouldn't work.'

"That was the difference between Red and Hope. Hope would go out there and give it everything he had. If it died, you'd know it was the joke's fault."

Judging from the way Red Skelton's "Scrapbook of Satire" was received by the American public, the jokes didn't "die" very often.

"The Scrapbook of Satire" was first broadcast from NBC's Hollywood studios, on the corner of Sunset and Vine, at 7:30 P.M. one Tuesday night in October of 1941. The reason for the early time slot was that Skelton's "Scrapbook," like most shows broadcast from the West Coast, was aimed at the more populous Eastern market, which received it at 10:30 P.M. Eastern Standard Time, immediately following Bob Hope's "Pepsodent Show."

The reviews were mixed, but then Skelton had never really appealed to the literati, who preferred the more sophisticated humor of Fred Allen, Bob Benchley, and Jack Benny.

But as far as the general public was concerned, Red Skelton could do no wrong. The audience in NBC's Studio A was in convulsions at Skelton's antics from his opening "warm-up," which was liberally sprinkled with pratfalls and mugging (as was the rest of the show), to his closing joke on the air. Amazingly, the radio audiences at home, who couldn't see Skelton, and therefore were unable to appreciate his sight humor, enjoyed the show almost as much as the people in Studio A. Even when a sight gag was taking place, the listening audience seemed to sense Red was doing something funny and would laugh right along with the studio audience. There was enough audio material, too, in his monologue and various characterizations to keep the folks at home in convulsions most of the time. For example, his "mean widdle boy," spouting the distressing phrase "I dood it," immediately won the hearts of middle-America when Red unveiled him for the first time in October of 1941.

An enormous help to Red that season, and the subsequent ones that they were with him, was the presence in the cast of Ozzie and Harriet Nelson.

Originally, this pair had been hired for what they could contribute musically. And this they did very well. Ozzie was one of the top band leaders in America and when paired with his vocalist wife, the former Harriet Hilliard, they were one of America's favorite singing combinations.

But when it became apparent to the show's writers that Ozzie and Harriet could also handle a bright line, they were soon doing more than just singing duets to America.

"Ozzie did all the male 'straights' for Red," recalls Harriet Nelson today, "and I did all the female 'straights' for him. In other words, if he did Clem Kadiddlehopper, I did Daisy June, obviously. And when he did Junior, I did Junior's mother. And whenever he worked with a man, he worked with Ozzie. For instance, Ozzie used to do the drunk along with Red when he did the two drunks together. In those days you doubled in brass. But I'll tell you one thing—it was an education in comedy to work with Red."

Within a month of the show's initial airing, the name Red Skelton was a household word; "I dood it" became a national catch phrase as frequently repeated as Joe Penner's "Wanna buy a duck?"; and the show established itself in the first ten national radio programs in the Hooper ratings.

Of course, it didn't hurt Skelton any that his "Scrapbook of Satire" was in the time slot immediately following Bob Hope—the Number One rated show in the land in 1941—and on the same network. Only a total disaster couldn't survive with such a high-powered lead-in. All that notwithstanding, Red Skelton had to be considered a major factor in making Tuesday night a time when most Americans wouldn't leave their homes and radios even to see the president. In fact, the Skelton meteor was rising so fast by the end of 1941 that nothing could stop Red—not even World War II.

By then he was so much in the public consciousness that when American planes, with General Doolittle in command, made their daring raid on Tokyo on April 18, 1942, the nation's headline writers printed, almost to a man:

DOOLITTLE DOOD IT!

On the day—December 7, 1941—that the Japanese were attacking Pearl Harbor, Red Skelton was standing at the front door of Gene Fowler's house, holding a copy of *The Great Mouthpiece*, which he was going to ask its author (whom he had never met) to autograph. Opening the front door, Fowler recognized Skelton, invited him in, and autographed the book for him. The two hit it off immediately, for each was an admirer of the other's work. Red stayed for about an hour, which was the beginning of a friendship that was to last until Fowler's death.

Hearing the news about the bombing of Pearl Harbor over the radio, Red rushed home to Edna, with the announcement that he wanted to join the Marines. He really didn't have to volunteer, for he was twenty-eight now and also married, so there was little danger of his being drafted, at least not in the immediate future. But Red was patriotic enough to want to do something for the country that had done so much for him.

Before Red could volunteer for the Marines, however, Louis B. Mayer got wind of his intentions and frantically summoned him to his office. There Uncle Louis sat Red down in a comfortable chair, bribed him with a dollar cigar, and then proceeded to give him a fatherly talk, the upshot of which was that Red could do more good for the war effort by remaining a civilian and entertaining the troops at the various service camps around the country. Keeping up "our boys' " morale, pointed out Mayer, was just as important as shooting a gun.

So Red deferred to the elder man's self-serving wisdom, and went on with his movie and radio careers, as well as doubling at camp entertaining, which was certainly more beneficial to Red financially than joining the Marines. Between movies, radio, and personal appearances, Red was earning an income in the neighborhood of $12,000 a week by 1942. Ample, it would seem, considering the average GI was only making fifty bucks a month. But wartime taxes took a large cut: 75 percent, and sometimes higher, give or take a few percentage points for business deductions. That meant that Red's take-home pay was considerably less than what he imagined he was making after reading in the "trades" how well he was doing. Which in turn meant that Red was in the red more often than he was in the black.

Part of the trouble was Red himself.

Even when he was grossing $3,000 a year instead of $300,000 Red had an almost childlike disregard for the value of money. As far as he was concerned it was for spending, not hoarding. At one time he had over 200 ties in his closet, all the same color: maroon. Why maroon? Because he liked maroon ties and didn't want to run out.

He'd order twenty-five custom-made suits at a time from the most expensive tailoring establishment in Beverly Hills—Marianni and Davies—then proceed to destroy them in a couple of months because he insisted on wearing a double-breasted suit while digging in the garden or doing a slapstick routine on stage that might require him to get soaked with paint or whitewash. His excuse for such profligacy was, "I'm just making up for when I couldn't afford to own pants that match the coat."

He paid two dollars apiece for the finest Havana cigars, but never smoked them—just chewed on one end for a few minutes and then dropped it into the gutter.

If Edna didn't keep an eye on Red's spending every moment, money would slip through his fingers like dry sand. When he first came into the blue chips Edna put Red on a fifty-dollar-a-week allowance. But after he was an important movie star he was no longer satisfied with that amount. To mollify him Edna placed $5,000 in a checking account for his personal use, the only condition being that he fill out each check stub properly and keep accurate track of his expenditures.

Five days later the bank phoned Edna to inform her that Red had overdrawn his checking account. That evening when Red came home from the studio Edna snatched the checkbook and examined the stubs. On them were such notations as: "For darned foolishness." "For rotten food." "Really wasted." On one entry for $1,000 Red had scrawled, "None of your business."

Until then Edna figured she was all the management Red would ever need to keep their financial house in order. Now she decided to put themselves in the hands of a professional business manager—not just to keep a rein on foolish spending, but to invest their money wisely so that they would have a financial cushion for the future.

From everything Edna had heard from other Metro stars who were his clients, Bo (pronounced "Boo") Christian Roos seemed to be just such a man.

Tall and heavyset, with dark hair and a moustache and a penchant for flamboyant clothes and mannerisms—he was one of the first to have a telephone in his car—Roos was considered the top business manager for people in the entertainment industry. From his offices on Camden Drive in Beverly Hills, Roos—with the help of a large staff of accountants—handled the financial affairs of about sixty important Hollywood high-earners, including John Wayne, Merle Oberon, Rita Hayworth, Orson Welles, Peter Lawford, and Fred MacMurray.

The name of Red Skelton was soon added to Roos's list of celebrated clients, to the mutual benefit of both parties.

Not only did Roos find tax shelters that enabled the Skeltons to keep Uncle Sam from eating everything they earned, but he put them into all kinds of profitable investments: oil wells in Bakersfield; a frozen food company; a dry cleaning establishment; a film studio in Mexico; income property in the high rent district on Wilshire Boulevard; and a hotel in Culver City.

As their relationship grew closer, Roos also took over as negotiator for most of Red's show business dealings, virtually eliminating the necessity for Red to have an agent.

Like Edna before him, Bo Roos also found it wise to put Red on a weekly allowance. It was the only way of coping with Red's penchant for carrying thousands of dollars in cash around with him.

Now that he was making big money Red felt he was entitled to walk into Tiffany's or some other purveyor of luxury items and buy a $10,000-bauble, or anything else that struck his fancy, simply by reaching into his pocket and pulling out the cash. And while Edna had convinced him a business manager was a necessary evil, he nevertheless resented having to ask Roos if he could afford it before he bought an expensive trinket, and this led to many an argument between the two.

Once, after a stormy fight in which Roos absolutely refused to release another dollar of spending money until the following week, he received a frantic distress call from the Hollywood police. "Mr. Roos," said the cop, "you'd better get down to the corner of Hollywood and Vine right away. Mr. Skelton is causing a traffic jam."

"What the hell are you talking about?" asked Roos, not anxious to take the eight-mile jaunt from Beverly into Hollywood.

"Never mind. Just come down here. We can't do a thing with him."

When Roos arrived at Hollywood and Vine he found the intersection swarming with people. In the center of the mob was Skelton's car, with Red sitting blithely on top of it in a director's chair, surrounded by large signs reading:

DOWN WITH BUSINESS MANAGERS
I WANT MORE SPENDING MONEY
75 CENTS FOR A TOUR OF MOVIE STARS' HOMES
CONDUCTED BY YOURS TRULY.

Frustrated policemen were trying to clear the streets and sidewalks but the throng wasn't paying attention. The fans were too busy trying to get Red's autograph and signing up for the offered tour.

Roos was the only person Red would listen to. And after considerable bargaining, they finally reached a *quid pro quo* agreement. Roos would raise Red's allowance to seventy-five dollars a week and Red would refrain from pulling any more stunts that would embarrass his business manager or otherwise harass him.

On the surface the Vine Street caper would seem nothing more than a crass publicity stunt. But Red claimed at the time that publicity had nothing to do with it. That was the way he really felt.

As Roos was swiftly learning, it was not easy to have a lasting relationship with a man as strange and inscrutable as his new client was.

How difficult Red was to live with was nothing new to Edna. Almost from the first day of their marriage she had been aware of the one show business truth—that being married to a comedian is no laughing matter. But their years of trying to get to the top had been filled with excitement, too, and that made up for the fact that life with Red wasn't always easy—or fun, either. Besides, she loved the big redheaded lunk with the heart of gold and had been willing to overlook his childish ways, which included moodiness and a hair-trigger temper, because she believed he loved her just as much and needed her advice and guidance.

But now that Junior had become Red Skelton the movie and radio star, he seemed to have lost that need for a "Mummy." Like a kid just reaching puberty, Red had suddenly discovered that there was a large world out there away from home—a world full of beautiful girls, booze, and other delicious temptations. And he wanted to taste them all.

When Edna was working with Red as a performer there had been little opportunity for Red to step out on her. Wherever Red went, Edna was sure to be close behind.

But in Hollywood it was a different story. At the studio he was thrown in daily contact with some of the world's most attractive women. Either he'd be working with one or he'd be mingling with beautiful creatures on the set between camera setups or sitting down to lunch with them in the commissary at the noon break. In any case, it was just a short step from those "business" relationships to desiring some of that same action after hours.

After hours, at Hollywood parties, there were more opportunities to get on familiar terms with unattached starlets. Now that Red's career was on the ascendency girls gravitated toward him. And why not? He was rich, cute looking, a barrel of laughs, and like most men, receptive to all kinds of female flattery. Especially after he'd had a few drinks.

As time went on in Hollywood, the "few" drinks became "many." "In the beginning," remembers Edna today, "Red never drank at all. It used to be our biggest private laugh that even though he didn't drink he did such great drunk imitations that drunks just gravitated towards him at parties because they thought he was one of them."

After the Skeltons became regulars on the Hollywood cocktail hour circuit, Edna realized that Red wasn't always just imitating a drunk—frequently he was one. Once he had made the switch from sodas to alcoholic beverages, Red acquired a prodigal appetite for the stuff. According to friends and associates of his during this period, Red didn't drink "like ordinary people." He could put a whole bottle of vodka to his lips and down three-quarters of it without coming up for air. Or he could knock off four gin martinis, downing them one after another, in about ten seconds flat.

"That was one of my reasons for wanting to get away finally," recalls Edna, with genuine sadness in her voice. "I refused to stand by and be a party to going down with him. I felt it could have been stopped but I didn't seem to be the one who could stop it."

Nobody knows with any certainty what was making Red

drink heavily, but it could be attributed to a variety of things. Possibly it was in his genes; after all, his father died of alcoholism. Perhaps alcohol bolstered his self-confidence when he was out socially. But more likely than anything, booze probably gave Red the courage to make the break from Edna, whom he'd feel guilty about leaving.

Red was still fond of her platonically and he admittedly needed her guidance in business. He was also grateful for what she'd already done in helping him reach the top. On the other hand, she was not as soft and cuddly as other girls and there was a little too much of the efficient "business manager" in her makeup. His sudden and unexplained preference for the pin-up kind of girl no doubt filled him with all kinds of guilt feelings, which he tried to assuage with booze.

Red started staying away from home later and later in the evenings. Sometimes he wouldn't blow in until early in the morning, more often than not with liquor on his breath and lipstick on his shirt collar.

"His excuses were really corny," complained Edna at the time.

Once, for example, when Red didn't arrive back in Tarzana until four in the morning, Edna was waiting up for him at the door. And when she heatedly asked him where he'd been, Red raised his right hand like a Boy Scout and said, "You probably won't believe this, Mummy, but I spent the night on Sunset Boulevard waiting for a red light to change."

Edna *didn't* believe it. In fact, she gave him the "mummy" treatment for several weeks, at the end of which Red promised to be a good boy. But the temptations of the flesh in Hollywood were just too great. In 1942 when Red was making *Du Barry Was a Lady* at MGM, he got a crush on one of the showgirls in the picture—a blond, leggy thirty-year-old named Muriel Morris Chase. A former "Sweater Girl" model for a clothing concern, Muriel was on the rebound from a defunct marriage to a Los Angeles businessman named Eugene Chase.

To Muriel, who was out to make a name for herself as a film actress, it was no trouble at all to bounce right into the arms of the star of the picture.

Red tried to keep his entanglement quiet but when their names became linked in the gossip columns and Edna found out about it, she unhappily concluded she'd stayed too long at the fair. As fond as she still was of Red, and as reluctant as she was to make the break, Edna decided she could not stand by and be publicly humiliated any longer. She filed suit for divorce in the Los Angeles Superior Court on December 28, 1942. Edna charged him with the standard complaint of "mental cruelty."

To established citizens of tinsel town, the Skelton divorce came as no surprise. It was a rerun of an old and predictable Hollywood potboiler: Struggling Actor, who finally strikes it rich, tires of First Wife, who stuck with him during his lean years, and trades her in for a Newer and Sexier Model.

What wasn't predictable was the friendly, almost Noel Cowardish manner in which the whole split was accomplished once Red and Edna had talked it over, and he had moved out of the house and taken up residence in the Beverly Wilshire Hotel.

There was no bitterness on either of their parts—no accusations in the headlines. What Red told the press at the time of the divorce announcement was absolutely true. He and Edna were still extremely fond of each other—they just didn't wish to remain man and wife any longer. But they would continue to be good friends and see each other often. As proof of this, Edna would continue handling Red's business affairs and to give him advice when he needed it.

For these services he would continue to pay Edna 50 percent of his income and give her half-interest in all of his holdings.

Once the financial arrangements were agreed upon and put into writing, Edna's attorney, Frank Belcher, submitted the document to the court, who awarded her an interlocutory decree in February of 1943. In those days it would take a year for a California divorce to become final.

So amicable were the proceedings that Red came to the courtroom in the Federal Building in downtown Los Angeles on the day Edna received the interlocutory decree and waited in the corridor, fidgeting and peering into the judicial chamber to see how Edna was getting along. Afterwards, he took Edna by the arm, led her out of the courthouse, then drove her to a good restaurant where the two of them had lunch together.

Now that Red's domestic affairs were temporarily in order he could get his mind back on his work—that is, until he got drafted. He'd lost his deferment in the divorce court.

As a civilian, however, he was doing his part for the war effort. From December 7, 1941, until he was inducted in 1944, Red put on over 3,000 camp show performances at Army, Navy, and Marine bases in various parts of the U.S. He also shortwaved weekly radio programs over Armed Forces Radio to servicemen in the European and South Pacific theaters of the war.

Simultaneously, he continued full speed ahead with his radio and movie careers. Judging from the frequency of Skelton films off the Metro assembly line between 1941 and 1944, the powers who were paying Red his salary seemed to be deliberately trying to wear out his welcome with the public.

Between 1941 and 1944 Red Skelton either starred, co-starred, or played a large supporting role in eleven more Metro films which included: *Dr. Kildare's Wedding Day* (with Lew Ayres and Lionel Barrymore); *Lady Be Good* (with Ann Sothern and Robert Young); *Whistling in Dixie* (with Ann Rutherford and Rags Ragland); *Du Barry Was a Lady* (with Lucille Ball, Rags Ragland, and Zero Mostel); *Thousands Cheer* (with Gene Kelly and Kathryn Grayson starring, and Mickey Rooney and Red playing comedy roles); *I Dood It* (with Eleanor Powell); *Whistling in Brooklyn* (with Ann Rutherford and Rags Ragland); and *Bathing Beauty* (with Esther Williams.)

Most of these films were successful at the box office—practically any film was during the boom years of World War II, which was why the majors kept grinding them out so unremittingly. But as far as the critics were concerned, they ranged in quality from poor to pretty good, with just a few out of the eleven actually pleasing them enough to be recommended to their readers. *Du Barry Was a Lady,* adapted from the Cole Porter Broadway musical which starred Ethel Merman and Bert Lahr, was far and away the most outstanding of the bunch.

In the Metro version, lavishly produced in technicolor by Arthur Freed and directed by Roy Del Ruth, Red played King

Louis to Lucille Ball's Du Barry. The combination of Lucy and Red had even the critics rolling in the aisles. "They have caught the humor of the original, with lots of Red Skelton's own thrown in," wrote the *New York Times* on August 20, 1943. "And they have added Rags Ragland and Zero Mostel to be funny when Mr. Skelton is not, which isn't very often, providing Mr. Skelton is on the screen."

Another Skelton picture that both the public and the *New York Times* enjoyed was *Bathing Beauty*. In this film Red portrayed a song writer who becomes a student at a girl's seminary in order to be near his wife, played by Esther Williams in her first important role on dry land. The results, if not hilarious, tickled enough ribs of Skelton and Williams fans to make it a hit.

Not so the sequels to *Whistling in the Dark—Whistling in Dixie* and *Whistling in Brooklyn*. These were hollow retreads of the original, as most sequels are. Both films were as uninspired in conception as they were in execution, although Red Skelton had some funny moments—particularly in a sequence in *Whistling in Brooklyn* when he somehow found himself in a baseball uniform and on the mound at Ebbet's Field, having to pitch against the Brooklyn Dodgers. "The rest of the doings are mildly amusing, but most are just plain nonsense," wrote the *New York Times* on March 24, 1944. "Better luck next time, folks."

The *Kildare* series, in which Red played a running character named Carlton Briggs, were not actually Skelton pictures. Casting Red in them was just the means by which Metro could amortize his large weekly salary when the studio heads couldn't find a proper vehicle in which to star him. But the series did nothing for his career beyond giving him dubious acting experience.

Maisie Gets Her Man, another Metro B-picture produced mainly for the purpose of filling bills, was another film that didn't utilize Red's talent to any extent. In fact, critics labeled it a disaster that even the presence of Red Skelton couldn't prevent.

Panama Hattie, taken from another Broadway musical, and produced by the same Metro team who brought America *Du Barry Was a Lady*, laid such a huge egg when it opened in New York on October 6, 1942, that the *New York Times* reviewer had to lapse into "nursery rhyme" in order to capture its full flavor:

Panama Hattie was finished last fall. At several sneak previews it cast a great pall. Metro revised it with scissor and pen, but couldn't put *Panama Hattie* back together again.

Finally, *I Dood It,* co-starring Skelton and Eleanor Powell, and directed by Vincente Minnelli, seemed to be little more than a blatant attempt on Metro's part to capitalize on the expression Red had made world-famous. As part of the publicity build-up for the film, the studio (in collaboration with the United States government) even had Red present a warplane to the Soviet Navy, and the plane was christened the Russian equivalent of "We dood it."

The picture succeeded in its mission of keeping the phrase "I dood it" before the public, but that was about all it accomplished. Wrote the *New York Times:*

> A lot of responsibility has been piled on Red Skelton's head by Metro in *I Dood It*. And that is to carry the whole picture, with a moderate assist from Eleanor Powell. The task is inhumanly on-erous, considering the tonnage of the load, and the title of the film.
>
> For the boy is a very funny fellow—you've got to hand him that—and when the moment requires inspiration, he would break his leg for a laugh.

Whether critics liked a film or hated it, the one recurrent theme in the reviews was that Skelton, in spite of having to carry one bad script after another, and usually without much help, was consistently a very funny fellow on the screen.

Considering the caliber of Skelton's early films, it's a wonder that MGM didn't succeed in killing off his motion picture career before it even got started. It's also a pretty good barometer of just how much American audiences needed to laugh in those bleak days of wartime shortages and American military defeats in the middle years of World War II.

Where was Edna while Red was getting bogged down in so many vacuous pictures? Why hadn't she been around to advise and consent, to pre-digest the scripts for Red and turn thumbs up or thumbs down on them, as the writing warranted? Had she lost interest in managing Red now that their divorce was about to become "final"?

In actuality, quite the opposite was true. He was as dependent on her for business advice as he ever was. Unfortunately, the czars running Metro could be fairly dictatorial when it came to choosing the "right" vehicles for their contract stars. Edna might offer Red her advice, but they held the purse strings and could put him on suspension for refusing to accept a role. So the upshot was that when Uncle Louie told Red he knew what was "best" for him, Red and Edna paid attention.

Edna, however, was still supervising Red's radio show, still acting as liaison between him and the press, and—along with Bo Roos—still managing his financial affairs when her divorce from Red became final on February 17, 1944.

In fact, Edna was still so much in Red's picture that it was beginning to be of considerable concern to Muriel Morris.

About a month after the divorce became final Red, with Muriel hanging on his arm, turned up at the Los Angeles County Hall of Records and applied for a marriage license. They wanted to get married that night.

"Where's your Health Certificate?" asked the clerk.

Red didn't know what the lady was talking about.

"The blood test," explained the clerk. "You can't get married without a blood test signed by your doctor. And that'll take three days."

"I thought you took the blood right here," complained Red.

"No, Mr. Skelton, your doctor has to do that. See you in three days."

Three days later, on a Friday, the frustrated lovers again turned up at the Hall of Records, this time with the medical documents that entitled them to get a license.

Their plans were to get married, in a private ceremony, the following Monday. Over the weekend, however, Muriel began having second thoughts, especially after the phone rang several times and it was Edna wanting to speak with Red about business.

Muriel was furious. She said she loved Red, but there was one thing about him she didn't understand—how could he be so helpless and babyish that he had to have his ex-wife managing his affairs and doling out spending money to him? Muriel resented it. Furthermore, she was jealous.

Red assured Muriel that it was purely a "business arrangement"—there was absolutely nothing to be jealous about. But the statuesque blond wouldn't buy that. "Either Edna goes or I go," she shouted at Red in their final showdown.

As far as Red was concerned, there was no contest. Muriel went.

And soon after that, so did Red—right into the Army. Without a wife, he lost his draft exempt status. And when that happened, not even the powerful Louis B. Mayer could prevent him from going off to war.

espite the fact that he had been living high on the Holly-wood hog for several years now, Red was still in good shape and sailed through his Army physical without any complications. Red joked about it when he exited the Army Induction Headquarters in downtown Los Angeles after passing the exam. Asked by an interested reporter how he had made out, Red said, "They told me I'm in A-1 condition." Then, with a take, he added, "or did they mean, 1-A?"

Red wasn't called up, however, for several months, which gave him a chance to finish out the radio season before putting "The Skelton Scrapbook of Satire" into mothballs for the duration of the war.

The delay also fit in nicely with Metro's plans to stick Red in one more picture before the Army got him—*The Ziegfeld Follies,* which went into production on the Culver City lot on April 24, 1944.

Ziegfeld Follies was an attempt on Metro's part to do a film version of the celebrated Broadway extravaganzas, following the original *Ziegfeld* formula. No interlocking story between scenes; just a straight variety show consisting of sketches and song and dance numbers featuring most of Metro's biggest stars who weren't in the service—Fred Astaire, Gene Kelly, Lena Horne, Fanny Brice, Judy Garland, Lucille Ball, Victor Moore, Esther Williams, and many more, including, of course, Red Skelton.

Each star was to do his own specialty or number for which he or she was famous: Astaire dancing, Fanny Brice impersonating "Baby Snooks," and, for the first time on film, Red Skelton doing "Guzzler's Gin."

Until then, it was assumed by most people that "Guzzler's Gin" was a product of the comic genius of the man who performed it, with perhaps some assistance from his clever ex-wife, who claimed she was his "writer." And neither Red nor Edna had ever done anything to discourage the notion that Red hadn't created it. In fact, before Metro could put "Guzzler's" in the *Ziegfeld Follies* script, Edna had insisted on being paid $5,000 for the "one-time" rights to their "Guzzler's" material.

The deception might have gone on forever if Harry Tugend, a screenwriter of note, hadn't been working on the Metro lot at the time *Ziegfeld Follies* was being shot.

Before coming to Hollywood, Tugend had spent twelve years in New York, knocking out sketches and clever lines for the "Fred Allen Show," one of NBC's top comedy radio programs. One of the sketches he had created had to do with a radio announcer who was pitching an alcoholic beverage to his listeners, and becoming drunker and drunker each time he took a swallow to demonstrate the "nice, smoooooooooth" quality of the liquid.

The one difference between the two versions was that Tugend's announcer wasn't working solo. An actor named Jack Smart had played the announcer, and Fred Allen, as the director of the commercial, had played straight to him, by asking him to try it "once more and let's see you really enjoying the drink this time."

The only other person working on the Metro lot who was aware of where the "Guzzler" sketch had been done originally was Irving Brecher, a close friend of Tugend's, and a former Marx Brothers writer. At the time Brecher was working on the *Ziegfeld* picture and in the course of his duties he wandered onto the set one day and saw Red Skelton doing "Guzzler's" before the Metro cameras. Later, while Brecher was having lunch in the commissary with his friend Tugend, he remarked, "Hey, Harry, congratulations. I see you sold your 'Guzzler's Gin' routine to Metro."

"I didn't sell them anything," replied Tugend, looking surprised.

"Then you'd better find yourself a lawyer, because I just saw Red Skelton doing it in the *Ziegfeld* picture."

Tugend had been aware for several years that Red Skelton had purloined his material and was claiming it as his own. In fact, one of the first to tell him about it had been his former boss, Fred Allen, who had phoned him one day and said, "Do you know, Harry, that some young comic named Red Skelton is going around the country doing your 'Guzzler's' sketch? I'd sue the son of a bitch if I were you."

Tugend had investigated and, sure enough, he caught the new comic doing his sketch, practically word for word, only without the second character. "However, I decided not to sue," relates Tugend, "because Red was doing 'Guzzler's' at Army camps and for a lot of fund-raising charity affairs, and doing so much good with it, I'd have felt like a heel stopping him."

But Metro-Goldwyn-Mayer was no "charitable organization," decided Tugend. If they wanted to use "Guzzler's" in a picture, they would have to pay him for it.

After lunch, Tugend phoned the Metro legal department and informed the lawyers that he was the author and owner of "Guzzler's Gin," and that they had no right to use it in a picture.

"There must be some mistake, Mr. Tugend," said one of the lawyers. "We own that material. We just paid Mrs. Skelton $5,-000 for it."

"That's unfortunate," said Tugend. "She stole it from me. I wrote it ten years ago."

When the lawyer demanded proof, Tugend said he'd show him his original Fred Allen pages, if he could see the script of the sketch Edna had sold them.

The lawyer agreed and several days later they exchanged scripts. The two sketches were basically the same, except that in Edna's script, Tugend noticed erasure marks where the name "Guzzler's" had previously been written. "Guzzler's Gin" had now been changed to "Gulper's Gin."

Trapped, the Metro lawyer asked Tugend, "How much do you want?"

Tugend, his own lawyer had informed him, could hold Metro up for anything at this stage, but he decided to be reasonable. "Well," said Tugend, "Edna got $5,000 for not writing 'Guzzler's.' I want $6,000 for writing it."

He got it, but that wasn't what really mattered to Tugend, who was extremely successful and wealthy by that time. He just wanted the injustice corrected. Tugend has never been too clear on just how Edna got her hands on his pages, but he surmises from what Red told him that it happened when the Skeltons were hanging around NBC in New York in the thirties, before they were successful and could afford to pay for material.

"In those days, it was the custom for radio actors to drop their pages to the floor after they'd finished reading from them," says Tugend. "After a broadcast, the studio floor would be littered with the discarded pages. Edna apparently wandered into the studio after the broadcast, picked up the pages containing the "Guzzler's" sketch, started reading them, thought they were funny, and decided it was something Red could use."

By the time of Fred Allen's death in 1956, Red had convinced himself of a whole new fairy tale regarding the birth of his most famous single piece of material.

As it happened, Allen expired on a Tuesday—the day of Red's television broadcast. But Red, who barely knew Allen, was so "moved" by the comedian's passing that near the end of his broadcast Tuesday night he suddenly turned solemn and spent the next five minutes eulogizing him. The gist of his lachrymose tribute was that not only had the world lost one of its greatest comedians, but he, Red, had lost one of his dearest friends—a friend so dear and generous that he had personally written "Guzzler's Gin" for Red and started him on the road to his first big success. Moreover, Allen had done it out of the goodness of his heart and not for any financial consideration.

Tugend's not bitter about the "Guzzler" saga, however. "In fact," he admits today, with a sly grin, "I have to say one thing about Red. He may have stolen 'Guzzler's' but he does it a hell of a lot better than we did it on the Fred Allen show."

It certainly was the only funny thing in Metro's *Ziegfeld's Follies*. When Bosley Crowther of the *New York Times* reviewed the picture after it was released in 1946, he labeled it a "backward step in film musicals." After picking on everything from the concept to the quality of the individual entertainment, Crowther wrote, "Red Skelton, making fun of radio sponsorship with his familiar gin-drunk scene, *was* fun."

Which proved one thing about Edna. She knew the right material for her husband, even though the way she went about getting it wasn't always within the rules of the game.

Red could expect no such assistance from the twenty-two-year-old actress and former Goldwyn girl he intended to make his second wife—Georgia Maureen Davis.

Georgia was completely different from Edna.

Tall and voluptuously built, with flaming red hair and a complexion like honey, Georgia was, in the opinion of one admirer, "almost illegally beautiful" when she first came to Hollywood.

A small-town girl, Georgia Davis was born in Glenwood Springs, Colorado, on September 17, 1922. Her goal in life was to become an artist. When she was attending Glenwood Springs High School, she did part-time work as a commercial artist for one of the local department stores.

Georgia's parents, Mack and Gladys Davis, wanted their daughter to attend the University of Colorado after high school, but she had her heart set on an artistic career and migrated to

Hollywood in 1940 to enroll in the Otis Art Institute. After two years in Los Angeles, Georgia qualified for a degree in Commercial Art, but after graduating found she couldn't make a living as an artist, so she supplemented her income with singing and modeling jobs, and other pursuits often available to extremely pretty single girls in a town like Hollywood.

A movie scout spotted Georgia in a magazine layout, liked her looks, and recommended her for a bit part in a film Howard Hawks was making at MGM.

Depending on who's telling it, there are a number of widely disparate accounts of Red and Georgia's first meeting, and when and where it took place. There are those who believe that Georgia, or "Little Red," as Skelton came to call his second wife, was the actual catalyst of the Edna–Red split. Certainly there was ample opportunity for Edna and Georgia to meet each other since they were working on the MGM lot at identical times before Red's divorce.

Edna herself refuses to shed any light on the matter at all.

The laundered version, bearing Skelton's official stamp of approval—the one Milton Weiss, his former publicity man, used to hand out to the press—had the comedian meeting Georgia for the first time a few weeks *prior* to his entering the Army in 1944, and about a month after he split with Muriel Morris.

Georgia was dressing up the scenery on a Howard Hawks picture at the time. Red thought she was beautiful and got someone to introduce them. The two hit it off, and Red invited her out for a date.

The date proved to be a bit of a disaster. Red threw a forward pass at Georgia, which she declined to receive. He then made some acidulous remarks designed to remind her that she couldn't possibly be all that innocent if she'd been knocking around Hollywood since she was eighteen, and working as a showgirl for people like Howard Hawks and Samuel Goldwyn.

Georgia responded by telling Red that he was the most uncouth, ill-mannered bum she had ever had the misfortune to come across, and she walked out on him.

A week later, Red phoned Georgia at her Wilshire Boulevard

apartment to apologize and to invite her out for another date. He promised to keep his hands off her. By this time the fiery Georgia had cooled off enough to warm up to Red. She accepted his invitation and they started seeing each other on a regular basis.

A couple of nights before his date with Uncle Sam, Red proposed to Georgia, suggesting that they elope to Las Vegas and tie the knot immediately.

Georgia, however, refused to be stampeded into one of those "hasty war marriages" that one, or both of them, might later regret. So she put him off, saying that she believed the formula for a "happy marriage" was for a boy and girl to know each other for at least a year before jumping into matrimony.

Thus, Buck Private Richard Skelton (serial number: 39 588 752) was still a single man when he reported for active duty at the U.S. Army Induction Headquarters on Spring Street in downtown Los Angeles early on the morning of June 7, 1944.

After he and about forty other confused draftees were sworn in by the Officer in Charge, they were herded onto the Red Car—L.A.'s now defunct trolley system—and taken to Fort MacArthur, the Army's processing center, twenty miles away in the port of San Pedro.

At Fort MacArthur, Red was given a uniform, the usual immunization shots, and a bunk of his own in an Army barracks.

After all those years on the road, Red was no stranger to discomfort, so it wasn't the Spartan life that bothered him during his basic training period at Fort MacArthur. What did annoy him—and it continued to eat away at his insides all through his service career—was the way he was treated because he was a celebrity.

Red didn't go into the service demanding or even expecting any special privileges because of who he was. He hadn't even tried to use pull to wangle himself an undeserved officer's commission, as so many big names in the film business had done. "I was the only celebrity to go into the service as a private and come out a private," he recalled after his discharge.

What nearly destroyed him was having to fill the jobs of two people—a lowly buck private and a professional entertainer.

As Private Skelton he rose at dawn with the other recruits,

drilled, trained, and hiked all day, did his share of latrine and K.P. duty, and otherwise contributed to the national defense.

As Red Skelton, the comedian, he was expected to eschew all rest and recreation periods, and pay not the slightest heed to taps. While the other exhausted recruits flopped on their bunks, Red was summoned to the officer's mess to entertain the brass. Sometimes he'd be up until two or three in the morning making the officers laugh.

After they released him, he'd crawl into his bunk, half dead, and close his eyes, hoping to catch a few winks before reveille. But often, the other fellows in the barracks would razz him after he got back from entertaining the officers and insist that he be "funny" for them too. Or some sergeant would stick a flashlight into Red's sleeping face and ask him to autograph an old T-shirt, or whatever else was available, for his kid brother or sick mother back home in Arkansas.

"I couldn't say no," states Red, "or they'd have thought I was trying to ritz them. It was a nightmare."

After basic training, Red was assigned to Field Artillery duty at Fort Ord, in Northern California, where Uncle Sam tried to teach him to be a gunner. Four months of gunnery training, plus the inevitable moonlighting chores entertaining the officers, drove him to the brink of a nervous and physical breakdown.

Finally, somebody in the upper echelons realized that a person of Skelton's talent was being wasted scrubbing latrines. Colonel Brubaker shipped our amiable redhead to the Army's Special Service School at Washington and Lee University, in Lexington, Virginia, for a two-month course in how to become an "Army Entertainment Specialist."

"Actually, I don't think the Army sent Red there to teach him anything," recalls Bob Schiller, one of Hollywood's Emmy-winning comedy writer-producers, who was working on his lieutenant's commission at Washington and Lee University at the time. "I think they just wanted to use Red to entertain the officers there—it was like the brass wanting their own 'private' comedian."

Arriving in the enlisted men's bunkhouse at Washington and Lee, Private Skelton barely had time to drop his duffel bag on his bunk and wash his hands before he received an order to put on a "command performance" at the Officers' Club after dinner that night.

The events at the Officers' Club turned out to be one of Skelton's more traumatic war experiences. Bob Schiller happened to be in the club the first night Skelton was brought in to entertain. "It was pathetic," recalls Schiller. "Red gave them his biggest guns, including 'Guzzler's Gin.' He knocked himself out to be funny. But nobody even watched him. There was no applause . . . not a single laugh, because all the officers were drunk and talking loudly among themselves. I think I was the only one in the entire room who watched him. He slunk off, feeling completely rejected."

Years later, when Schiller was one of Skelton's writers, he reminded his boss of the incident. Red turned grim, and said, "Those bastards—can you blame me for hating officers?"

To a comedian, especially one as sensitive and insecure as Red Skelton, being ignored by an audience, and not hearing any laughs, is torture worse than death.

Although, according to Schiller, Red's audiences didn't improve much during his matriculation at Washington and Lee University, he managed to get through his course in Athletics and Recreation without cracking up, and to graduate as a Private First Class, with the official designation of Entertainment Specialist beside his name in his Service Record.

By then it was March of 1945, and the war in Europe was winding down. Red was assigned to the Army Transportation Corps. More specifically, troopship duty. It would be up to him to entertain the GI's sailing between the U.S. and Europe. Not bad duty, as wars went.

Before reporting to the USS *General Altman,* the troopship that was to have the pleasure of seeing "Guzzler's Gin" seventeen times a day seven days a week, Red was given a fourteen-day furlough.

This he chose to spend on the West Coast, for two reasons. First of all, he had been troubled by tonsillitis during his year in the service and he wanted to have the infected membranes removed—but by his own throat specialist, Doctor Karl Lewis, and not one of the Army medicos. Second, he had known Georgia for about a year now, and over the long distance phone she had agreed to marry him before he left for the European theater.

Because both Red and Georgia were Catholics, the two redheads naturally wanted to be united in a Catholic Church. Unfortunately, the Church of the Good Shepherd in Beverly Hills didn't believe in sanctioning a marriage involving a divorced person. So after the license was taken out, the setting had to be switched at the last minute to the Beverly Vista Community Church in Beverly Hills.

The wedding took place on March 9, 1945, and was performed by the Reverend Dr. James Stewart in front of a small group of Red's and Georgia's closest friends. Among them were Patty Hope, a friend of Georgia's, who was the maid of honor, and Bo Roos, Red's business manager, who was best man.

Red delivered his lines perfectly straight, and he even refrained from saying "I dood it" when the reverend asked him if he took Georgia to be his lawfully wedded wife.

Immediately after the ceremony, Red quaffed a glass of champagne, kissed the bride good-bye, and checked into St. Vincent's Hospital for his tonsillectomy, which was scheduled for the next morning.

10

The history of Red Skelton's overseas adventures in World War II will never make a war film to rival the General Patton story, in either excitement or volume. In fact, it's questionable if there's even enough there for a short subject.

On April 5, 1945—just twenty days before the Germans capitulated—Entertainment Specialist Red Skelton boarded a troopship in Hampton Roads, Virginia, and along with about 3,-000 other GI's, sailed for Naples, Italy.

In theory, Red's job should have been no more demanding or dangerous than that of a social director aboard a cruise liner. All he had to do was keep the GI's laughing and free from boredom until they reached their destination. But in reality, it was a nightmare because he hardly had a moment to himself. He was on twenty-four hour call as the ship's Court Jester. Just wind him up, and he was supposed to go into his act.

In the evenings, and far into the night, he'd be entertaining up in "officers' country." Often the brass would be swacked on beer, or hard liquor they had managed to smuggle aboard, and would be paying more attention to the pretty nurses sitting beside them, or on their laps, than they would to Red's jokes.

In the daylight hours, Red would be staging shows for the GI's on one of the hatches forward of the bridge. Because all 3,-000 of the troops couldn't be squeezed into one area simultaneously, Red would have to stagger his show times. To accommodate so many men, ten or twelve shows a day would be necessary.

This left little or no time in between performances for Red to take a break. If he could find the time for one, he'd retreat to his bunk in the hold down below. But that was no place to rest. Bunks filled with noisy GI's were tiered six high, and so close together there was barely room to walk in the aisles between them. Day or night Red found it impossible to get away from the mob of soldiers who were either snoring, writing letters, reading, playing cards, or just shooting the bull out of boredom.

The moment Red would crawl into his sack, some tough GI with a chip on his shoulder could be counted upon to shout out, "Come on, Hollywood movie star, get up and be funny." And if Red refused, claiming weariness, chances were that the bully would say, "What do you have to rest about? You just tell jokes. We gotta fight a war when we get there." And then Red would be rousted out of his sack and forced to put on a show right there in the crowded, smelly, stuffy hold.

What made his position even more untenable was that no matter how stringently he rationed out his routines he didn't have enough to keep serving the GI's and officers fresh material every time he had to get up and entertain.

The disheartening result was that by the third or fourth day out his audiences started hooting and jeering when Red gave them something they'd heard or seen before.

It was the same problem he'd had to face at Fort MacArthur

and the Special Service School, only a hundred times worse. In those places the audience changed with the day-to-day movement of the personnel; on board a troopship audiences were always the same for the length of the voyage.

Besides, on a dry land base there were places to hide, and occasionally he could even talk an officer into giving him a weekend pass. Not so on board a troopship. The only way to escape the masses was to jump over the side.

Finally, a mess sergeant, who was a Skelton fan, took pity on Red, invited him into the galley, and gave him a place to sit down in a quiet corner of a pantry where he wouldn't he hounded twenty-four hours a day.

He also handed Red a cup of some high proof, two-day-old whiskey he had personally distilled, and told him there was lots more where that came from. The homemade booze would never rival "Guzzler's Gin" for pure "smooooothness," but it proved enormously effective for easing Red's tension and giving him the courage to face hostile audiences. As a result, these whiskey klatches became a daily occurrence. Not just daily, but even between shows Red would retreat to the galley for a drink of his favorite pick-me-up. When he would emerge, he would have the courage of a lion.

Obviously, the sergeant believed he was doing Red a favor by lavishing his home brew on him. Unfortunately, Red began to rely on the stuff to get him through his daily tribulations. By the time the USS *General Altman* put into Naples—nine days after it had left the States—Red was close to a nervous breakdown.

Red's ship was slated to stay in port for three days, unloading and loading troops. This, Red figured, would give him a brief respite from his shipboard duties. Perhaps he would even be allowed to go ashore and see the sights.

He was allowed ashore, all right, but not as a sightseer. His superiors had him scheduled for three days of shows at the various Army camps in the area.

After the first show, Red cracked up and had to be hospitalized. The Army doctor diagnosed his problem as a "nervous breakdown," and recommended that he be returned to the States.

He was on a hospital ship that sailed for the States on April 17 just three days after Red had arrived in Italy.

The hospital ship put into Hampton Roads, Virginia, on April 29, 1945. By then the war in Europe was over and Hitler had blown himself up in his bunker.

But the war was not over for Red.

He spent the next four months recovering his physical strength and his sanity in an Army Hospital at Camp Pickett, Virginia.

During this period the A-bomb was dropped on Hiroshima, and the war in the Pacific also came to an abrupt halt.

There was no longer a need for Uncle Sam to detain Red Skelton in the Army. So, on September 18, 1945, at Camp Pickett, Virginia, the Army gave Private Red Skelton a Medical Discharge, a lapel button shaped like a duck, a Good Conduct Medal, $300 in mustering-out pay, $140.50 in travel expenses, and said he was now free to return to Hollywood, where there was more of a need for a man of his unique talents.

11

With the war behind him, his position as one of America's top entertainers still secure, and a beautiful, brand-new wife to come home to, Red Skelton seemed to have the world on a string when he arrived back in Hollywood late in September of 1945, to resume his radio and film careers.

And unlike many returning GI's, Red didn't even have to be concerned about a place to live, in spite of the fact that he no longer owned the ranch in Tarzana and the severity of the housing shortage in Southern California due to the war.

Thanks to Bo Roos's expert managing, Red and Edna jointly owned the Wilshire Palms, a luxury apartment complex of about twenty-four low-rise units spread across several rolling acres fronting Wilshire Boulevard, just slightly west of Beverly Hills. The Wilshire Palms had just about everything to make Red feel as if he were living in his own home—beautiful gardens, a large swimming pool, a championship tennis court, and Edna for a landlady.

Edna occupied the penthouse suite, from which she reigned, with her usual efficiency, as live-in landlady. But she had kept one of the most desirable apartments on the premises vacant and waiting for Red. This one had three bedrooms, a large living room, dining room and kitchen, and was in a building of its own, on a secluded section of the property farthest away from the traffic noises of Wilshire Boulevard.

Red could reach his and Georgia's apartment through an entrance off Comstock Avenue and few of the other tenants even knew a celebrity was living there. Altogether, it seemed the perfect place for two people who'd scarcely spent any time together since they were married half a year before, to begin honeymooning.

Metro was already preparing two pictures for Red, both adapted from hit Broadway plays of another era—*The Show-Off* by George Kelly, and *Merton of the Movies,* by George Kaufman and Marc Connelly. The producer in both cases was Al Lewis, and the conversion of the plays into Red Skelton vehicles was put in the hands of George Wells, one of Metro's most dependable contract writers.

Although the first of these pictures, *The Show-Off,* wasn't scheduled to go before the cameras until early in 1946, Red, with Edna by his side, had to attend frequent meetings on the Culver City lot with the film's creators.

More immediate was Red's radio show. NBC informed him shortly after he returned to civilian life that Red's "Scrapbook of Satire" was to return to the air in December, in his old time slot following Hope on Tuesday nights. The only changes were his sponsor—Procter & Gamble's Tide Detergent instead of Raleigh Cigarettes—and the show's title.

A December air date didn't leave much time to do all that

had to be done, which included hiring an entire new cast, except for Red, and putting a script together that would get "The Red Skelton Show" off to a fast start.

Popular as they had been, Ozzie and Harriet Nelson would not be returning to the line-up. Before Red went into the Army, he had allowed Ozzie and Harriet to cut an audition transcription record for a show of their own in his studio one night after he had finished performing. The studio audience loved the audition. So did a sponsor, who put Ozzie and Harriet on the air the following fall, playing a husband and wife. They caught on with radio audiences immediately, and when they had kids the program evolved into *The Ozzie and Harriet Show* that became one of the first big hit family situation comedies on TV.

As a result of Red's generosity, he wound up losing not just an orchestra leader and pretty vocalist, but his two favorite straight men as well.

It was now up to Fenton Coe, the producer NBC had assigned to the show, to find both an orchestra leader and some competent bit part players who would not be thrown by Red's ad libs and usually unreliable cue lines.

Red had his heart set on David Rose for his orchestra leader. He had come to admire Rose's music when they had played some Army camps together during the war. Rose had fronted the band stationed at the nearby Santa Ana Air Base, which was composed of the best studio musicians culled from Hollywood.

Red loved the "big sound of all those strings Davey Rose used," recalls a friend. "I think he was beginning to have dreams of becoming a composer himself."

Unfortunately, Rose was getting married to Judy Garland in 1945, so Red had to settle for another popular band leader of the period, David Forrester. Forrester had a thirty-five piece orchestra, and like Rose, employed a large string section.

Actually, Red could have gotten along with a five-piece band, but he insisted on all those violins and the symphonic sound.

David Forrester and his vocalist could not double in character acting, however, as Ozzie and Harriet had. So after auditioning dozens, Edna and the producer finally settled on Verna

Felton, Lurene Tuttle, and Pat McGeehan, three of radio's most gifted comedy character performers, to play straight for Red.

Luckily for everyone concerned, Red would be able to have the same writing staff he had when he left for the Army in 1944—Benedict Freedman, Jack Douglas, and John Fenton Murray, the last to be hired.

That this talented trio was still available after the war wasn't due to luck so much as it was to Red's fear of losing them when he went into the Army, and Edna's ability to anticipate a problem. She persuaded Red to keep all three writers on salary while he was in the service.

The extra expenditure was returned to him a thousandfold when the new "Red Skelton Show" was broadcast for the first time in December of 1945. His first program was a typical Skelton broadcast, featuring his opening monologue and many of his familiar characterizations but freshened up with new material. He also made use of his war experiences by doing riotous imitations of the Army and Navy brass, which the GI's in the studio audience ate up, of course.

As a bonus, purely for the studio audience, Red put on a second show after his regular broadcast that laid everyone in the aisles who wasn't already there. The after-show not only included Red's favorite risqué material, but every wild sight gag in his bag of tricks—from squirting actors in the face with seltzer to throwing a coat over his face, inserting his arms in the sleeves, and imitating two elephants in love.

Red's after-show was such a success that he included it in the program every week, and audiences started coming for that as much as the broadcast. It wasn't unusual for radio comedians of that day to throw in an extra twenty or thirty minutes for the studio audience. But other comedians did their bonus spots before the show, and called it a "warm-up." The purpose, of course, was to get the audience in a mood for laughing.

"But Red's warm-up was so hilarious," recalls Johnny Murray, "that the broadcast wasn't strong enough to follow it. Which was why Red had to do his warm-up afterwards."

A member of the studio audience who never stopped laughing that first night was author Gene Fowler, who had recently become one of Red's closest friends. Fowler, who had been on intimate terms with such luminaries as John Barrymore, William Fallon, W. C. Fields, and written best-selling biographies about them, was one of the few intellectuals who appreciated Red's comedy. He never missed a Skelton broadcast if he could help it.

Red, of course, appreciated Fowler, too. He considered him a fatherly "good luck charm"—especially after the way his first broadcast was accepted by the majority of radio listeners.

Within three weeks, the new "Red Skelton Show" shot to the Number Three position in the ratings race, just behind Jack Benny, who was being nosed out for Number One position by Bob Hope.

Such swift public acceptance should have renewed Red's faith in the human race, and made his and Georgia's first Christmas together a very happy one. Unfortunately, it wasn't. Their marriage was already in trouble. And the trouble was Edna.

No matter how open-minded Georgia tried to be about the presence in Red's life of the ubiquitous Edna, there was something deeply disturbing about living in such proximity to a woman whom Red still referred to as "Mummy," and on whom he was dependent for practically everything.

Georgia had never been exactly wild about moving into the Wilshire Palms, where Red and Edna would have such easy accessibility to each other. She had felt that the presence of Edna on the scene, popping in and out of their apartment for whatever reason she deemed necesary, would make her feel "uncomfortable."

But she had acquiesced under the logic of Red's argument that Edna certainly posed no threat to Georgia from a romantic point of view. Red had demonstrated he wasn't interested in Edna that way when he left her. Moreover, Red had pleaded, Edna certainly wasn't interested in him, either—except for what he could earn a week. Edna had demonstrated that by becoming engaged to their mutual good friend and the man responsible for bringing Red to Hollywood in the first place, director Frank Borzage, whom she planned to marry in November.

Red could intellectualize about it all he wanted, but Georgia was a very emotional woman. Nothing Red could say could reconcile her to having Edna play such an important role in their lives.

It was bad enough to have to sit back and have her husband's first wife advising him on business matters, masterminding his radio show, handling his studio problems, acting as a buffer between him and the press, holding his power of attorney, and getting 50 percent of his income. But because Georgia still loved Red very much, she was willing to accept his word for it that he needed Edna. "Look, Little Red, Edna brought me up from fifty bucks a week to $7,500. If it weren't for Edna, we couldn't be living this way," was Red's usual line of defense.

Georgia could accept that—at least in the early stages of their marriage. But what she found almost impossible to bear was how deeply Edna was involved in their personal lives.

Not only did Edna live just a few yards and up a few steps away, but she kept Georgia on a strict personal household budget, dictated to her where to market to get the best bargains, told Georgia and Red how much spending money they could have every week, hired their household help, and even chose the suits Red wore.

What exacerbated the situation even more was Red's apparent insensitiveness to his wife's viewpoint.

His first Christmas home, for example, he walked into the shop of Jack Bender, the Beverly Hills furrier, and blithely picked out two identical mink coats, in the $5,000-range, and had one sent to Edna and one to Georgia. While Edna wore hers, Georgia burned.

Such behavior, while generous, is definitely not recommended by marriage counselors.

What added more salt to the already festering wound was that Georgia could hardly avoid seeing Edna in *her* mink coat, because of the way Red was always ringing his first wife in on their social affairs.

Since Edna was Red's manager, and an integral part of his radio staff, a certain amount of social contact was inescapable. Dinner with their wives or husbands and business associates at the Vine Street Brown Derby right after a broadcast was a ritual most NBC radio stars observed in those days. And Red wasn't any different from the other stars, except that when he invited his head writer to join them, he was also inviting his ex-wife.

And every week there'd be a coffee klatch with Edna and the writers after a preview of the radio show—often without Georgia—to discuss what went wrong and how it could be fixed.

But Red was not satisfied with that. Often he'd include Edna when he took Georgia to Chasen's or Romanoff's or some other expensive Hollywood hangout.

Even if Red had to go to New York on business, and decided to make it a pleasure trip as well by inviting Georgia to accompany him, there would be no escaping Edna. Chances were good that she'd have the suite next to theirs at the Hampshire House or the Sherry Netherland. He needed Edna along, Red explained, to keep him from making ill-considered or hasty business commitments, and to be his public relations contact with the media.

But did he also have to invite her along to the theater, or to dinner?

No, he didn't have to, but it would seem kind of unfriendly to make her eat alone. After all, Edna wasn't just another head writer. "Edna's practically 'family,' honey. She and I raised each other."

So Georgia would have to be a good sport about it, and smile for the photographers who caught the three of them together at The Stork or "21" or Chasen's or the Derby.

The rest of the show business community thought this quasi–*ménage à trois* a pretty unique arrangement. Even those who had witnessed all kinds of strange behavior and combinations in their lifetimes had to marvel when they saw the three of them dining together so compatibly. But a few close friends wondered how long the arrangement could last before the whole thing erupted into open warfare.

Georgia wondered, too. She couldn't get Edna out of her life even after Edna married Frank Borzage in November of 1945. The threesome simply became a foursome.

Possibly Georgia would have been more willing to put up with Edna after she married Borzage if she hadn't believed it was just a "rebound" marriage, hastily conceived and consummated to save face, and that Edna was still in love with Red and hoping to win him back if she stuck around long enough. Since Georgia and a great many others believed Edna never had stopped loving Red, it was understandable that she was jealous.

Yet if Georgia dared open her mouth to ask Red why it was necessary to see quite so much of his first wife, she would risk getting into a bitter fight with him—a fight that would generally culminate with the two of them drinking heavily, and Red storming out of the apartment and moving into a hotel until he cooled off.

Red never stayed angry for long, which was one of his nicer characteristics, according to Edna. "He'd generally be the first one to apologize and want to make up," she says.

But each incident chipped away a little bit more from the bonds that were holding their marriage together. And the incidents multiplied, and became a little bit more stormy with each passing day that Edna stayed on.

According to people who were intimate with the Skeltons in the late forties, the period of the joint Edna–Georgia regency coincided exactly with the period in which Skelton did some of his most spectacular carousing.

However, even when he was sober, Red's many moods were a difficult thing for a wife to cope with. Georgia never knew from one moment to the next whether he would be clowning, or sullen, obstreperously belligerent, or the helpless little boy who needed his Mummy.

Red, on the other hand, complained vociferously that Georgia was a nag, and too demanding—especially in wanting him to dump Edna. "Just leave me alone," he used to tell Georgia. "I just want to make people laugh. How can I concentrate on my work if you keep bothering me about Edna?"

Somehow, and despite their differences, Red and Georgia managed to keep their marriage from going on the rocks during Red's first year out of the service. And in the fall of 1946, Georgia surprised Red with the news that she was going to have a baby the following spring.

Red was delighted, and hoped it would be a boy. He even had the name picked out—Richard.

As so often happens with a foundering marriage, Georgia's pregnancy seemed to be just the incentive the two of them needed to try a little harder to make theirs work.

Georgia was willing to give up a promising acting career to make a good home for Red and their forthcoming heir or heiress. And Red, though unwilling to give up Edna entirely, was willing to stop giving her $5,000-mink coats.

So for the next couple of years, at least—through Georgia's first and second pregnancies—there was a definite feeling, even among the couple's most intimate friends, that the Skeltons' marriage was finally heading out of the shoals.

On May 5, 1947, Georgia announced that she was starting to feel labor pains. Reacting with more composure than one would believe a man with his anxieties capable of, Red calmly helped her pack and then rushed Georgia to St. John's Hospital, in Santa Monica. There, not many hours later, Georgia gave birth to a seven-pound-four-ounce red-haired girl, whom they named Valentina Marie.

Ironically, it was Edna who informed the news media that Red Skelton had finally achieved his lifelong ambition of becoming a father.

Although Red was disappointed at begetting a Valentina instead of a Richard, he was not so discouraged that he didn't try again. Just a year and a few days later—on June 14, 1948—Georgia gave birth to a second child. The new addition tipped the scales at exactly seven pounds, also had red hair, and was of the appropriate gender to be named Richard. He was also given the middle name of "Freeman," in honor of Freeman Keyes.

Although Red dearly loved his little red-haired Valentina, he was overjoyed at the news that Georgia had finally given him a boy, and he was all smiles when he showed up in his wife's hospital room the next day and posed beside her and baby for the newspaper photographers—who had been alerted to be there by the ubiquitous Edna.

From the way Red stood beside the bed, with his chest thrust forward, beaming proudly down at the bawling, red-faced infant in Georgia's arms, looking like an old fashioned tin-type, it was apparent to all that this was the happiest moment of Red Skelton's life.

The irony of it was that before many years would pass this baby boy, through no fault of his own, would turn Red and Georgia's life into a nightmare.

12

For the immediate future, however, fatherhood seemed to have a leavening effect on Red. It settled him down. He was less temperamental, not quite so wrapped up in himself, and in general, easier for Georgia to get along with.

Motherhood matured Georgia, too. In many ways now she was a better influence than Edna on Red.

She worked hard to improve his diction and manners. She reconciled him to putting on his shoes before coming to the table, and even to answering the telephone occasionally.

She even got him interested in good books, art, and music, and because of her own artistic leanings, in taking up painting as a hobby.

One thing about Red that she couldn't cure was his penchant for doing anything for a laugh.

Department stores seemed to bring out the devilish in Red. One day, after the birth of their second child, Red went on a shopping trip with Georgia to Saks Fifth Avenue in Beverly Hills. While Georgia went to Ladies' Dresses on the second floor, Red ambled around the street level. When Georgia returned, she couldn't find Red anywhere. Finally Georgia asked a saleslady if she had seen her husband.

"I think he's over there, Mrs. Skelton," said the saleslady, pointing to a large crowd of women in the Hat Department. Peeking over a shoulder, Georgia saw that Red was the center of attention. He was trying on women's hats—as riotously as he would if he'd been performing on the stage of the New York Paramount.

Once, while Georgia and Red were at Macy's in New York, Red had wanted some silly knickknack that was much too expensive for what it was. When Georgia told him not to waste their money on it, he had thrown himself down on the floor, and kicked and bawled until a crowd gathered.

On the same trip, at the intersection of Fifty-seventh Street and Fifth Avenue, Red lay down in a puddle of water so that a dachshund could cross onto the sidewalk without soaking its paws and belly.

Back in Los Angeles, Red took Georgia to lunch one noon at Romanoff's, an expensive bistro of the forties and fifties no longer in existence. On his way out, Red stopped at Milton Berle's table to congratulate "Uncle Miltie" on having the first really big successful comedy show on television.

While Berle was smilingly accepting Red's compliments, Red picked up a glass of water, poured it inside the front of his own gray flannel trousers, and exited, shaking his leg, to Georgia's complete mortification.

Red's imagination for practical jokes knew no bounds—and certainly not the bounds of propriety, especially when he was on the sauce, which was a good deal of the time in the early 1950s.

When Red was drinking he sometimes ran stag movies in his apartment at the Wilshire Palms for the benefit of his guests. And when he was really bombed he liked to turn the projector around and flash the dirty movies on the wall of the apartment building next door, so that everybody driving west on Wilshire Boulevard could see them.

Since those were the days when the only way one could see a pornographic film was to attend a stag party, most drivers either slowed or stopped their cars completely in order to witness the forbidden lewd entertainment. Frequently Red's stag showings would cause a traffic tie-up large enough to bring out the cops. The moment the police appeared, Red would turn off the projector, and the images would instantly disappear from the next door apartment wall. Often the bewildered drivers would wind up in the Purdue Avenue Police Station, making their explanations to a judge.

But sometimes the cops would be too quick for Red, and come knocking on his apartment door. "At those times, while Red was stalling them at the front door, I'd have to run out the back door with the stag films and burn them in the incinerator," confessed the late Marty Rackin, who was a frequent guest at Red's place after the war.

Most of Red's gags weren't quite so elaborate or notorious, however. Like the time in 1947, when he was on a train returning from a nationwide personal appearance tour that Metro had sent him on to promote *Ziegfeld Follies*. Accompanying him on this junket was Milton Weiss, his faithful and subservient publicity man. As the two got off the train in Pasadena, which was the customary disembarkation point for returning movie stars, they were met by a mob of newspaper reporters and photographers.

Feeling impelled to give them a laugh, Red suddenly turned to his publicity man and said, "Gee, Milt, you've been so nice to me that I'd like to do something for you. I'm going to give you the shirt off my back."

Before Weiss could object, Red stripped to the waist, handed his shirt to his flack, and stepped into the waiting limousine Metro had sent for him.

When he walked onto the MGM lot an hour later, and into Louis B. Mayer's office, Red was still shirtless but a tie was knotted neatly around his neck.

*   *   *

The pictures Metro was saddling him with in those days should only have been as funny as Red's off-screen antics.

The Show-Off, in which he co-starred with Marilyn Maxwell, was Red's first film after the war. To the Metro brass, which was always hard pressed to find good comedy vehicles, it must have seemed an inspiration to remake George Kelly's hit play for the fourth time. Paramount had filmed it twice, and Metro had made it in 1934 with Spencer Tracy portraying the leading role of an incorrigible braggart. If it had been a hit three times, why not try for four?

There was nothing wrong with Red's performance, or Marilyn Maxwell's, either, but judging from the grosses there were very few film fans who hadn't seen *The Show-Off* its first three times around. It was a dismal failure, and the critics didn't care for it much, either. "*The Show-Off* if just too creaky a vehicle to satisfy customers in these highly charged post-war years," wrote the *New York Daily News.*

Merton Of The Movies, when it was released in 1947, did nothing to enhance Red's reputation as a motion picture star, either. The film's creative credentials seemed important enough to insure a blockbuster success. It had a screenplay by George Wells and Lou Breslow. And that was adapted from George S. Kaufman and Marc Connelly's hit play which in turn had been taken from a best-selling novel by Harry Leon Wilson. And for a director it had Robert Alton, who had done some of Metro's biggest musicals.

Something, however, went terribly awry between the drawing board and the theater. "*Merton Of The Movies,* presented yesterday at Loew's State, is a brutishly slapstick prank, and so help us it's not the least bit funny," wrote the *New York Times'* Bosley Crowther. "Mr. Skelton's true comic personality never comes to the surface, chiefly because the script is unashamedly inane."

With Hollywood's most prestigious studio turning out films of that quality, it's not surprising that the movie business was heading for trouble—serious trouble—in 1947.

During the war, movie attendance had boomed. The people

on the home front, anxious to forget their worries, would go to see practically anything that was being shown at their neighborhood theaters, and what's more, enjoy it.

But by 1947, film-goers were becoming more selective. There was less money around. Twelve million ex-servicemen had suddenly been dumped on the job market, creating unemployment and the beginning of Harry Truman's first post-war recession.

And to further compound the ailing film studios' problems, a little box containing an electronic tube that could receive pictures right in people's homes, and presumably entertain them, had suddenly raised its ugly antenna.

At first the movie producers were inclined to look at TV as a novelty that the public would soon tire of—especially the way weekly TV programs voraciously ate up material, dragging the quality of its entertainment down the longer it went on. They figured they could win the public back simply by making better pictures and showing them in 3-D or on taller and wider screens such as Cinemascope, Vistavision, and Panorama.

But when the public even started to stay away from quality pictures, starring some of Hollywood's biggest names—Clark Gable, Jimmy Stewart, Robert Taylor, and Gary Cooper—panic set in at the major studios.

Even Louis B. Mayer was beginning to look worried as he wandered around the Metro lot, and he instituted all kinds of emergency economy measures to cut down on his overhead: making fewer pictures; putting contract people not actually assigned to a film on "lay-off" (in accordance to a standard "lay-off" clause in most contracts); and even putting less white meat in the renowned Louis B. Mayer Chicken Noodle Soup, which up until then had been a favorite on the commissary menu.

Some of the top radio stars of the day—Hope, Benny, Burns, Cantor—were also concerned about losing their audiences to TV, and spent many a sleepless night pondering whether to switch over to the visual medium.

It was inevitable, of course, that eventually they would all have to succumb. But each of these high-wage earners wanted to postpone the day of reckoning as long as possible, because in most of these comedians' minds, there was no easier way of making a living in show business than to be top banana of one's own radio show. There were no lines to memorize, no sets to be built, and very little acting to be done. All they had to do was show up at the broadcasting studio, perhaps twice before the show went on the air: once for a rehearsal, and once for a preview (though not all shows even bothered with previews). At the broadcast they'd simply read off lines that a dozen gag writers had slaved over for the past six days. In radio, the star's work was minimal.

But television meant longer working hours for everyone—star, director, and writer alike. The production schedule on most shows in the inchoate years of TV usually called for a six-day work week. Unlike radio, producing a weekly TV show was tantamount to putting on a brand new stage play or vaudeville act every seven days. Even the simplest Broadway play required three and a half weeks of rehearsal, plus another three and a half weeks on the road trying out the material.

TV allowed its participants no such luxury. The moment a show was finished, preparations began for the next one. What also struck fear into the hearts of most radio actors was the visual aspect of TV. For example, many of the characterizations and famous radio bits that relied on the audience's imagination were likely to fall flat when actually seen—Jack Benny's basement vault, for example, or his Maxwell automobile. On radio, Bob Hope would say, "Well, Colonna, here we are on the moon," and the imagination of the listeners would go to work and construct a complete set in their minds' eyes. On TV, you'd have to show them on the moon, and that might not be so funny.

Of all the radio stars popular in those days, Red Skelton was considered to have the best chance to make it on TV, because as everyone had been saying for years, he was basically a "sight" comic rather than a "line" comic, and "born for TV." Even his "mean widdle boy" characterization, though dependent on the radio listener's imagination in order to visualize the grown man as a kid, had been accepted in a visual medium such as vaudeville. So Red's future seemed assured.

Nevertheless, and despite the TV clause in his contract, Red was not sure he was ready to jump into the new medium and take the chance of failing. At least not while his radio show was still drawing healthy ratings and his sponsor was willing to pay him $8,500 a week for a firm thirty-nine-week commitment, and he was still popular in films.

One thing Red was sure about was that he didn't like the last three pictures he had made for Metro. Under its new policy of making fewer but better pictures, Metro was biding its time and being more selective about what to star Skelton in next.

While Metro was making up its mind, Columbia Pictures was solving Metro's problem for them. Under the auspices of producer Edward Small, Columbia was preparing a new comedy called The Fuller Brush Man, which Sylvan Simon, who had been associated with many of Red's earlier successes at Metro, was going to direct. Written by Devery Freeman and Frank Tashlin, The Fuller Brush Man was about a timorous street cleaner who gets a job as a brush salesman to please his girl-friend, who wants him to elevate himself in the world. In the course of his new job he becomes involved in a murder plot, resulting in the usual number of visual bits.

The role seemed tailor-made for Skelton, and Columbia, at Sylvan Simon's request, started making overtures to Louis B. Mayer to acquire the comedian on a loan-out deal.

In palmier days, Mayer would have told his arch-enemy Harry Cohn what he could do with his overtures. In no way would he have considered loaning out any of his superstars—even if they were lying around the lot doing nothing but drawing their huge salaries, eating his famous chicken soup, and adding to studio overhead. But Mayer was faced with a daily bombardment of unpleasant words over the long distance phone from Nicholas Schenck, President of Loew's, who was vociferously demanding that Mayer cut every penny of excess overhead or risk getting replaced by Dore Schary (which eventually did happen). So the Lord Mayor of Culver City decided to let Columbia have the pleasure of paying Red's $3,500-a-week salary for the ten weeks or so they would need him for The Fuller Brush Man. He even managed to make a $1,000-a-week profit on the deal by charging Cohn $4,500 a week for the use of Red while continuing to pay him his regular $3,500.

It was like old times working under Sylvan Simon's direction again, and in a script specifically tailored to Red's comedic dimensions. Moreover, Simon always managed to bring out the best in Red—perhaps Red sensed how much the director admired his talents. Of course, he didn't have to sense it. Simon was very outspoken on the subject. "Red," he used to insist while sitting around the huge luncheon table with Harry Cohn and the rest of the studio brass in the executives' dining room, "is probably the greatest living comic. The funniest sequences in all the pictures we've done together have come as a result of his split-second inspirations. He's the only comic I know who can get laughs and heart-tugs from the same audience."

Motivated by Simon's positiveness on the subject, and also by how wonderfully funny the "dailies" of *The Fuller Brush Man* looked to him, Harry Cohn, never one to let integrity stand in his way, started a campaign, halfway through the filming of the picture, to lure Red away from MGM by making him all kinds of fabulous offers. Cohn promised Red a weekly salary twice what Metro was paying him, and in addition threw in all kinds of tax gimmick inducements to further sweeten the deal. At the same time he filled Red's ears with words to the effect that only Columbia knew how to make a Skelton comedy the way it should be made, and that if Red continued appearing in pictures of the caliber of the last three he made for MGM his film career would soon be as dead as Anna Sten's. By night, Cohn wined and dined Red and Georgia, either in his Beverly Hills mansion, or in Los Angeles's finest restaurants.

By the time Cohn had finished romancing him, and he was back on the MGM lot, Red was convinced he ought to make the change, and through his various managers, agents, and Edna, he sent word up to the MGM brass that he wanted to be freed from his contract. He would actually be doing them a favor, he explained, since they were having such a difficult time finding strong properties for him.

It was a nice try, but Metro wasn't interested in losing their Number One comic. However, to appease their unhappy clown, the Metro bigwigs gave him a $500-raise in salary, and assigned Paul Jones to produce his next picture. Jones had a good track record for comedies, having produced many of Hope's successes at Paramount, and Metro was hopeful he could do the same for Skelton, which was one of the reasons they had signed him.

With Jones as the bait, Red reluctantly returned to the Metro lot and went to work in *Southern Yankee,* a comedy about the Civil War in which Red played a goofy spy for the North. This film had a screenplay by Harry Tugend, which was based on an original story by Norman Panama and Mel Frank, who had scripted many of Hope's and Crosby's better *Road* pictures.

According to Tugend, Red "deliberately dogged it" during the shooting of the picture. He was hoping Metro would get disgusted with him and let him out of his contract. "But the odd thing was," says Tugend, "even when he was dogging it he was brilliant, and nobody even noticed it."

At Metro, that is. Around the country both critics and the public noticed it and gave *Southern Yankee* a lukewarm reception. And they were right.

The Fuller Brush Man, however, was screamingly funny all the way through (when Red wasn't going for pathos, that is), and was a spectacular success at the nation's box offices, in a market that was generally considered soft.

The reviews weren't spectacular, but then Red Skelton has never been a critic pleaser, except on rare occasions. Opined the *New York Times* on May 15, 1948:

> *The Fuller Brush Man,* for all its limpness, especially at the start, is a pretty good sample of slapstick in the latter-day Keystone style. Mr. Skelton is a clown with obvious talent for the moments of frantic distress, and he gives a good show of hysteria in the ultimately concluding chase.

That *The Fuller Brush Man* was a hit merely compounded Red's dissatisfaction with Metro. As a result, he was in a state of constant rebellion, which manifested itself in outlandish, and usually hilarious, practical jokes aimed at his boss, Louis B. Mayer.

A favorite gag of Red's was to drop a gold money clip containing as much as $20,000 in large denominations on a studio street, then wait behind a corner for someone to pick it up. Then he would appear and accuse that person of stealing the cash from him.

Red pulled it on Mayer one day, and after the mogul counted the bills and then started back into the Irving Thalberg Building to turn in the clip to the lost and found, Red dashed after him, shouting at the top of his lungs to the studio policeman, "Stop that thief!"

Another of Red's capers that is still being talked about occurred during the making of *Neptune's Daughter,* another Esther Williams aquatic extravaganza, in which he supplied the comedy.

The sets for the picture were, as they were in most Esther Williams musicals, opulently spectacular, with one of them featuring a gold-leaf grand piano constructed in the shape of a large sea shell. It was the kind of thing that definitely couldn't be picked up at your local piano store; it had to be specially designed by MGM's finest artisans, for this one picture.

The piano wasn't built for just ornamental purposes; it was to be featured in several numbers, including one in which Miss Williams and Ricardo Montalban sang Frank Loesser's "Baby, It's Cold Outside," and another, when Red and Betty Garrett reprised the tune.

Halfway through the filming of *Neptune's Daughter,* its director, Eddie Buzzell, walked onto the set one morning and discovered that the piano was missing. Furthermore, nobody in the prop or set dressing departments could explain what had happened to it. Panic immediately set in among the film's makers.

Because this was the only piano of its kind extant, and it had already been filmed in several scenes prior to now, there could be no simple substitution. Either the sequences already shot would have to be remade, with another piano, or production would have to be shut down until a twin of the missing one could be constructed. Either alternative would cost the studio thousands of dollars, in a picture that was already over-budget.

As head of production, Mayer was summoned to the set to make the decision. He, of course, was absolutely livid that security on the set had been so poor that someone could get away with something so cumbersome as a piano.

Suddenly Red piped up, and with a completely innocent look on his face, said, "I have a piano just like it at my house, Mr. Mayer. Maybe you'd like to rent it from me."

Mayer couldn't believe there were two such pianos in the world, until Red drove him to his apartment at the Wilshire Palms and pointed out what was presumably its twin in his living room. Only it wasn't a twin; it *was* the missing piano, which Red had hijacked from the studio in the middle of the night with the help of a couple of prop men from M.G.M.

Mayer was so delighted at the windfall that it never occurred to him that it was the same piano.

"How about fifty dollars a day?" bargained Mayer.

"How about $1,000 a day?" replied Red, completely deadpan. "It's the only one of its kind in the world."

"What!" sputtered Mayer.

Red shrugged indifferently. "Well, if you don't want it, let's forget it. I could use a vacation while you're building a new one."

Needless to say, Red got his $1,000 a day, which he later split with his accomplices.

Red's pranks notwithstanding, *Neptune's Daughter* turned into one of Metro's rare hits of the post-war years. In addition, Frank Loesser's "Baby, It's Cold Outside" wound up winning the Oscar for "Best Song in a Motion Picture."

Nevertheless, Red was still unhappy about being attached to Metro. *Neptune's Daughter* may have been a success, but Red Skelton wasn't the main attraction. He merely had supplied the laughs, while Esther Williams and Ricardo Montalban, two relative lightweights, were considered the stars.

This had been his fate in a half-dozen Metro films of late, but after the success of *The Fuller Brush Man,* he was beginning to resent, all over again, being just another member of the MGM repertory company. If he didn't feel this way, he wouldn't be an actor with superstar potential. But what added further fuel to his resentment was that he already was the star of his own radio show, where he was boss (with the usual assist from Edna). Moreover, NBC was anxious for him to start thinking seriously about making the conversion to TV.

According to the NBC executives, many important radio

personalities had already made the cross-over, and if Skelton didn't get into the new medium soon, he might miss the boat entirely. As a result of their prodding, Red started making noises around Metro that he was thinking of quitting films to devote all his time to radio and TV. Upon hearing this, Louis B. Mayer turned his usual apoplectic green, and shouted, "Absolutely not!" As far as he was concerned, no Metro star was going to cheapen his or her image by working in an upstart medium designed primarily for selling soap and underarm deodorants.

"But I have a contract that says I can," Red reminded him.

"I don't remember that," sputtered Mayer.

Whereupon Red pulled out his contract and showed Mayer the clause he had insisted on when he signed with Metro back in 1940.

Cornered, Mayer tried another tack. He reverted to the character of the lovable patriarch who cared about nothing but the welfare of his family of stars. Wearing this disguise, Mayer asked Red if he would consider postponing his debut into TV for another year *if* Metro could come up with a starring vehicle for him as good as *The Fuller Brush Man.*

Since Red wasn't that anxious to get into TV (despite what NBC wanted), he said okay, and Mayer and Dore Schary, who by then was right under Mayer in rank, ordered the story department to start searching for vehicles for Skelton that would satisfy him enough to keep him around for another year.

Imitation being the sincerest form of flattery in the movie business—correction: the *only* form of flattery—MGM decided to tailor-make a vehicle in the same exploitable mold as *The Fuller Brush Man.*

One of the things that made *The Fuller Brush Man* successful was that it involved an exploitable subject. There was a natural tie-in for free publicity between the picture and the Fuller Brush Company. For example, they utilized photographs of Red as a brush salesman in all their newspaper and magazine advertising, and Fuller brushes were given away as door prizes in theater lobbies.

Metro's answer to *The Fuller Brush Man* was a little pastiche by Devery Freeman called *The Yellow Cab Man.* Red drove a hack for the Yellow Cab Company, and of course got into all kinds of scrapes with the usual comedy heavies.

The Yellow Cab Man wasn't quite the smash that The Fuller Brush Man was, for the simple reason that it wasn't as fresh as its predecessor. However, with Red's name above the title, The Yellow Cab Man succeeded in earning a substantial profit for the studio, which made the stockholders happy, and Red reasonably eager once again to go on performing under the trademark of the regal MGM lion. Just find him another Fuller Brush or Yellow Cab man-type role, and there'd be no complaints from him. As far as Red was concerned, there was a limitless vista of those kinds of roles in his future—such as The Good Humor Man, The Bell Telephone Man, The Adohr Milk Man, and The Garbage Man.

Thus it came as a shock to Red when he started hearing rumors around the lot that the front office was considering him for the part of Harry Ruby in Three Little Words, a proposed film biography of the pop tune writers, Bert Kalmar and Harry Ruby. Kalmar's and Ruby's song hits included "Nevertheless," "Who's Sorry Now," "I Wanna Be Loved By You," and, of course, "Three Little Words." They'd also written the scores for many Broadway musicals and films including the Marx Brothers' classics: Animal Crackers, Horsefeathers, and Duck Soup.

While Kalmar and Ruby were not so widely known as Irving Berlin, Jerome Kern, Cole Porter, Rodgers and Hart, and some of the other giants of Tin Pan Alley, their story had one thing going for it that the biographies of these other song writers didn't have: an entertaining tale with unusual characters. Kalmar had started out to be a dancer, but was forced to switch to lyric writing when he injured his knee. After Kalmar and Ruby wrote their first hit, "I Wanna Be Loved By You," which Helen Kane (the boop-boop-a-doop girl) made popular, Kalmar decided he wanted to be a magician and worked seriously at it.

Ruby, by the same token, had a mania for baseball, and would rather be playing on a minor league team in Mingo Junction, Ohio, than be elected to Double-A ASCAP or win an Academy Award. What made their collaboration difficult and also amusing was that when Kalmar needed Ruby to write the music to one of his lyrics, Ruby was generally working out with the New York Yankees (who sometimes allowed him to take part in their pre-game warmup), and when Ruby needed his lyricist, Kalmar could generally be found in some small vaudeville theater or nightclub sawing a young lady in half. They weren't nearly as accomplished in their avocations as they were at composing pop tunes.

Under Jack Cummings' aegis, George Wells had written an amusing screenplay about the tribulations of the Kalmar and Ruby collaboration.

The only thing holding up production was that Metro, after reading the script, was afraid to put a couple of million dollars into bringing it to the screen, because the public was suddenly turning cool on film biographies, as attested to by the box office failures of *Words and Music,* the story of Rodgers and Hart, and *The Cole Porter Story.*

Cummings, whose pet project it was, argued that Kalmar and Ruby, while lesser known than the others, were more colorful characters than Rodgers and Hart and Cole Porter, all of whom were successful when young and had relatively few problems or complications in their careers.

The Metro moguls, while conceding all that, still were wary of the project until Cummings came up with the enterprising idea of casting Fred Astaire as Bert Kalmar, Vera-Ellen as his wife, and Red Skelton as the baseball-daffy composer. With Skelton and Astaire as box office insurance, the Metro brass believed that the picture might just have a chance, so they gave Cummings the word to try to get them in his cast, if he could.

Now for Fred Astaire, a consummate straight actor, playing Kalmar wasn't much of a reach, and Fred didn't have to be talked into the role. But it was difficult for anyone who'd ever seen Red perform in *The Fuller Brush Man* or *The Yellow Cab Man* to visualize him playing the more or less straight role of Harry Ruby. Skelton couldn't visualize it, either.

After years of doing broader comedy, it frightened Red to make such an abrupt departure from the farcical, bumbling boobs of the *Fuller Brush* and *Yellow Cab* pictures.

Throughout Red's most active years, his dependence on old

material and his fear of trying something new has been perhaps his only shortcoming as a performer. As a result, Red didn't even want to read the script when Jack Cummings called him into his office and told him about the Kalmar and Ruby project. It sounded amusing, Red conceded, but it didn't seem like his cup of tea.

"Just read the script," urged Cummings. "Then make up your mind."

Red agreed to do that much, but the next day decided to pass on the project anyway.

This turn-down was a blow to Cummings, because he knew that without Skelton in the picture, the front office wouldn't let him make it.

"So I went over to Red's and Georgia's place that night," recalls Cummings, "and I pinned Red down as to exactly what was troubling him. Didn't he think the script was funny? 'Oh, yeah,' he said, but he didn't think it was his kind of funny. There wasn't much chance for him to do any *schtick,* like in his other pictures. 'That's exactly why you should do it,' I told him. 'If you don't do something different soon, instead of that half-assed imitation of Bob Hope, you'll soon be washed up in the movies.' Red looked shocked that anyone would talk to him that way, and still resisted. But then Georgia piped up and said, 'You better listen to Jack, Red. He knows what he's talking about. Better than Edna. Try something different.' Well, with the two of us ganging up on him, Red finally agreed. But it was one of the hardest sells I've ever made."

When Harry Ruby, a mild-mannered, introspective intellectual type, heard that Red Skelton was going to play himself, he was more alarmed than Red was. He figured the story of Kalmar and Ruby would turn into a typical Skeltonian farce, with Red mugging all over the place, taking pratfalls, and ad libbing his own dialogue. Ruby's first inclination was to tell Metro to forget it.

"Don't worry," Cummings assured Ruby. "It's offbeat casting, but at least you'll get it made."

So Ruby took the money and ran—as it turned out, for a touchdown. Thanks to Astaire and Vera-Ellen's dancing, and

Red Skelton's characterization of Harry Ruby, *Three Little Words* was an enormous hit, both with the critics and at the box office where it opened in New York on August 10, 1950. Under Richard Thorpe's direction, Red surprised everyone—Astaire, Ruby, and even himself—with his ability as a straight actor.

The acceptance of Red as Harry Ruby should have been a lesson to him to be more adventurous in his choice of roles in the future. But his career, it seemed, took the proverbial two steps backward when, shortly after completing *Three Little Words*, he allowed himself to be cast as a camera nut in *Watch The Birdie*, a farce that didn't make a great deal of sense or money. In this comedy he once again reverted to his moron character, and though he obviously felt more comfortable doing that sort of thing, *Watch The Birdie* wasn't very inspired film making, and when it was released late in 1950, it only served to tarnish Red's reputation as a box office draw that he had worked so hard to achieve in *Three Little Words*.

Although few of Red Skelton's MGM films, funny as some were, will be very long remembered as artistic achievements by cinematic historians, the demise of *Watch The Birdie* could not be blamed on its star.

The film business was actually at a dangerous crossroads when *Watch The Birdie* was produced. Most studios were struggling to find a formula to woo audiences away from their TV sets and back into theaters, so it was small wonder that most of the major studios didn't know quite what to do with their stars, outside of not picking up their options when they came due.

Having been the colossus of Hollywood during the twenties, thirties and early forties, MGM was among the last to concede victory to that piece of talking furniture (as Fred Allen labeled it).

As a demonstration of their faith in the future of the film industry, Dore Schary and Louis B. Mayer decided to make great publicity capital of MGM's twenty-fifth anniversary year—1949—by hosting a gigantic studio luncheon on one of the sound stages on the Culver City lot. Everybody who could possibly mean anything to Metro's future—motion picture exhibitors, critics, gossip columnists, and local politicians—was invited to the commissary to partake of Metro's renowned chicken soup while sitting in serried ranks with Metro stars, as news cameras clicked frantically away.

As part of the Silver Jubilee hoopla—but also to preserve its impressive galaxy of stars on film for future generations to behold and wonder at—Louis B. Mayer and Dore Schary ordered all their acting talent to congregate on one of Metro's sound stages to pose en masse for one huge family portrait.

Fifty-eight of MGM's eighty stars and featured players showed up, and were seated, side by side, in five rows of elevated tiers. Although several important names were among those unavailable that day—Elizabeth Taylor, Lana Turner, Jimmy Stewart, Margaret O'Brien, William Powell, Cyd Charisse, and José Iturbi—those who did pose for the family portrait, which today hangs in the foyer of MGM's Irving Thalberg Building, were a veritable Who's Who of the Golden Years of the film industry: June Allyson, Leon Ames, Edward Arnold, Fred Astaire, Mary Astor, Ethel Barrymore, Lionel Barrymore, Spring Byington, James Craig, Arlene Dahl, Gloria De Haven, Tom Drake, Jimmy Durante, Vera-Ellen, Errol Flynn, Clark Gable, Ava Gardner, Judy Garland, Betty Garrett, Kathryn Grayson, Edmund Gwynn, Van Heflin, Katharine Hepburn, John Hodiak, Claude Jarmon, Jr., Van Johnson, Jennifer Jones, Louis Jourdan, Howard Keel, Gene Kelly, Christian Kent, Angela Lansbury, Mario Lanza, Janet Leigh, Peter Lawford, Jeanette MacDonald, Ann Miller, Ricardo Montalban, Jules Munshin, George Murphy, J. Carrol Nash, Reginald Owen, Walter Pidgeon, Jane Powell, Ginger Rogers, Frank Sinatra, Red Skelton, Alexis Smith, Ann Southern, Dean Stockwell, Lewis Stone, Clinton Sundberg, Robert Taylor, Audrey Totter, Spencer Tracy, Esther Williams, Keenan Wynn, and last but by no means least, Lassie.

Fifty-seven of the fifty-eight were already seated and facing the still photographer when Red Skelton, the last to arrive, bounded breathlessly into the scene.

Taking a quick look at the imposing assemblage, Red jumped up on a table facing the group, raised his hand for silence, and announced, completely deadpan, "Okay, everybody! The part's already been filled, you can go home now!"

The house in Vincennes, Indiana where Red Skelton was born "on time." His mother wanted him to arrive before his older brothers came home from school. *(Photo by Paul Willis)*

The cast of *As Thousands Hear* at the W. E. Tebbets Walkathon in Atlanta, Georgia during the depression. Red Skelton is sixth from the right in the back row. *(Photo by Elynas Wood)*

Probably taken during his vaudeville days, this photograph is from an old album.

Dubarry Was a Lady was one of the many films Skelton made during World War II, before he joined the army. (MGM photograph)

With Lucille Ball in *Du-barry Was a Lady*. The two redheads would compete for television ratings in later years. *(MGM photograph by Clarence S. Buli)*

(OPPOSITE TOP) *The Yellow Cab Man* was MGM's answer to Columbia's successful *The Fuller Brush Man*. Red is shown here with Gloria de Haven.

(OPPOSITE BOTTOM) Red with his first wife, Edna, Ozzie and Harriet Nelson, and Jack Douglas at the Brown Derby in the late thirties.

With Fred Astaire, Red in one of his few straight roles as Harry Ruby in *Three Little Words* which opened in 1950.

Red's television career spanned seventeen years and viewers saw him performing in a variety of roles such as:

The Mean Widdle Boy of
"I dood it" fame

Cauliflower McPugg

Clem Kaddiddlehopper

Red Skelton at Rockefeller Center with his children Valentina and Richard during a tour of New York City in the spring of 1957. *(World Wide Photos)*

Red and his son Richard at the Pierrot Statue in the Trivoli Garden in July 1957. *(World Wide Photos)*

The Skeltons try out an Italian motor scooter in front of the Colosseum. *(World Wide Photos)*

The Skeltons—Red, his wife Georgia, ten-year old Valentina and nine-year old Richard checking out of the Savoy after the British have labeled Red's gift to his dying son a publicity stunt. *(World Wide Photos)*

The Skelton's returning to Los Angeles after the world tour for Richard. Eight months later the boy would die from leukemia. *(World Wide Photos)*

Red rests between takes; his wife Georgia is to his right. *(Photograph by Henry Fitzgerald)*

In the early sixties, Red and Georgia at the home in Bel Air.

Valentina as a teenager at the Bel Air estate.

Red on the lawn of the Sorbonne estate with his photographic equipment.

Pictures used on a program for Red's nightclub act at the Sands Hotel in the late sixties.

Red's exhibit of his paintings at the Sands Hotel in Las Vegas in the mid sixties. Note that one of the "oils" is really the performer himself.

Red and Georgia in the Japanese Garden of their Palm Springs house.

Red with the Scarlet Macaw who lived in a tree in the yard in Palm Springs. *(CBS Portrait by Gabor Rona)*

13

Although Red was to make six additional highly forgettable films before Metro dropped him, his thoughts, as 1950 ushered in the new decade, were mostly about television. And they were not particularly happy thoughts, either. Despite what everyone told him about being "born for TV," Red was still scared stiff to put that birthright to the test.

Other radio comedians had tried it and were making good: Benny, Hope, Martin and Lewis, Fred Allen, Jackie Gleason, Milton Berle, Eddie Cantor, Jimmy Durante, Sid Caesar, and Groucho Marx. Yet to Red there were just too many things about TV that worried him:

Having to memorize a whole new script every week.

Having to stick to markers so he wouldn't be constantly wandering out of camera range.

Having to deliver cue lines reliably so that other performers would know when to speak.

Having to be *seen* in his characterizations rather than imagined.

Overexposure.

Being well aware of Red's apprehensions, his two most trusted advisers—Bo Roos and Freeman Keyes—suggested he not do a regular weekly comedy show for a while, but instead get his feet wet in the new medium by accepting some guest appearances—with Uncle Miltie, perhaps, or on the *Colgate Comedy Hour,* or with Benny or Hope. Any one of those people would have been happy to pay Red "top of the show" to bolster their own ratings.

Red, however, was even more afraid of risking his reputation doing guest shots than he was of appearing in a weekly show of his own, if such a thing were possible. "He never felt he would be treated properly in terms of material on somebody else's show," remembers John Fenton Murray, who was still writing for Skelton when he arrived at the TV crossroads. "He felt he'd be at the other comic's mercy, and that he wouldn't have any creative control of what he'd be doing. And another thing—despite who he was, Red was afraid to go up against people like Benny and Hope and Berle.

"He looked up to those people like gods, and he was sure he'd come off second best. If you recall, he had very few guest stars on his own show, when he finally did go on.

"But even before TV, Red was afraid of doing guest shots. I remember this big radio special for charity—kind of like a Jerry Lewis telethon—that he was supposed to be on, along with just about every other big name there was: Danny Thomas, Jack Benny, Bob Hope, Bing Crosby, Groucho Marx, Eddie Cantor, Burns and Allen, Dinah Shore, etc. And they were all supposed to come on and do their own thing. This was just before Red went on TV—around the spring of 1951. Now I'll give you an insight on how he felt, how insecure he was. The day of the show he came to me—his face was pale—and he said to me, 'Boy, they sure gave me a shitty deal. I have to go on *last*.' Last on a two-hour show meant half the audience would be asleep by then.

"Well, he was scared to death to have to follow all those other stars. And he wouldn't have . . . he was trying to think of a way of not showing up at all—when I reminded him that the reason they scheduled him last was because none of the others—Hope, Benny, Danny Thomas, and the other biggies—would follow *him*. They'd told the producer, 'If we have to follow that guy, we don't go on.' Because when Red did go on—and even though the audience was all pooped by then—he broke them up. Of all those comics, he was the only visual guy, and the studio audience just went bananas.

"But in Skelton's mind, they—the Bennys, Hopes, and so on—were bigger than he was. Up until the time I left him that was his attitude. He used to say, '*Someday* I'll be as big as they are.' He just idolized them. For example, if Hope would walk on Red's stage while he was doing his warm-up or 'after-show' that was a thrill to Red like God had just appeared. Red was overwhelmed by those people. And they were overwhelmed by him.

"Ed Gardner once told me out in the corridor outside our broadcasting studio—he did his show, *Duffy's Tavern*, right across from us—he said, 'That son of a bitch Skelton. His timing is greater than any comic I've ever known, and he doesn't even know it.' "

There could be no greater tribute than to be held in such high esteem by a man as talented, egomaniacal, and filled with professional envy as was the late proprietor of *Duffy's Tavern*.

Yet, judging by his fear of failure, Red seemed to have no idea of how good he was. No matter that he had killed 'em in vaudeville for years; no matter that he was a veteran of twenty-six MGM films, some huge hits; no matter that he was the star of his own highly successful coast-to-coast radio show. To him, he was still a comedy weakling, who had about as much chance of making it in TV as he had of climbing Mount Everest barefooted.

Red Skelton had none of the miserly hang-ups common in the hazardous and ephemeral profession of show business. The more he earned, the more he wanted to spend. That was his security blanket. He loved Rolls Royces, and at one time owned five of them, one of which he *gave* away to a friend who admired it. He thought nothing of walking into Harry Winston's—one of New York's top jewelers—and letting Georgia pick out a $50,000-gem, which he'd pay for on the spot with cash he'd pull out of an attaché case. He made one such visit to Winston's just about every time he and Georgia were in New York together.

And he loved living in princely surroundings.

In 1950, Red decided that he and Georgia had been apartment dwellers long enough, and shelled out $175,000 to purchase Noah Dietrich's imposing hilltop estate at 801 Sarbonne Road in Bel Air, Los Angeles's highest rent district. In 1950, few people except millionaires paid that much for a house.

There were several reasons for the move away from the Wilshire Palms and the comforting presence of "Mummy."

First of all, the situation between Edna and Georgia was not getting any better. In fact it had been deteriorating since 1949, when Edna's short marriage to Frank Borzage terminated in a Las Vegas courtroom. Being a single gal again left Edna with even more opportunity to interfere. It was important to get out of that atmosphere if Red and Georgia hoped to preserve their own marriage.

Second, Valentina and Richard were three and two years old respectively by 1950, and were beginning to need more outside playing area than an apartment could provide. As they became more mobile, additional servants were required to look after them, which in turn meant more living quarters to house the help.

And third, Red was becoming more of a recluse—in fact, almost misanthropic—the longer he lived in Hollywood. To be happy, he needed the kind of privacy he could find only on his own walled-in estate. Red socialized extremely selectively. He didn't have stooges constantly hanging around him, as other celebrities did, and the few close friends that he and Georgia had between them could probably be squeezed into a booth for four. Occasionally they'd have another couple to dinner, or perhaps Red's mother, Ida Mae, who had moved west since her son had become successful and into a house in Brentwood that Red had bought her. Georgia's mother and father, Mr. and Mrs. Mack Davis, had also moved to Southern California, and of course, they'd come to dinner occasionally, too. But outside of those people, few others were invited to the house.

So by Hollywood standards, Red led an almost monastic existence. He avoided so-called "Hollywood parties," and never went to opening night bashes or attended premieres. Moreover, he never attended, or performed at, the testimonial banquets the other comedians were constantly throwing for each other at the Friar's or Masquers or one of the posh country clubs. Red avoided the company of other actors, especially comedians, claiming that "they are the worst people in the world to hang around with. They never listen to you or care about what you're doing. They spend all their time thinking of ways to top you."

801 Sarbonne Road provided the perfect sanctuary for the anti-social Red. It was located on the highest mountain peak in the hills of Bel Air, with a commanding view of the city in the smog-shrouded distance, and of the rolling, verdant fairways of the Bel Air Country Club directly below. The estate had four and a half acres of beautifully landscaped grounds, a magnificent swimming pool, a greenhouse, and the whole thing was protected by a twelve-foot stone wall. Access to the grounds was through imposing wrought iron gates imported from Europe and electrically controlled from either the main house or the interior of one of the Skeltons' fleet of Rolls Royces and Cadillacs.

Inside the stone walls, and up a long, tree-bordered driveway, stood a two-story Georgian colonial mansion, with stately white pillars, green shutters, fourteen rooms, including two master suites—one for Big Red and one for Little Red—separate suites for each of the children, and seven bathrooms.

The 7,500-square-foot house, replete with paneled walls and terrazzo floors, was decorated by William Haines, one of the movie colony's top interior designers. But its fifty-foot living room, done in green and white, reflected the eclectic tastes of its two owners. Its furnishings were a mixture of eighteenth-century English antiques collected by the Skeltons in their five years of married life—mahogany breakfronts, drum tables, Victorian hat racks, and several pump organs—combined with custom-made contemporary pieces, including two huge white sofas, with a coffee table between them, and a grand piano. Along the entire length of one wall, from floor to ceiling, ran bookcases filled with reading matter.

Between the dining and living rooms was a stately entrance foyer, from which a curved banistered stairway led upstairs along marbled wallpaper to Red and Georgia's and the children's private living quarters.

Red's suite contained, among other things, a nine-foot-square bed, huge walk-in closets, and three full-sized television sets, so that the master of the estate could monitor more than one channel at a time. Attached to the bed was a complicated control panel to raise and lower the blinds automatically, turn on recording machines or regulate the TV sets, and a master switch to light every room in the house simultaneously, as well as illuminate the grounds of his estate in order to discourage any nocturnal sneak attacks by burglars.

Red's bed was usually piled high with books and papers and scripts, and sometimes his gray miniature poodle Nicodemus. (The Skeltons had four other poodles which didn't sleep with Red. For security reasons, Georgia would have preferred German shepherds, but Red's health wouldn't permit it. In recent years he'd been plagued by asthma; The French poodle was the only breed of dog he wasn't allergic to.)

"I do a lot of my writing in bed," Red once told a reporter who came to interview him. "I got all that equipment because I always forgot the 'great' ideas I'd have at night. I remember one night I had a particularly bright idea and I wrote it down on a pad. Next morning, I couldn't wait to see the brilliant thing I'd written. I grabbed the pad and it said, 'Write play.' "

If Red's home was his castle, his bedroom was his private fortress, for it was there that he kept his collection of fifty guns that he'd been accumulating since his days in the Army, when he'd become fascinated with firearms. Although the main collection was in a separate alcove, Red kept a high-powered pistol and a 16-gauge shotgun, both loaded, by his bed at all times, in case the Skelton household was invaded.

Over the years Red had been the victim of several hold-ups.

Ironically, he once was robbed because of his interest in acquiring guns. It happened shortly after he had been discharged from the Army and he was living at the Wilshire Palms. Coming home from the studio one day Red stopped his car at Santa Monica Boulevard and Doheny Drive to pick up a hitchhiking GI, which was the patriotic thing to do in those days. As they were driving along Santa Monica, the chatter got around to guns, and Red confessed that he had always wanted a .38 caliber pistol.

"I've got one I'll sell you," offered the hitchhiker, pulling one out of his pocket. "Seventy-five bucks'll take it."

Red liked the looks of the weapon, but because he didn't have seventy-five dollars on him, drove the GI to his apartment to obtain the cash.

Nobody else was home when the two men arrived at the Wilshire Palms. It was the maid's day off, and Georgia was working at the studio that day.

"All I've got around the house is fifty-one dollars," Red told the hitchhiker.

"Thanks, I'll take it," the GI replied, pocketing the money and backing out of the apartment while he covered Red with his gun.

In spite of the fact that he had small children in the house, Red kept all his guns loaded twenty-four hours a day. When asked by a visitor if he didn't think that was a dangerous habit, Red's reply seemed like something out of *Catch-22*. "I noticed years ago," he said, "that people are always getting hurt with guns they think are *unloaded*. When someone picks up a firearm at my house and asks if it's loaded, I say, 'Sure.' Why, right away he drops the gun like a hot potato. That way, no one gets hurt."

Red's eclectic interests were not confined to just dangerous firearms, however. The Sarbonne house was a repository of Red's many and varied collections: cameras, coins, hats, paintings, oriental jade, carved ivory figures, two dozen briefcases, first editions of some of the world's greatest classics, and twenty-two rare and antique Bibles, including one that he claimed was a "genuine Gutenberg."

Although he had little talent for photography, Red owned just about every kind of camera made, from sound movie cameras to Nikons and Rolleis and Leicas, and bought practically every new one that came out on the market, plus thousands of dollars worth of accessories. He carried a miniature "spy" camera in his pocket at all times, and was always snapping candid shots of everyone who visited the house. But according to those who have been victims of his camera wizardry, Red took the worst pictures imaginable. "He never could get the exposures right or the focus correct, and has no idea of composition," says John Fenton Murray.

One thing Red did do well around the house was keep the two littlest redheads entertained. Not only did he read stories to them, but he acted out all the animal parts. When Valentina would say, "Do a bear, Daddy," Red would waddle about with the perfect rolling gait of a grizzly bear, knocking over a lamp or two in his enthusiasm. When Richard would say, "Now do the bunny," Red would drop to his knees, and hop wildly around, until the children were convulsed with laughter, and the house was in a shambles.

Red's hat collection—containing just about every hat style ever devised by the headware profession—was also a source of merriment around the house, starting early in the morning. The first thing Red would put on after he awoke and brushed his teeth would be a top hat or a homburg or a battered brown derby, which he'd wear to the breakfast table. Such headware, he claimed, put him in a humorous mood for the rest of the day, not to mention that it amused the entire family of redheads during breakfast.

About the only luxury item actually missing from the Sarbonne estate was a tennis court. But since Red had never had the time to learn, or engage in, such rich man's sports as golf or tennis, it was no hardship to him. He dunked himself in his pool occasionally—in the shallow end—but for the most part he got his exercise wandering along the flower-bordered paths of his estate, in as few clothes as possible, romping with the children, and dreaming up new comedy routines, which he'd set down on a battered typewriter in his cottage workroom, a retreat away from the main house. Because of the way he maintained it—with papers and books and samples of his various collections scattered about—most of the time his workroom resembled the aftermath of Hurricane Mabel. Red wasn't the neatest person in the world, and like most men resented having the help fussing around in his private sanctuary.

Georgia was an excellent housekeeper, but to keep such a large ménage functioning properly required a retinue of servants—two live-in maids, a governess, a chauffeur, an Italian gardener, a pool man, and a butler, who was built like a tackle on the Rams, and who doubled at being Red's bodyguard.

That much help meant a large monthly outlay, but Red no longer had to worry about paying bills. In addition to his many profitable investments, for which Bo Roos was chiefly responsible, Red still had three years to go on his MGM contract, and in 1949 had signed a new radio pact with CBS for approximately $10,000 a week.

Red, along with a number of other former NBC stars, had been enticed over to CBS by its president, William Paley, who at that time was determined to make the Columbia Broadcasting System the Number One network. Over the past two years, Paley had perpetrated a series of raids on the NBC star roster, his chief weapons being money and capital gains deals, and had succeeded in signing not only Red Skelton but Jack Benny, Burns & Allen, and Desi & Lucy as well. Red's deal did not include television, however, so by early 1951, when it became evident that he was about to make the jump into TV, both major networks began vying spiritedly for the privilege of presenting Red on television for the first time and were dangling all kinds of golden carrots, plus assorted fringe benefits, in front of him in order to persuade him to sign.

Although Red could never be accused of not wanting to squeeze the maximum amount of money from a potential employer, his main consideration was not *what* he was going to be paid so much as which network could offer him the most solid guarantees against failure.

That's what he told his two chief negotiators, Freeman Keyes and Bo Roos, as they went into a series of meetings that spring with the heads of both networks.

NBC apparently offered him the most assurances, for on the

morning of May 3, 1951, both Hollywood trade papers carried news of the deal.

The deal, which was made through Red's mentor, Freeman Keyes of the Russell Seeds Company, called for the comic to star in a series of live, half-hour-long television shows over NBC, starting in the fall of 1951. Procter & Gamble was to sponsor the show, with Red reportedly being paid the tidy sum of $5.5 million for his services on the network over the next seven years.

When he first started negotiating, Red was insisting that his show be filmed rather than broadcast "live," because he felt it would be courting trouble to attempt his kind of comedy, with its dependence on props and sight gags, in front of live TV cameras. There were just too many opportunities for boo-boos, such as lines being forgotten, props misfiring, cues being missed, and sketches failing to play. On film, mistakes could be re-shot and scenes completely edited before being broadcast to 50 million home viewers.

However, there were some valid arguments against filming, too, the main one being that Red worked best in front of an audience, responding to their reactions with ad libs and impromptu bits, and that his comedy would probably suffer greatly without that kind of stimulation. Moreover, filming was more expensive and time-consuming. A live show didn't take any longer to shoot than the length of time it was on the air.

In the end, Red bowed to network pressure to do the show "live," for thirty-nine weeks, beginning September 30.

The one thing Red insisted on, and got, was that he be allowed to keep doing his weekly radio program.

That Red should wish to take on the additional burden of doing a radio show while attempting to make his much-heralded TV debut a success is surprising only in retrospect.

In 1951, "Nobody," according to writer Ben Freedman, "knew how television was going to go over with the public. Many people didn't have sets yet, reception was poor in many areas, and don't forget, Red still had a tremendous radio audience, which he did not want to lose in case he failed on TV. Also the money. He liked money."

* * *

Early that spring, while Red's army of negotiators, including Freeman Keyes and Bo Roos, were busy winding up the details of his deal with the network heads, Red accepted an invitation to play the London Palladium with his opening there set for July 2.

Red had always wanted to play the Palladium, having been told that his kind of pantomime would probably go over big in Britain, the birthplace of the greatest pantomimist of all, and one of Red's idols, Charlie Chaplin.

Also on Red's itinerary were some commitments to entertain U.S. troops still stationed in France and Germany, and an audience with Pope Pius XII, which had been arranged for June 27. The person responsible for this audience was Father Edward Carney, a Jesuit Priest from Massachusetts, who had been a friend of Red's for many years, and who was one of Red's traveling companions on this trip.

Others in Red and Georgia's party, when they took off for Rome on June 20, were Bo Roos and Gene Fowler. The latter was contemplating a biography of his favorite comedian and figured that accompanying him on a trip would be a painless way to collect some biographical information.

The audience with Pope Pius XII was mostly Georgia's idea, for she was the only member of the Skelton family to take her Roman Catholicism seriously. Red was not *irreligious*, but he considered himself nondenominational rather than a member of any particular group of worshipers. In addition, he didn't like to be bothered with the formal obligations of religion, such as attending church regularly. Notwithstanding, he claimed he read at least one chapter of one of his many Bibles every night before going to sleep; he had an eight-foot statue of Christ of the Sacred Heart standing in his garden on the Sarbonne estate; and he seemed to enjoy the company of rabbis, ministers, and priests. "They just like me, and I like them," he used to explain. "It's that way with everybody. I love people—just people—anybody—everybody. They're wonderful. That's why I clown. It's simply that *I love to make people laugh.*"

As it turned out, the audience with the Pope was not a private one. There were two or three hundred other people in the room as well. So neither Red nor Georgia had the satisfaction of being able to converse personally with the Pope, and had to settle for a "group" blessing.

However, even the Pope's group blessing paid off—on the flight from Rome to London several days later.

As the airliner soared over snow-capped Mont Blanc in the Alps, two engines sputtered and died. Then a third engine caught fire and the plane started to go down.

Understandably, panic began to break out among the passengers, among whom were a large number of children of various nationalities and religions, including Hindu. Red wasn't too happy about the situation either.

Suddenly Father Carney, in the seat next to Skelton, turned to his comedian friend and said, "Okay, Red, you take care of your department, and I'll take care of mine."

The two men quickly unstrapped their seat belts and while Father Carney prepared to give the last rites to all who wished, Red started running up and down the aisles of the plane, clowning and miming even more frenetically than he had for his Walkathon audiences.

Few of the children in Red's audience that day could understand a word he was saying, but the beauty of pantomime is that they didn't have to. He was able to make them laugh and forget the impending crash, despite the language barrier.

"None of us ever expected to get out of there alive," recalls Red. "It was the most wonderfully satisfying performance I ever gave."

But just when a crash seemed unavoidable, the pilot was able to slip the powerless liner past the last remaining craggy peak and glide it to a shaky landing in a cow pasture on the French side of the border. There were no injuries—just a few frightened cows and worried passengers, who converged on the pilot to thank him for bringing the plane down safely. But as far as Red was concerned, their escape was not so much a result of good piloting (though that helped) as it was a "miracle performed by the Guy Upstairs," as he often referred to his Maker.

After the passengers were safely out of the plane and were standing around in a concerned group in the cow pasture, Red turned to them with a grin and said, "All right, now you can forget those noble resolutions and go back to all the bad habits you had before!"

Apparently the Pope's blessings were still covering Red when he opened at the Palladium in London two nights later.

Although it was a sweltering July night, with no air-conditioning in the Palladium, there was a capacity turnout to watch Red perform the act they'd heard had been killing them in America for years—which, of course, included the doughnut dunking bit, "Guzzler's," and his various other drunk imitations.

Understandably, Red was extremely nervous about facing a London audience for the first time, because many other American comedians, including Martin & Lewis and the Marx Brothers, had bombed in their initial attempts to capture the British. But according to just about every one of the London critics who saw him perform, Red had nothing to fear.

In spite of the intense heat in the Palladium, Red managed to capture the British audience with what one of the reviewers called his "backwoods charm, manifest sincerity, and a large amount of absolutely genuine unsophistication." Another critic wrote, "There was never a dull moment during the fifty minutes that Red occupied the stage." But the strongest kudos of all came from a critic who wrote, "I noticed for the first time during a dumb act [pantomime] the musicians did not walk out for a smoke."

From a London critic, that was the ultimate in praise.

14

From the way Red Skelton's television career took off in the fall, he had no more reason to fear video than the Palladium.

Either Red had lucked into it, or else he or his advisers were gifted with some kind of precognition, but he had somehow succeeded in stalling his television debut until the day when the coaxial cable became available to the networks, enabling them to take advantage of coast-to-coast transmission and the resulting wider audiences.

Transcontinental radio programs had of course been routine for years because ordinary telephone lines could carry the shows. But television signals were considerably more complex and required a much wider band of frequencies, which only the new coaxial cable could provide.

Until 1951, all the major early TV hits—Milton Berle, the *Colgate Comedy Hour,* and Sid Caesar's *Show of Shows*—had originated in New York City, in order that sponsors might reach and hawk their wares to the most densely populated areas of the United States—namely, the Eastern seaboard. The Middle and Far West received the same shows on a delayed broadcast, usually a day later, by kinescope.

But by the fall of 1951, both NBC and CBS were announcing, in large newspaper ads, the availability of the coaxial cable on their networks, and heralding its obvious advantages of reaching all advertising markets simultaneously.

As a result, many of the important television shows moved their bases of operations to Hollywood, in order to accommodate their stars, most of whom lived in Southern California, and to take advantage of the fact that there was more talent of every kind—writing, acting, and directing, plus all the technical know-how—available in the film capital.

For a time, the move west resulted in a severe shortage of broadcasting space in Hollywood.

In the fall of 1951, for example, NBC had just one theater on the West Coast set up for television broadcasting, and that was the former legit playhouse, the El Capitan, on Vine Street, just two blocks up from its main radio broadcasting studios on the corner of Sunset and Vine.

Formerly the home of Ken Murray's *Blackouts,* the long-running stage review in which the late Marie Wilson's bosom first achieved the kind of recognition it deserved, the El Capitan had been purchased by NBC specifically to house the television broadcasting needs of the *Colgate Comedy Hour,* which featured rotating comedians each week, among them Eddie Cantor, Fred Allen, Abbott & Costello, Donald O'Connor, Danny Thomas, and Martin & Lewis. Later the El Capitan was used for the *All-Star Review,* which on different weeks featured Jimmy Durante and Martha Raye.

Realizing that the El Capitan was already being used seven days a week, either for rehearsing or broadcasting, and that it could not possibly accommodate any more traffic, NBC bought a large tract of land in Burbank, a few miles outside of Hollywood, late in 1951, and started making plans for building a brand new broadcasting complex there.

Their initial plans called for the erection of one building containing dressing rooms, administration offices, and two studios for broadcasting.

These two studios were to be tailored to order to fit the requirements of NBC's two main comedy powerhouses—Bob Hope and Red Skelton.

In those days, nobody was quite sure what was the best design for a theater for "live" broadcasting, because everyone working in television was more or less a beginner. The major complaint of most performers was that it was difficult, if not impossible, for the audience to see what was taking place on the stage because the cameras, lights, and other technical equipment stood between them and the action. About the only way the studio audience could see the action was over the monitors—small TV sets distributed throughout the studio overhead—but that wasn't very satisfactory.

In his new studio, Bob Hope wanted an orchestra pit in front of the stage, because that had been a characteristic of all the great vaudeville theaters. But then Hope decided a pit was inappropriate to the new medium and would put the spectators too far away from him. So the pit was omitted. The orchestra was put to one side, and seats for the audience were placed close to the apron of the stage, with a ramp in the middle for cameras.

But the highly resourceful inventor of the renowned Skelton De-Fogging device believed he knew a better arrangement. He specified that a balcony for the spectators be built opposite the stage, but at a slightly higher level. That way the cameras could be placed under the balcony and not be in the line of anybody's vision.

Unfortunately, even the ground-breaking for the Burbank facilities couldn't begin until early in 1952. In the meantime Red, whose first television broadcast was scheduled for September 30, needed a studio. So in late summer of 1951, coinciding approximately with the time that Red returned from his trip abroad, NBC started converting Studio D, the largest of its radio studios, in the complex at Sunset and Vine, over to television. But that was merely a facelift to take care of temporary expediencies and not a complete new design like the one Red had ordered for Burbank, so audiences still were forced to catch the show on monitors until the winter of 1953.

With the technical problems out of the way, Red, whose NBC deal also called for him to be his own producer, was now free to concentrate on how to get the best show on the air.

For the creative end, Red stuck basically to the same writing staff that had served him so reliably in radio—John Fenton Murray, Benedict Freedman, and Jack Douglas. Red also took a writing credit that year, although how much actual writing he contributed is debatable. Nevertheless, he did include his name in the credits with the other writers, a practice he continued for the rest of his television career. Like Bob Hope and a number of other television stars, Red apparently felt that his presence at story conferences, plus how he enhanced the material in the actual playing, justified his name on the crawl.

According to most of the writers who've toiled for Skelton over the years, there is little doubt that he could take an ordinary piece of material, and in the playing, occasionally turn it into something "brilliant." Nevertheless, most writers resent the practice of a star taking a writing credit, feeling that the star gets enough of the glory, plus the lion's share of the loot, without having to horn in on their domain as well. "But if you wanted to work for Skelton, it was just something you had to live with," says Marty Ragaway, one of television's top comedy writers, who served a long stint with Skelton in the sixties.

Red also wanted to direct his television show. He felt that most of his recent MGM films could have been better if he'd been the director, and he had a point. But Freeman Keyes, who controlled the whole package, was able to talk Red out of taking on that additional burden, claiming that it would be impossible for him to be both in front of, and behind, the cameras simultaneously.

So in the end Red settled for the titles of star, producer and writer, and NBC hired a young man named John Gaunt to direct.

"Not that anyone really directed Red," recalls John Fenton Murray. "He pretty much did everything the way he wanted, and it usually turned out damn good. In those early days he was pretty nice about letting us show him in rehearsals how we felt a sketch ought to be done. In fact, he insisted on it. I remember, he'd sit in the front row of the studio during rehearsals and make us enact what we'd written. That way he'd study it, get it set in his mind, and then go up there on the stage and really take off with it."

Red had to get acquainted with the material that way because Edna was no longer around to read and explain the TV scripts to him. Not that Edna was completely out of Red's life—she was still overseeing his Wednesday night radio show—but that was secondary in importance now that he was doing TV. So there's little doubt that by the fall of 1951 Edna's power was beginning to wane dramatically. This didn't happen accidentally.

Georgia more or less insisted that Red start cutting himself loose from Edna's umbilical cord. And what better way to begin than by easing her out of the operation of the television show. Besides, television required more professional, exacting writing, which Edna wasn't qualified to handle. "In radio, she'd give us outlines, and we'd punch them up with jokes," recalls Ben Freedman. "But on the television show, we'd write full sketches and have to tie the whole thing together in one script that was supposed to make sense from start to finish."

Since the radio show was being done at CBS, Edna wasn't even working in the same building with Red and the TV staff, and after a while she was no longer allowed up at the Sarbonne house to listen to "first readings."

Murray, Freedman, and Douglas continued to write Red's radio program, so Edna didn't even have to break in anybody new or make any decisions about hiring and firing. Ordinarily, it would have been impossible for writers to do both television and radio for someone as demanding and jittery as Red Skelton—without heading for nervous breakdowns themselves, that is. But the Skelton radio setup had a unique system of operation once Red started doing television. "We weren't actually writing anything new for the radio show," recalls Freedman. "Not that Red was doing old stuff on the air. It was simply that Edna and Red had accumulated so much extra material over the years that we'd written but which they'd never used that all Edna had to do was to go through the files, dig out the best of the discarded stuff, and put it into thirty-minute script form. We'd write new lead-ins, but hers was mostly an editing job."

With Edna missing from the front lines of the TV action, there was no one on the staff to act as a buffer between the writers and Red, who frequently balked at doing new material.

"Someone had to control Red and talk him into trying something new," remembers Ben Freedman. "Neither John nor I were in a position to do it. So they hired Marty Rackin to act as head writer."

Marty Rackin, who had been a buddy of Red's from their vaudeville days, was by 1951 a successful Hollywood writer and about the only one in town Red trusted and would listen to, outside of Freeman Keyes, that is. But Keyes did not contribute anything creatively to the comedy; he was a businessman, and only in that capacity would Red accept his advice.

The only other person on the staff whom Red trusted and liked was the highly talented musician, arranger and orchestra leader, Dave Rose. Rose and his forty-piece orchestra finally joined the Skelton TV program in 1951. That started a relationship, both professional and personal, that was to last throughout the entire eighteen years Red was on the air. It was one of the few relationships in Red's life—including his marriages—that didn't eventually turn sour. In fact, the pair is still extremely friendly today, and whenever Red needs a musical director for a very special event, Dave Rose is the first person he tries to draft.

With Dave Rose supplying the music, the Skylarks, one of the most popular singing groups of the time, supplying the vocal numbers and singing commercials, and three of the best writers in the laugh-making trade supplying the comedy inspiration, the *Red Skelton Show* seemed to have "the sweet smell of success" about it as September 26 rolled around, and a series of very clever full-page ads touting the show appeared in both Hollywood trade papers.

The first ad showed a large portrait of Red Skelton dressed

as San Fernando Red in white top hat and a white vest, debonairly flicking an ash from a large cigar in his hand. The text below read:

THE RUSSELL M. SEEDS COMPANY,
Freeman Keyes, President
IS PRIVILEGED TO PRESENT
San Fernando Red on his TV debut on
the full NBC-TV network, starting Sept. 30,
KNBH, Channel 4, 7 P.M.

The second ad showed Red as Deadeye, dressed in a Mexican sombrero, playing the guitar. Its text read:

THE BEVERLY MANAGEMENT COMPANY,
Bo Roos, President, is
proud to number among its distinguished clientele
DEADEYE

The third ad featured a photo of Red dressed as Cauliflower McPugg, the punchdrunk prize fighter:

BENTON AND BOWLES, INC.
congratulates
CAULIFLOWER MCPUGG
on his TV debut on NBC-TV network starting
Sept. 30, 1951

Ad number four showed a photograph of Clem Kadiddlehopper and beneath it:

THE NATIONAL BROADCASTING COMPANY
congratulates
CLEM KADIDDLEHOPPER
on his TV debut on NBC-TV network starting
Sept. 30, 1951

And on the last page, a portrait of Red as his most dignified self, wearing a suit and tie, and the following text:

PROCTER & GAMBLE
Presents
THE RED SKELTON SHOW
starring
Red Skelton

Directed by	written by	Produced by
John Gaunt	JohnFenton Murray	Red Skelton
	Ben Freedman	
	Jack Douglas	
	Red Skelton	

Musical director
DAVE ROSE

A Russell M. Seeds Company Production

A format of the Red Skelton television show was not dissimilar to his radio program. It opened with Red in a tux doing a stand-up monologue of topical jokes in front of the curtain; this was followed by a musical interlude, which led into a number of short blackout sketches featuring his various characterizations: Clem Kadiddlehopper; San Fernando Red, the corrupt politician; Willie Lump-Lump, the drunk; Cauliflower McPugg, the pugilist; Deadeye, the Mexican bandit, and whoever else he had time for.

The first show was a pleasant mixture of new and old material, with the emphasis on the latter. As usual, Red insisted on hitting the audience with old material his first time out because he felt it was sure-fire and most people in the vast TV wasteland hadn't seen it before, and therefore it was safe. And it was. He had the audience in convulsions.

But some of his new bits were just as funny, if not funnier. One, dreamed up specially for his TV debut, occurred at the end of his monologue. While Red was standing in front of the curtain taking a bow and smugly acknowledging audience applause, two hands reached out from under the curtain, grabbed him by the ankles, and whisked him out of view under the curtain.

This surprise conclusion to Red's monologue threw the audience into hysterics. The bit would be repeated on subsequent programs. Flat out frontwards is perhaps the most dangerous way to take a fall, however, and though it never failed to get a huge laugh, Red later wound up having to go to the hospital to correct internal injuries he sustained from being thrown forward and dragged under the curtain week after week.

Another new show-stopper featured Clem Kadiddlehopper, as an Irish tenor, singing some classical piece, to the accompaniment of Dave Rose and his entire ensemble.

As he had been doing for years on his radio show, Red turned serious just before the closing sign-off to tell the audience:

"Ladies and gentlemen, I want to thank you for putting up with my nonsense. I sincerely hope I haven't said or done anything to offend anyone. If I have, I didn't mean it. I hope you have had as much fun as I have had. It is a lot of fun to try to make people laugh. Regardless of what your heartache might be, while laughing for a few seconds you have forgotten about it. Thanks for coming, and good night."

A touch of corn, perhaps, but Red meant every word of it, which his fans seemed to sense and loved him for. As a result, they were on his side. Red could get away with things that in most comedians' bags of tricks would be considered in atrocious taste.

As Leo Rosten once wrote in a magazine article about Red shortly after his television debut, "Skelton draws his best characterizations from the half-world of illiterates, imbeciles, and inebriates. He has insight and compassion, and a kindly respect for those who are not quite 'all there.' He has an inner feeling for the naïve and slow-witted, the unbright, and the schlemiels. To imitate a lunkhead without malice or derision is quite a feat—and Skelton brings it off every time."

Unlike Broadway, television reviews have a minimal effect on a program's eventual success or failure. The show's time slot, its competition from the opposing networks, luck, and the taste of the American public are what count the most.

A bruised ego is about the most damage a TV critic can inflict on his subject.

In the case of Red's first television outing, his ego didn't have to worry about being bruised. The returns from most of the nation's television critics ranged from good to raves, with *The Hollywood Reporter* waxing the most ecstatic.

> Move over, Mr. Berle—Mr. Skelton has arrived. The redhead took to television last night with all the ease of a genuine pro, and the new medium has found its newest—and perhaps greatest—comedy star.

> The brief half-hour of Skelton's debut seemed to zip by in something under five minutes. Two sketches, a musical interlude by the Skylarks, a wonderfully integrated commercial, and it was all over, leaving the viewer crying for more.

Hard-boiled Jack Gould of the *New York Times* trumpeted the only note sour enough to spoil Red's breakfast the morning the reviews broke in their respective papers.

Gould accused Red of everything from sloppy production to stooping to bad taste to breaking up unnecessarily at his own jokes to resorting to wearing funny hats in order to evoke a laugh.

Built into Gould's review were the usual signs of Eastern chauvinism, which makes it difficult for some critics to admit, even in this enlightened age, that anything worthwhile creatively could possibly originate west of the Hudson. On the other hand, some of Gould's criticisms were justified. Throughout his career, for example, Red has always had the unfortunate habit of breaking up at his own jokes, and pretending that lines already written in the script were ad libs.

Another of Gould's complaints that one could hardly take issue with was Red's wanton use of funny headware. But according to Red's writers, there was a reason behind this madness; he didn't just put on a funny hat because he thought it would be easier to get a laugh that way. "What it was," explains Marty Ragaway, "is that Red just couldn't get inside one of his characterizations unless he was wearing the headgear of that particular person. He just didn't feel comfortable playing Deadeye without his cowboy hat, or Clem Kadiddlehopper without his farmer's hat, or the drunk without his punched-in fedora with the brim pulled down over his ears. Whenever he tried to play those characters without the hats, the spot died. That's why his monologues were the worst part of the show. He came out and delivered it in a tuxedo. He had no hat protection."

Regardless of what Jack Gould thought, the *Red Skelton Show* took off like a rocket after its initial airing and soon reached the top of the ratings, where it remained for most of the season.

Along the way to proving *The Hollywood Reporter* correct, the *Red Skelton Show* picked up sixty-two separate awards for comedy, and on February 19, 1952, in ceremonies at the Ambassador's Coconut Grove, before most of Hollywood's top stars, Red won the Emmy for "Best Comedian on Television," and against fairly stiff competition—Sid Caesar, Lucille Ball, Imogene Coco, Jimmy Durante, Herb Shriner, Martin & Lewis, and Milton Berle, who wasn't even nominated that year. As the show's producer, Red picked up a second Emmy for "Best Comedy Show," and if the Academy had been giving writing awards in those days, he no doubt would have won in that category as well.

Zsa Zsa Gabor presented the award to Red, with Georgia looking on proudly from a ringside table. Red was truly touched as he accepted his trophy, thanked the Academy for voting for him, but added humbly, "If you want to know my opinion, I think this should have gone to Lucille Ball."

Perhaps he would have been wise to keep that opinion to himself, because by the end of that same television season *I Love Lucy* had taken over the top of the ratings and Lucy was on her way to winning her first of many Emmys.

15

After such a glorious first season, who could have predicted that in just a little over a year the same Red Skelton would be on the verge of being totally washed up in show business, dropped by both NBC and MGM; that his wife would be leaving him; and that he'd be playing Willie Lump-Lump for real.

Perhaps Jack Gould could have predicted this, for he was the lone person, among all the TV critics, to question whether or not Red could keep up his opening show's pace for more than a few weeks.

On the way to his TV Waterloo, Red used up 162 of his best comedy routines—the ones he had played and perfected over his years in vaudeville and nightclubs. These were sure-fire spots that most of his TV fans had never seen before.

One of Red's greatest sketches had him playing a starving tramp who was mistaken for an actor dressed as a tramp. The actor didn't show up, and Red was shoved into the scene, which took place at a table in a restaurant. Starving, the tramp tried to eat the food that had been placed on the table for the scene, but the director kept insisting that he forget the food and concentrate on his role, which involved welcoming a girl who played a starving waif. Red finally went berserk from hunger and did one of the funniest bits of pantomime in his repertoire when he picked up the girl's hand and mistook it for a piece of chicken. His business of separating the fingers as if they were chicken bones and picking out the imaginary pieces of meat from between them became a comedy classic, reminiscent of Chaplin.

As long as he had that kind of material to rely on, Red was the hottest comedian on the tube. However, classic bits like that one can't be invented every week. Once Red finished feeding the last of his tried and true material to the voracious electronic monster, and he and his writers had to start coming up with something new each week to replace it, he was no longer so funny, and the show started going downhill.

This was no reflection on Red's writers. No comic could hope to have a more competent staff batting out jokes and sketches for him than Freedman, Murray, and Jack Douglas. Indeed, many of Red's newest and best characterizations—San Fernando Red, Cauliflower McPugg, Deadeye the cowboy, Willie Lump-Lump, and J. Newton Numbskull—had been dreamed up by this trio.

And some of his new bits were better than many Red had brought with him from vaudeville. Skelton satirizing breakfast food: "Junior is getting bored with cereals that merely crackle; he wants cereals that explode." Skelton satirizing a drunk, who has to drive home because he is in no condition to walk. Skelton, as a new father, bathing a baby in a pan of water that's too small to accommodate the infant. Finally, he becomes so frustrated that the baby won't fit into the pan that Red gives him a Karate chop in the stomach, causing him to bend inward and into the pan of water.

Then there was the poker game sketch that saw all of Red's characters pitted against each other at one table, with Red hopping from chair to chair to play their respective hands. This, too, became a classic bit that was repeated on many subsequent Skelton shows over the years.

The Topsy Turvy Room, written by Ben Freedman, was another audience favorite. The idea behind that sketch was that Willie Lump-Lump's wife, in order to cure him of drunkenness, arranged with a carpenter to have his room built on its side. The floor, with chairs and tables nailed to it, was at right angles to the wall, which was where the floor normally was. When Willie passed out, his wife put him in his favorite chair, which was now halfway up the wall. When he came to and saw the room on its side, he thought he'd gone nuts from booze and promised to lay off the stuff in the future.

Such unusual ideas were not easy to come by, and frequently Red had to go on the air with new material he was not particularly happy with, which was reflected in his performances. The self-assurance he had when doing bits he liked and was familiar with seemed to vanish. He stumbled over lines and missed cues, upsetting the whole production.

But the problem was not only the struggle to find fresh material. Every comedian was in that same boat. It was compounded by also having to get the show on the air "live"!

One of Red's most vexing stumbling blocks was the instant costume changes that live television demanded of its performers. Since Red relied heavily on funny costumes for his various characterizations, and because he was in every sketch from start to finish, he'd have to race off the stage after every blackout to get into fresh clothes. In his hurry, he'd sometimes trip over a cable or bump into a prop or piece of furniture, and wind up injuring himself and having to play the next scene nursing a fractured toe or a bleeding gash on his face.

Another thing Red hated about "live" TV was having to learn new routines and lines every week. As a result, he'd frequently resist any new material offered him under the guise that it wasn't funny, simply so that he wouldn't have to memorize it.

The Topsy Turvy sketch became one of his favorite routines,

and one he used over and over again during subsequent years. But when Ben Freedman first submitted it, Red nearly threw it out on the pretext that he might get hurt climbing into the chair, a strange argument to come from a man who used to finish his vaudeville acting falling off a stage and into the orchestra pit. Red wasn't afraid of physical punishment. At the end of an average TV season Red had more welts, bruises, lumps, sprains, fractures, and internal injuries than you'd find in the average emergency ward.

Of course, the Topsy Turvy sketch did present certain hazards, as its creator will allow. It couldn't be done with trick photography, or a double playing Red's part, as it could if the show were being shot on film. Red actually had to climb into a chair that was jutting out from the wall at a right angle about five feet off the stage floor.

Claudio Guzman, one of the finest talents in the business, had designed the set, and had the chair rigged so that Red couldn't possibly fall and get hurt. But when Red first walked out on the stage for a rehearsal, and saw where he was supposed to sit while doing the scene, his face turned white and he balked at having to climb into his precarious perch.

The only way he would even consider it, he said, was if the writer who'd thought of it would climb into the chair first, to prove that it could be done without getting hurt. "I didn't want to do it, either," says Freedman, "but it was either that or see the sketch I'd been working on all week go down the drain. So I climbed up into it, and showed Red how, and after that he did it—reluctantly."

It wasn't, however, just a question of climbing into the chair and not falling out that had bothered him. Red had to learn new lines to go with the physical business. And that always threw him. Of course, he could do as other comedians did and read his jokes off "idiot cards" or a teleprompter. But Red didn't care for idiot cards. He felt they inhibited his clowning, which they did. He didn't object to using a mechanical prompting device for drawing room comedy, but not for the kind of wild farce that Red's fans expected from him. How could he read lines from a card while he was hanging from a chair on the wall, or falling on his face, or getting hit over the head with a break-away vase that refused to break and wound up giving him a mild concussion?

Not very well. But because the strain of committing an entire new script to memory week after worrisome week was beginning to tell on Red, both physically and emotionally, he eventually let his staff talk him into using idiot cards.

Red never stopped resenting having to rely on them, however, and he was always kidding himself about it in front of other staff members—mostly to cover his embarrassment. One day, during a break in rehearsal of a show in which Red had to rely more heavily than usual on his idiot cards, he stepped into the Men's Room next door for the usual purpose.

As Red entered the lavatory, John Fenton Murray was just stepping away from one of the urinals. Noticing Murray, Red suddenly effected a befuddled expression.

"Oh God, I haven't got my idiot card!" he exclaimed. "What did I come in here for?"

However, Red's biggest barrier to continuing success in television, outside of finding new material and learning it, was having to stick to the stage "markers"—spots chalked out by the camera crew and the director which were the perimeters inside of which every performer had to work while doing a scene.

"Red simply could not adjust to being in a certain place so that the cameras could get the action," remembers John Murray. "Red was a freewheeling performer. He could take off and do an hour show for you completely ad lib without a TV camera around. But to tell him he had to go here on the stage or there in order to achieve a certain effect scared hell out of him. And to have to remember new lines at the same time really threw him. Sometimes in the middle of a new routine, he'd just forget it and go into an old routine."

Luckily, Red received strong back-up support from his stock company of supporting players who'd moved over from radio to television with him—old pros like Benny Rubin, Hans Conried, Mel Blanc, Verna Felton, Peter Leeds, Shirley Mitchell, Pat McGeehan, and a few others.

"If Red gave the wrong cues or switched to an old routine in the middle of a new one, Pat or Verna or Benny would go right along with him and usually save the sketch from being a complete disaster," recalls Murray.

But as most of the reviewers never failed to point out, Red Skelton was the backbone of the *Red Skelton Show,* so the burden of being good was mostly on him.

As a result, Red was a physical and emotional wreck by the end of the first season, and though his ratings were holding strong, he was not. The strain of putting on thirty-nine weekly half-hour "live" television shows, plus an equal number of radio programs, plus having to argue with Georgia about Edna when he got home nights—providing he went home nights—had exhausted him mentally and physically. To help him relax and forget how hard he was working, Red started going to the vodka bottle a little more frequently than was good for either his health or the show.

On Sunday, June 10, 1952, for example, Red passed out in his dressing room from a combination of asthma, booze, and exhaustion, and had to be revived with oxygen in order to go on that night and do his last show of the television season.

From that and similar incidents, it was apparent to everyone close to him that there would have to be a change in the way the shows were done in the future or else Red would wind up in a sanitarium from a nervous breakdown.

Filming the show—as Red had originally wanted—seemed to be the answer. Not only would it be easier on his jangled nerves than doing a show "live," but it would enable him to get five or six shows ahead in the "can," which would allow him the luxury of a few weeks off from television, either to vacation or finish out his contractual obligations to MGM. So Bo Roos and Freeman Keyes passed the word to NBC's top programming executives that Red insisted on switching to film the coming season, or else he'd go to another network.

Afraid of losing Red to CBS, NBC agreed and leased shooting and office space for Red and his staff at Eagle Lion Studios, next to the Goldwyn lot, on Santa Monica Boulevard in Hollywood. There, starting in the fall of 1952, the *Red Skelton Show* was done on film, using the "three-camera" technique that had been perfected by Desi and Lucy on their hit series.

The three-camera technique was designed to provide the best of both the "live" and "film" TV worlds. The shows were played straight through, in front of an audience, with three cameras grinding away simultaneously to cover long shots, medium shots, and closeups. But the advantage it enjoyed over "live" was that the filming could be stopped between scenes to allow Red to change costumes without breaking his neck in the process. In addition, the show could be edited before it was broadcast, so jittery performers such as Red didn't have to be quite so apprehensive about making mistakes and could relax more and concentrate on just being funny.

The new technique might have worked for Red—except for one thing: Red refused to do his show in front of a regular audience. His theory was: what's the use of having an audience if they couldn't see him perform? And with the big Mitchell movie cameras that were being used, which blocked the action from the spectators, there was no way the people could ge close enough to watch the show. It was more difficult than trying to see him perform in NBC's Studio D, because on film, there could be no monitors.

As a result, Red's only audience on the filmed shows consisted of the technical crew, his managers, and as many invited friends as he could persuade to come down to Eagle Lion Studios. Two dozen people at most, and not enough to fill up the laugh track. As a result the show had to be "sweetened" with "canned laughs," which always sounded artificial, even though the man working the laugh machine claimed he took his cues from the few people actually watching the filming on the sound stage.

Red tried hard that season, and on occasion was his old brilliant self. But most of the time the show suffered from a lack of spontaneity, which the critics seemed to detect.

A consensus of the reports from "Murderer's Row" was that while the Skelton show was basically the same in format as it was the previous year, it lacked inspiration, possibly because there was no studio audience; its slapstick sketches went on too long; most of his material was "pretty sad" and appeared to be "merely a rehash of last year's weaker programs."

Not quite the handwriting on the wall, but it was an indication that the wall was starting to crumble.

Aside from a material problem, which was to plague Red all season, his biggest bug-a-boo continued to be the markers. His inability to heed them was also of considerable concern to the cameramen and Marty Rackin, who was serving as director of the show the second season, and whose Herculean job it was to keep the perambulating Red's image in their view finders.

On one occasion, remembers John Fenton Murray, two of the cameramen, while trying to keep Red in their sights, forgot where they were on stage and collided into each other's cameras head-on.

It was a scene worthy of a Woody Allen or Mel Brooks satire on Hollywood. It was just unfortunate that Red's fans, viewing the show on their home screens, weren't privy to the fun. Because according to the few people who did witness the collision, it was probably the most hilarious bit on the Skelton show during the entire 1952–53 season.

The first ratings of the season, published on October 24, were another barometer of just how rapidly Red was losing favor with the public. The top ten were:

I Love Lucy
Martin & Lewis
Arthur Godfrey's Scouts
Texaco Star Theater (Milton Berle)
Life with Luigi
Dragnet
Godfrey's Friends
Prizefights
Gangsters
The Nixon (Checkers) Speech

Red not only didn't show up in the first ten, but lost out to the Nixon "Checkers" speech as well. On the front page of the November 7 *Variety* came an even more ominous reminder that the Skelton show was in serious trouble.

RED SKELTON TO FOLLOW STORY LINE IN VIDPIX
AS SPONSOR TOUGHENS UP

Red Skelton will try out a new comedy format for television, at the suggestion of his sponsor, Procter & Gamble, and filming is slated for Nov. 15. Formula will have a story line.

If situation comedy piece fails to pass muster, Skelton may test a variety format, with him as head comic and ringmaster. P & G has advised Skelton and the package owner, Freeman Keyes, that they are dissatisfied with the present run of comedies, of which five are still to be shown, and are demanding better quality for their TV outlay, around $60,000 a week.

Understood P & G has adopted a toughened attitude toward Skelton, who is under a firm 39-week contract with the Cincy soapmakers. Sponsor is insisting the comic devote more time to his own comedy and the writing and let others worry about the production and filming.

Nobody, from Skelton to his sponsors, from the writers to the network heads, knew exactly what was ailing the show, but everyone in Hollywood was speculating wildly, without coming up with a practical answer.

Many, even among those who'd previously stated that Red was "born for television," were now declaring that television wasn't his medium, that he was too undisciplined, couldn't stick to the written word, and that he probably needed the freedom of a large stage, such as at Loew's State or New York's Music Hall. As proof of his total lack of discipline, they pointed to the fact that he couldn't even do his most oft-repeated routine— "Guzzler's Gin"—the same way twice in a row.

Some claimed television wasn't the problem; otherwise he wouldn't have been a hit the first year. It was more likely that he had simply shot his bolt the first year, as had several other flash-in-the-television-pans, and that his kind of comedy probably wouldn't stand up over the long haul.

Still others blamed it on the fact that he was doing a "filmed" show with "canned laughs." They maintained that the real Red Skelton personality couldn't be captured on film. Not playing to an audience took away from his spontaneity. As proof of this, they pointed to his last six MGM releases, all of which had been lambasted by the critics and avoided by the majority of movie-goers: *Excuse My Dust* with Sally Forrest and Monica Lewis; *Texas Carnival,* in which Red played the supporting comedy role to Esther Williams and Howard Keel; *Lovely To Look At,* a rewrite of the thirties' Jerome Kern stage musical; *Roberta,* in which Red co-starred with the Metro stock company—Ann Miller, Zsa Zsa Gabor, Kathryn Grayson, and Marge and Gower Champion; *The Clown,* a nothing little story about an alcoholic comedian and his divorced wife and their little son who inspired "Dad" to make a comeback, and which exuded the distinct whiff of an old Wallace Beery–Jackie Cooper sobber; *Half a Hero,* a light comedy about a man whose wife (Jean Hagen) has him constantly in debt because she is vainly trying to keep up with the Joneses; and finally, *The Great Diamond Robbery,* another lackluster comedy in which Red starred and had James Whitmore and Cara Williams for support—but not enough to do any good.

Anyone who'd seen his last movie outings probably wouldn't argue with the theory that Red wasn't at his best on film, and that he needed to go back to doing his TV show "live."

In his desperation, even Red was driven to the point of making jokes about the kinds of films Metro was putting him in. After *Half a Hero* opened to bad reviews, he commented bitterly to a reporter, "They were afraid to show it at Grauman's Chinese for fear the footprints would get up and walk away."

Finally, there were those who blamed Red's fall from TV grace on his tumultuous personal life, and the fact that he no longer had Edna around to advise him and guide him. As best as it can be pinpointed, Edna faded completely out of Red's life sometime in the winter of 1952–53, and became something of a recluse forever afterward.

The two most influential gossip columnists, Hedda Hopper and Louella Parsons, who claimed to have the inside dope on everybody's personal life, were inclined to go along with the last theory.

"It is said," wrote Louella, in one of her columns, "that

Georgia objected to Red working with his ex-wife, and that Edna, not wishing to make trouble, gracefully bowed out."

Louella went on to say that she believed the reason Red's shows weren't so good that season was because of "overwork, combined with excessive drinking, plus the fact that he probably needs Edna."

Hedda echoed all this in her columns, plus her theory that Red "didn't care whether he lived or died."

Red neither confirmed nor denied any of this. Much later in his life, Red was to state that Edna had absolutely nothing at all to do with his rise to the top, but in those days he still became defensive whenever Georgia started nagging him about her, and that always led to stormy arguments and more sessions with the bottle.

In fact, things got so bad between Red and Georgia by the middle of November that Red took off with Bo Roos for a meeting with NBC's top executives in New York City, without even telling Georgia that he was going, or for that matter, *where* he was going.

While Georgia was frantic with worry, Red and his business manager checked into suites at the Hampshire House, and spent the better part of a week having conferences with NBC programming brass who were concerned about Red's falling ratings, his drinking, and the all-round sloppy look of the show.

After intensive diagnostic huddles, NBC decided that Red was at a disadvantage doing a "filmed" show and they insisted he should go back to performing "live," as he had done his first year, when he had won two Emmys. Now that the Burbank studio, which Red had designed specifically to fit his needs, was nearing completion, he could do his show in the new facility and wouldn't have to worry that his audience couldn't see him. NBC removed more of the pressure from Red by saying he could shoot the show the "stop-and-go" method. In other words, stop between scenes, and allow him time to change costumes and compose himself.

Under those conditions, Red agreed to resume doing a live show, and he and Bo Roos flew back to California, very much relieved.

* * *

If his show was "live," his marriage now appeared to be dead.

After arriving in California, Red packed his bags and officially moved out of the Sarbonne estate and into the Beverly Wilshire Hotel, which had served him so well as a retreat during past marital difficulties.

Red never divulged the exact cause of this particular dispute with Georgia, but it's safe to assume it must have had something to do with his going to New York without her during the holiday season and without even letting her know why.

But whatever motivated the split, Red was fairly adamant that "this time it's for good." In fact, he was so sure of it that the moment he moved into his hotel suite, he phoned New York to tell his friend Earl Wilson about it.

"Why are you splitting?" asked Wilson.

"Because I am ruining my life and she says I'm ruining hers," replied Red.

"Did you talk to Georgia before you left?" asked Wilson.

Typically, Red tried to make light of what was basically a very sad situation. "Talk to her?" he quipped. "I not only talked to her—I yelled at her."

Earl Wilson broke the story of the Red–Georgia rift in the *New York Daily News* on December 3. The rest of the media picked it up, of course, and converged upon Red outside his hotel room door, to learn from him the exact reason for the marital disharmony.

"I just can't take it any longer," explained Red. "I've taken all a man can expect to take. I'm so much in love it's pitiful, but she does not want to be in love."

Georgia was more furious than ever with Red—not so much because he had walked out on her, but because he had been in such a hurry to tell the world about it. When the media caught up with Georgia the next day and pressed her to reveal her side of the battle, she denied that they were having trouble at all.

"We haven't split," she told reporters who were waiting for her outside the gates of their Sarbonne estate. "Of course, Red's a difficult person to live with," she finally admitted, when pushed by the reporters to explain why her husband had taken up residence in the Beverly Wilshire, "but it'll blow over. It always does."

Red's lawyers then confirmed that there had been a split and that they were proceeding with the business of filing a divorce action. In confirming that Red was serious about a divorce, his lawyers speculated that perhaps the reason Georgia was denying it was because she was trying to spare the kids, who were old enough now—four and five—to understand what straits their parents were in.

This was like waving another red flag in front of Georgia, who promptly phoned her errant husband at his hotel and informed him that he might as well come home because she wouldn't give him a divorce under *any* circumstances. She was Catholic.

Red shot back that he would not come home under any circumstances, and accused Georgia of ruining his career because of her refusal to let him concentrate on the thing he could do best— being funny. However, he seemed to have retreated somewhat from that position by the next day, when Milton Weiss, his publicity man, issued the following convoluted statement to the press.

Stated Weiss: "After much consideration, in talks between Red, Mrs. Skelton, and close friends, no further steps will be taken and no moves for a divorce are contemplated at the moment."

It was now Georgia's turn to speak, and speak she did:

"A divorce is out of the question. I don't believe in it. I've had plenty of trouble with this boy, only before it just never got into the papers. If I was going to quit, I would have quit a long time ago. I'm not going to quit now because we have two wonderful kids. The only reason we're having trouble now is because Red is *overworked,* because he's *artistic,* and because he's a high-strung *genius.*

"When he gets ready to come home, he'll cool down. I'm sure he'll come back. He always does."

Georgia knew what she was talking about. Five days later, Red had second thoughts about the divorce and decided he wanted to return home.

At any rate, he made a number of telephone calls to the Sarbonne house to try to make up with Georgia, but the help would never let him get through to her. Either the phone would be answered by the housekeeper, who would say, "Mrs. Skelton says she can't come to the phone right now—what is it about?" Or he'd have to deal through the butler, whose stock reply was, "Mrs. Skelton tell me to tell you that she isn't in."

Strangely enough, Georgia really wanted Red back, but she had an uncommon amount of pride, and after he'd walked out on her and told the press he'd had it, embarrassing her in front of the whole world and possibly her children, she wasn't about to kiss and make up so quickly. She was going to let him squirm on the hook a little longer.

Red, however, wasn't in any shape to do much squirming, except possibly in a hospital bed.

Although only Georgia, his personal physician, Stanley Immerman, and a few close friends were aware of it, Red had been quietly suffering from a ruptured hernia in his diaphragm for about six months. Apparently the result of years of physical abuse on stage, the hernia permitted Red's stomach to press against his heart and lungs, causing breathing difficulties and other unpleasant symptoms that at times required the emergency intake of oxygen to revive him. Red's condition became acute at about the same time he was having the most difficulties with his television shows, many of which he filmed while in excruciating pain. Immerman had recommended surgery previously, but Red had resisted.

But two days after Red's final and unsuccessful attempt to effect a reconciliation with Georgia, he was walking through the lobby of his hotel, when he collapsed on the marble floor and, in a coma, had to be rushed by ambulance to St. John's Hospital in Santa Monica.

At St. John's, Red spent the next two days undergoing tests and being x-rayed, and complaining to doctors and nurses alike that he couldn't waste any more time in the hospital as he had a radio and TV show to do. Finally, forty-eight hours later, Dr. Immerman decided to operate.

Red retained his sense of humor, however, and just before he was wheeled into the operating room, he stuck a piece of adhesive tape to his chest. He had printed on the tape: DO NOT OPEN UNTIL CHRISTMAS.

With three assistants at his side, Dr. Immerman performed the operation, which took nearly five hours to complete, and which kept Red out of television action for about a month while he was recuperating. Fortunately, there were about six Skelton shows already in the can, so NBC would have no problem filling his Sunday night time slot until he recovered.

As was to be expected, news of the operation brought Georgia out of seclusion and to her ailing husband's bedside at St. John's.

Georgia remained by his side all during the post-operative period, and when Red was discharged she allowed him to return home to their mansion on the hill. But that didn't mean he was completely forgiven. She gave him the silent treatment for days.

Being both an invalid and the fellow who was paying the bills, Red was deeply hurt that Georgia wasn't welcoming him home with all the enthusiasm he felt he deserved after what he'd been through. But because he enjoyed his home and loved being around the children, he put up with Georgia's behavior.

Meanwhile, he spent about a month and a half lying around the house, recuperating, dabbling with his paints, worrying about his future, and trying to make up with Georgia. In February, he was ready to go back to work, when he became mysteriously ill again and had to be hospitalized. His doctor told the press that "it was a virus infection complicated by a severe case of neuralgia."

With Red out of action again, the network had no choice but to put reruns of the shows he had filmed in the fall on the air. Since they hadn't been any good the first time, on their second showing his ratings took an even more severe plunge.

By March, he had recovered enough of his strength to report to Burbank, to try out the new "stop-and-go" method of taping his shows, "live." He tried it for the first time on March 22.

Unfortunately, this didn't work out as well as everybody had hoped.

From purely a technical standpoint, broadcasting from Burbank was an improvement. Though Red was no architect, the design he had recommended for his studio was quite ingenius.

The problem now was that the audience *could* see the show.

According to home viewers and critics alike, Red was suffering from a drought of fresh material, and people not familiar with the operation of the Skelton show were coming up with all kinds of helpful suggestions like, "Why don't you get new writers?"

But according to Jack Douglas, who was doing his monologue, that wasn't the problem at all. They were writing new material, but Red was refusing to perform it. "He just didn't feel comfortable doing anything that he hadn't been using in his repertoire for years. Once he knew it by heart, and had honed it to perfection, like "Guzzler's" or his doughnut bit, he could be as relaxed in front of the cameras as Jack Benny. But make him do something new and right in the middle he'd switch to something old, and there was nothing any of us on the sidelines could do about it."

Red's reluctance to tackle new material had nothing to do with his ability to memorize. Laziness was partly to blame, probably brought on by his weakened physical condition. Often he didn't show up for rehearsals, and when he did, he'd frequently not be paying attention, "but clowning around for the benefit of the camera crew or perhaps a couple of pretty showgirls he was trying to impress," recalls one of his associates.

As these pressures persisted and the show's ratings continued to plummet, Red started seeking more solace in the bottle. Perhaps, as people were saying, he had shot his bolt his first year out. Perhaps he was through, and would soon start the long slide back to small-time vaudeville and nightclubs and perhaps even carnivals where he had begun.

By the spring of 1953, even Red's staunchest backers at MGM had given up on him and his erratic behavior. One day it became Bo Roos's sad duty to inform Red that MGM was not picking up his option. As far as they were concerned, he was through in pictures.

After that his binges started occurring with more and more frequency. Sometimes there didn't seem to be a place where one ended and a new one began. When this happened, it would be up to Marty Rackin, who doubled as Red's guardian now that Edna wasn't around, to find Red and see that he got to NBC in time to rehearse and do the show on Sundays. Frequently Red wouldn't go home nights when he'd finished working, so Georgia wouldn't know where he was, either. Rackin knew most of Red's favorite haunts, however, and after locating him, would haul Red to NBC in the back of his station wagon, or in an ambulance, with a tank of oxygen handy to bring him around. Then he'd take him to the gym and steam him out and get him a rubdown and into fresh clothes.

"All day long after Marty got him to the studio, and we were rehearsing, we had to keep buckets of ice water and wet towels all over the place," remembers one of Red's co-workers at NBC during that period. "We also had a doctor on call who used to come down and give Red shots to revive him, if necessary. Red was a pretty good pro, though. Somehow we always managed to get the program on the air those first two seasons."

But judging by the latest ratings, it was obvious that just getting on the air wasn't good enough. Lucy was again on top, by far, with another "Red"—Red Buttons in tenth position. But there was no Red Skelton anywhere near the top ten.

Red's sponsors, Procter & Gamble, who were picking up the $60,000 a week tab, were now so disgusted that they were dropping hints about dropping the show. NBC was already talking about who to put in Skelton's Sunday night spot the following season.

And Red, who lived only for audience applause and approval, was in a state of depression so deep that the only way he could think of ending it was to drink himself to death. Moreover, the two most influential people in his life, Bo Roos and Freeman Keyes, were absolutely powerless to keep the vodka bottle out of his hand.

As proof of how bad his dipsomania had become, even Red, who refuses to face he ever was much of a drinker, will at times admit, "I only drank heavily once in my life, and that was for about three months in the spring of 1953."

As is the case with every show that is about to feel the sponsor's or network's ax, the morale of all the people connected with the show had sunk lower than a snake's belly, to borrow a phrase from Clem Kadiddlehopper. Especially the writers' morale. Not only did they have to take the brunt of the criticism, but they had to stand by and watch material they knew was good be ruined in the playing, because Red either "dogged it" to prove it was worthless, or refused to rehearse it, or else had it thrown out before the show because he was afraid to try anything new.

Moreover, Red had fallen into the habit of insulting his writers every time he didn't get a laugh, with ad libs like, "I told the writer that wasn't any good," or "Who wrote that—remind me to fire him after the show." A cheap laugh at the expense of the writers, and it didn't make him any more popular. Fortunately, the real pros of the business—Jack Benny, for one—respected Freedman and Murray's talents, and knew enough not to blame them for what was really Red's fault. Benny, in fact, made several overtures to Freedman and Murray during the last part of the season to try to persuade them to quit the Skelton show and go to work for him immediately at a higher salary.

Since it was apparent that Freedman and Murray didn't have much of a future with Skelton, they confided in Freeman Keyes, who was still in charge of the package, that they were thinking of accepting Benny's offer.

Keyes eyed the two Judases reprovingly, and snapped, "You wouldn't kick a man when he's down, would you?"

Being honorable young men, they didn't. They stuck it out through the show's final death rattle, only to discover that when their positions were reversed and it was Red's turn to show the same loyalty to them, he couldn't have been more disinterested.

16

After NBC axed the Skelton show, Red's prospects for employment couldn't have been bleaker. Not only had his popularity as an entertainer reached an all-time new nadir, but his confidence in himself was completely shattered, he was nearing hopeless dipsomania, his stomach was half-eaten away from alcohol, and he had cut himself off from the rest of the world—and also his family.

Reports from unimpeachable sources around Hollywood had him, in his worst moments of paranoia, retreating to a high branch of a tree on his estate, with a bottle and a gun, and defying anybody—Georgia included—to make him climb down. In his saner moments he collapsed inside an oxygen tent, or checked into a hospital to cure some mysterious ailment labeled "exhaustion."

"Georgia was at the end of her tether," states a producer of Red's from that period. "She didn't know what to do. In fact, nobody knew what to do. There was nothing anybody could do."

In spite of Red's widely recognized condition, Bo Roos had not given up completely on palming his famous client off on one of the other networks, and he made his availability known to the people in the higher echelons at CBS and ABC even before Red had severed his ties with NBC. Evidently Roos was still operating under the standard Hollywood agent's maxim that if you have a client who is flopping at one studio, you quickly sign him up to a new and better deal somewhere else—*before* the first flop becomes generally known.

But how could Red's NBC flop have been kept under wraps when what was passing for a television show was being seen by millions of people every week, and those embarrassing ratings, with the Skelton show close to the bottom, were being published in all the trades and daily newspapers? That was really taking a bath in public.

All that notwithstanding, CBS showed immediate interest in talking about a deal, to Red's great joy.

The reason for this was that CBS was still in the thick of the competition with NBC to see which of the two major networks could sign up the most big names. Howard Meighan, an executive vice-president whom the network's programming chief, Hubbell Robinson, had recently installed for the purpose of boosting CBS's television programming on the West Coast, apparently didn't care if Red was drinking heavily or not, or if he had temporarily lost favor with the fickle public. As far as Meighan was concerned, Red was still a big talent who, if properly controlled, could add luster to the CBS fall line-up.

But then just when it seemed that a deal would be signed, reports of exactly how bad Red's condition was reached Hubbell Robinson's ears, and, temporarily at least, he had second thoughts. Robinson, never particularly a fan of Red's brand of slapstick comedy anyway, evidently felt that even if Red could stay sober through a whole season, there was still an extremely "iffy" question to be answered: whether or not Red was funny anymore.

None of Roos's assurances that Red was "funnier than ever"... "that he had matured in his approach to comedy"... and that reports of his drinking had been "grossly exaggerated" satisfied Robinson. He decided to pass on Red Skelton.

With his hopes for a comeback smashed to smithereens, Red, once again, sought solace in the bottle.

When ABC also showed no interest, even the normally ebullient Bo Roos was on the verge of giving up.

Only Marty Rackin still had faith in Red. He got Red down from his tree long enough to tell him that the only way he believed CBS would go through with the deal now would be if Red could prove he was the brilliant clown of old by showcasing his talents someplace where CBS's doubting executives could come and see for themselves that he was sober and performing better than ever.

Red agreed, but doubted if anyone with his present reputation could get a decent booking anywhere.

Rackin suggested Las Vegas. More specifically, the Sahara Hotel, which he'd heard was desperate for some big names who'd never played the desert resort before to lure in some fresh customers.

Red immediately balked. Playing Las Vegas scared him, because he wasn't sure if his kind of comedy would go over with the gambling element.

Rackin assured Red that he had nothing to worry about—that Vegas also catered to the "family trade," which was sure to love Red's act. "Just do your regular old *schtick* that you did in vaudeville—"Guzzler's," the doughnut bit, all your imitations—especially your drunks. They'll love it."

Reluctantly Red said okay to Vegas, and Rackin contacted the Sahara's management and arranged a booking for him to open in mid-July.

In the meantime, Rackin helped Red throw an act together, using the best of all his famous bits, but with some fresh introductions to fit the Las Vegas milieu, and this seemed to ease Red's apprehensions.

But at the last minute, Red had one of his irrational fears about appearing in Las Vegas. Desperate, Rackin loaded Red's vodka glass with sleeping pills. After Red passed out Rackin put him in a sleeping bag and drove him to Las Vegas in the back of his station wagon.

Prior to going on the stage opening night at the Sahara, there were enough butterflies in Red's stomach to fill a lepidopterist's trophy room. But after his initial few minutes on the stage, looking healthy, sober, and well-groomed in an expensive tux, Red overcame his attack of the jitters and turned into the confident yock-getting Skelton of old.

Red's opening monologue, kidding about his new job in a gambling resort, where it was impossible to hold on to one's money, struck home with the audience. Following that, Red reverted to his stock routines of the past, including bringing out of retirement all the characters he had made famous. He also did bits from his famous MGM screen test in which he satirized how different movie stars died on screen. Finally, for a smash finish, he treated the audience to as fine a performance of "Guzzler's Gin" as he had ever done.

Red's face was dripping with perspiration as he took his bows at the end of his forty-five-minute show. There was also a huge grateful grin on his puss as the audience, really taking Red into their hearts, gave him a standing ovation, as they kept yelling for "more."

The result was smash reviews in all the trades and daily papers, and word of mouth that was even better. Consequently, Marty Rackin had no trouble persuading a delegation of important executives from CBS to come to Vegas to watch his charge perform. His hardest job, of course, was to keep Red on the straight and narrow until they arrived. Once they did arrive and saw Red fracture an audience, Rackin's mission was accomplished.

Shortly after his successful Sahara stand, Red signed with CBS for $12,000 a week for thirty-nine "live" weekly broadcasts. For those days, that was an unbelievable sum for someone who'd just bombed on another network and whose reputation for reliability was not exactly outstanding.

Evidently the powers running CBS felt that by implementing some important changes in the way the Skelton show was run that Red could be a hit again.

The new game rules for the Skelton show were: first, Red's programs would be broadcast absolutely "live," in the belief that this would bring back some much needed spontaneity into Red's television performing. Red wouldn't even be allowed the luxury of "stop-and-go" taping that he had enjoyed at NBC. That was too costly and time-consuming, and judging by the way his ratings took a nose-dive the previous season, it wasn't much help. As a concession to Red, however, there would be an attempt to write into the scripts small bits involving other characters between the main sketches in order to give Red opportunity to change costumes without breaking his already bruised neck.

Second, control of the show would be taken away from Red and turned over to a producer and director who knew what they were doing and who could handle their star. The men hired for this were Ben Brady, a veteran CBS staff producer and former writer, to produce; and Seymour Berns, a new, hot young talent who had come highly recommended by Harry Ackerman, one of the network bigwigs, to direct.

Third, there would be a completely new writing staff. John Fenton Murray and Ben Freedman found this out after Red had made the move to CBS and they approached him one day to find out when they would begin their new assignment. "Sorry, fellows," explained Red, "but I'm hiring all new writers. CBS told me I've got to get rid of the writers who ruined me last season." As the two men who'd been the mainstays of his writing staff for over ten years looked at their former boss in disbelief, Red smiled sheepishly and added, "But don't worry—I'll try to bring you back as soon as the heat's off."

But they never heard from Red again. Which was the thanks they got for not accepting Jack Benny's offer the previous spring.

The new writers on the show were Artie Stander, Howard Leeds, Artie Julian, and Arthur Ross. All had impressive credits in the comedy writing field, and it was hoped they could bring to the show an entirely new look.

And last, there would be a different format. Instead of the

show being just a chopped-up series of unrelated sketches and wild gags, Hubbell Robinson wanted the writers to try to inject some continuity into the half-hour by weaving a thread of a story line through it. Robinson also believed that a little more "heart" and a little less "slapstick" in the show would be an improvement, too.

One thing Hubbell Robinson couldn't get on demand that first season was a legitimate sponsor. "As far as most sponsors were concerned," says Ben Brady, "Red, after his debacle on NBC the previous season, was as untouchable as a carload of poison ivy. And if I hadn't had a friend, Walter Craig, who was the head of Benton and Bowles, we would have gone on the air sustaining. When Craig heard I was producing the show, he said, 'I'll go on the air with one of my products, Geritol. But my client won't pay the regular sponsor's fee—we'll just pay for the air time.' That's how far-reaching Skelton's reputation for unreliability was in those days. They figured there'd be no ratings, so if they couldn't buy Skelton for practically nothing, why bother?"

As a result, Pharmaceuticals, Inc., the company that manufactured both Geritol and Serutan ("natures" spelled backwards) made a deal with CBS to allow them to put their name on the show to give it the appearance of true sponsorship, and Skelton was slotted into the 8:30 to 9:00 P.M. time spot on Tuesday nights, beginning September 22. Red felt good about that, at least. Tuesday night had been lucky for him when he first went on radio back in 1941, and perhaps it would happen that way again.

Unfortunately, Red still didn't feel good about going on the air "live," despite assurances from the network that they had the best technical crews in the business to assist him, and a director who had practically grown up in live television. Red not only didn't feel good about going on the air "live," but as the first script came out of mimeo and the September air date approached, he seemed to be struck with an irrational fear of going on the air at all. "Since his debacle of the year before, he had completely lost confidence in himself," says Brady, "and he had a fear that audiences no longer loved him, which is all these people live for."

Red started drinking and missing rehearsals again; if not

missing them completely, then not taking them seriously, so that nobody else could rehearse properly.

"I'd known before then that Red was no ordinary drinker," says Brady. "Drinking to him wasn't a couple of martinis with an olive in them—it was taking a bottle of vodka and raising it to his lips and gulping the entire contents down. The way he drank would kill the average man. But this man was built like a battleship. He could withstand anything.

"When he was drunk you could take him and drop him out the window, and he'd fall down and come right back in the house again. But when I got him he was really attempting to destroy himself. He was so ossified that at one point he actually thought he had done a show when we hadn't even been on the air yet. Another time he came into CBS all cut up. He had gotten so drunk at home that he had fallen through a glass shower door. He was so bad we had to keep oxygen on the set to revive him after he passed out."

Two days before the show went on the air there still hadn't been one complete run-through. Berns, the director of the show, hadn't even been able to get a "timing." Under the circumstances, it seemed that it would be virtually impossible to put on even a preview performance Monday night, much less meet the September 22 air date.

Hearing reports of the approaching calamity, Hubbell Robinson placed a conference call in New York to Ben Brady and Harry Ackerman on the West Coast. And when the two of them apprised him of just how serious the situation was, Robinson said, "Let's just swallow the contract. We'll lose a million, but so what? We can't do a live show—not with this bum. Let's just cancel him out next Tuesday, and we'll stick something else in there."

Brady asked for one more chance to get Skelton under control, and Robinson, mainly because he had no other show to substitute, told him he was welcome to try.

"So I went up to Skelton's house," recalls Brady. "I found Red in bed with a bottle of vodka—completely ossified. I told him, 'Red, you want to go on the air or don't you? Because if you do, you'll have to come down off this hill and rehearse.' Red looked at me with glazed eyes, but it seemed to sink in. Finally, he said, 'I'll make it.' While I waited, he sent for his doctor ... Stanley Immerman, I think ... who came and gave him a shot. This seemed to sober him up, and he came down to the rehearsal. But he rehearsed mechanically, and he did the preview mechanically. He simply wasn't giving the show anything himself. Finally, we went on the air."

The results were what one might expect. What *Variety* wrote about the show on Wednesday morning pretty much reflected what the rest of the nation's critics, and also the public, thought about it: "It's going to take better than what Red Skelton served up on his live opener last night if he's to get back on the first team."

The so-so reviews were reflected in the ratings which continued a downward trend, along with Red's morale. Now Red was thoroughly convinced that audiences no longer loved him.

By the third week, Red's drinking and paranoia had reached such proportions that he felt *everybody* was against him—his wife, his writers, his producer, his director, the network, and the public. But he blamed his writers in particular, and suddenly refused to have any direct contact with them. Any discussions concerning script changes had to be done through Brady and Berns, who transmitted Red's thoughts to the writing staff. This was the beginning of a habit that was to continue through the next sixteen years of his television life.

"I'll tell you one story about Red that is absolutely pathetic," recalls Seymour Berns. "Ben Brady and I were down at the office one day. It was a rehearsal day—but so far Skelton hadn't showed. Then we got a call from his house—Georgia said, 'Red's up a tree and he won't let anybody come near him, because he's got a gun. So we go up to the house, this magnificent mansion up on top of a hill. And sure enough, after we drove in and parked the car, there was Skelton, up a tree—with a rifle, a bottle, and his joke file. And he won't let anybody come near him. If anybody came near him, he said, he'd shoot them. We told him we didn't want to hurt him. . . . We just needed him for a rehearsal. But he kept saying, 'I don't need anybody. I've got my jokes up here.'

"Finally, we told him that we wouldn't take his jokes away from him if he'd just come down and go to rehearsal. We pleaded and cajoled for about an hour, and finally we got him to come down and attend rehearsal. But that'll give you an idea of the kind of man we were dealing with in those days."

Somehow Brady, Berns, the writers, and the technical crew managed to get the first five programs of the season on the air. But the shows remained mediocre and the ratings were so low that even a nonpaying sponsor like Geritol was thinking of pulling out. "He was like a wraith," recalls Brady. "He would come out and go through the show, but mechanically. It was in his nature to function when he got on the stage, in front of an audience, but the results were anemic. The audience seemed to sense something was wrong. They didn't laugh or applaud spontaneously. They had to be 'cued' into it."

Then, just when it seemed as if nothing in the world could prevent Red from having another disastrous season on TV, one that unquestionably would spell *finis* to his career, there came a reversal of his fortunes.

The exact turning point for Red was a trip to New York to appear on *The Ed Sullivan Show.* CBS had arranged this appearance in the hope that the additional exposure might improve Red's ratings. Sullivan not only had one of the top rated shows on CBS, but a simple plug from him in those days was often enough to turn a flop play or book or even another TV program into a hit. Perhaps he could perform the same magic for Red.

As long as he was going to New York for that purpose, CBS arranged for Red to do his own show from New York as well. It was hoped that a change of venue to a city where Red once had many fans, might snap him out of his slump.

In theory it seemed like a splendid idea, for in addition to possibly being a tonic to Red, the trip east would give everyone connected with the Skelton show—Ben Brady, Seymour Berns, Dave Rose, and some regulars in the cast—an opportunity to have one of those "business" vacations.

Unfortunately, the business-vacation turned into a Lost Weekend when Red, now faced with the prospect of having to do *two* live shows in New York, started attacking the vodka bottle the moment he took up residence in his suite at the Hampshire House. And he still hadn't let up by the Saturday before his Sullivan appearance on Sunday night.

Berns and Brady performed yeoman service in mother-henning Red around New York on Saturday and preventing him from becoming too stoned and passing out completely. They even put him to bed before midnight so that he wouldn't have bags under his eyes the next day. But Red was too frightened to fall asleep, and after an hour of tossing and turning, he summoned Berns and Brady to his suite so that he wouldn't have to drink alone.

About one-thirty in the morning, Red, bleary-eyed from both fatigue and alcohol, announced that he was hungry and insisted that Brady and Berns get back into their clothes—they were all in bathrobes and pajamas—and accompany him downtown to a hot dog joint in the Village that, according to his memory, made the best "chili dogs" in the world.

Traveling to the Village at that hour to load their already queasy stomachs with garbage wasn't exactly what Berns and Brady felt like doing, but since Red was their star and had to be catered to—not to mention the fact that some food in *his* stomach might be a good antidote for all that liquor—they put their clothes back on and climbed into a cab with Red, who directed the driver to take them to some address in the Village.

"I don't remember the name of the place," says Brady, "but it was a dump, there wasn't much light, and it was absolutely empty except for the guy behind the counter. And then this miraculous thing happened."

While the three of them were waiting for the counter man to fill their order, people—evidently loyal fans of Red's who had seen him alight from the cab in front of the place—started drifting in one by one. As he or she entered, each was doing an imitation of one of Red's characterizations—Freddy the Freeloader, Clem Kadiddlehopper, Willie Lump-Lump, Cauliflower McPugg, Junior the "mean widdle boy," Deadeye the Texas cowboy, San Fernando Red, and even the TV announcer of "Guzzler's Gin" fame.

Among the group were a couple of typical Village derelicts who didn't have to do much acting in order to become Freddy the

Freeloader and Willie Lump-Lump. One of these bums picked a cigar butt out of the gutter and stuck it in his mouth as he paraded around in front of the astonished—and greatly pleased—Red.

"It was like some kind of a miracle," believes Brady. "This nocturnal, eerie, almost ghostly ad lib performance put on by these people, who seemed to appear from out of the woodwork, suddenly made Red realize that there *were* people in the world who still loved him."

As the emotionally charged Red watched the parade of all the characters he had made famous pass before his eyes, it occurred to him that this was some kind of a message from God—a message trying to tell him not to give up, that the people still cared about him. Maybe not the critics or the eggheads or the ratings-takers, but the "little people" of the world, who always made up the bulk of Red's fans, anyway.

Suddenly his old confident self again, Red jumped off his counter seat and put on an ad lib performance of his own for nearly an hour in the eerie, pre-dawn light of the hot dog parlor.

Red returned to his hotel a changed man. He didn't touch another drop of liquor during the rest of his stay in New York, and he was a huge hit on the Sullivan show, where he received such a standing ovation at the finish of his act that it brought back memories of the halcyon days of his first big success at the New York Paramount.

Tears of joy filled Red's eyes as he stood on the apron of the stage bowing and listening to something he hadn't heard very much of in recent months—the *spontaneous* clapping, cheering, and whistling of a studio audience. It wasn't something they had been "cued" into by an assistant director holding up cards telling them when to laugh and when to applaud.

Overcome with emotion, Red waited for the din to die down. Then with a weary smile, he leaned into the mike and for the first time ever signed off with the benediction that from that moment on became his trademark—"Good night and God Bless."

Red had suddenly found religion. Like the Pope, he never made another public appearance without blessing his audience at the finish of his act.

Red didn't go on the wagon entirely after his brush with God and subsequent renascence in New York. But he did pare his intake down to the point where he could conceivably be labeled just a very enthusiastic "social drinker." At least he no longer allowed his drinking to interfere with his work. He showed up for rehearsals; he paid attention to the script; "and occasionally he even listened to me," recalls his former director, Seymour Berns.

As a result of his renewed enthusiasm there was a noticeable improvement in the quality of the Skelton show, starting with the one he did from New York following his appearance on the Sullivan program.

Notwithstanding, Red's ratings continued to linger in the

substratum all through the 1953–54 and 1954–55 television seasons. At one point in 1955, in fact, he was as far down the list as number eighty-six. Any other comic would have been on his way to Sheboygan with a rating like that. But luckily for Red, CBS was stuck with a three-year contract with him from which it couldn't very well extricate itself without risking a messy lawsuit.

That CBS didn't dump Red turned out to be a good thing for both of them, because by 1956 his television career took a significant turn for the better again and he eventually wound up being their Number One star.

The interim period, however, was a trying couple of years for Red and all the people who had to work with him. New producers, directors, and writers came and went with the regularity of the daily mail.

Dissatisfied with his low ratings, Red sought a scapegoat other than himself. His writers, of course, were the handiest target, so, like most comedians in trouble, he started with them. Immediately after his return to California, Red fired Artie Stander, Howard Leeds, Artie Julian, and Arthur Ross, and replaced them with David and Bob Ross.

The two Rosses hung on until the following May, at which point Red had them fired.

At the same time, Red also fired Ben Brady and Seymour Berns. "That made no sense to us at all," says Ben Brady, who today heads the Television Writing Arts Department at Cal-State Northridge. "After all those good things happened to him in New York and we brought some order back to the show, he fires the two of us. Why? Well, he accused me of planning the New York trip just so I could take one of the actresses on the show to New York so I could have an affair with her. That, of course, was totally false. But that's the kind of a strange man he is. It's not even fair to call him paranoid. He's stranger than that."

Skelton gave no reason for firing Seymour Berns. "I think he fired me," says Berns, "because he wanted to fire Ben, whatever his reason was for that. So he figured he'd fire everybody and make a clean sweep. That way it wouldn't look as if he was playing favorites."

According to both Berns and Brady, Red cannot remain loyal to anyone for very long—even those who helped him the most. For example, Red wound up hating Marty Rackin, who was not only a good and loyal friend of Red's, but who was also at least partially responsible for his salvation at a time when he appeared to be heading for Skid Row. Yet for some reason known only to himself, Red blames Rackin for the entire downfall of his NBC show. "Red wouldn't allow you to say one good thing about Marty," recalls Brady. "You'd say, 'Look, Red, Marty didn't do anything deliberate.' And Red would turn mean and say he was a 'no good dirty bastard.' "

"When I first went to work for Red," says Berns, "he used to give Edna a lot of credit for getting him where he was. But as the years went by, he blotted her out of his consciousness. Finally Red reached a point where he would barely acknowledge that she had ever existed."

It was no skin off Berns's back to have to leave the madness of the Skelton show. As soon as he completed the last program of the season, CBS signed him to direct the *Shower of Stars,* an hour-long weekly special featuring rotating stars, that was a pet project of Hubbell Robinson's. *Shower of Stars* became a hit, "and I was suddenly one of the hottest young directors around," recalls Berns, with a pleased grin.

Brady and Berns were immediately replaced by Doug Whitney and Jack Donahue. Whitney, a former agent for MCA, didn't have the qualifications or experience to produce a television show with as many built-in problems as the Skelton show had. But Whitney had a good gift of gab, was a pleasant fellow to be around, and Red took a liking to him, so he was hired as the show's producer. Donahue was better qualified, having directed a number of Red's film comedies at MGM, but this was one of his first TV assignments, so he had much to learn about the new medium.

Hal Goodman and Larry Klein, a bright young writing team with many successful radio and television shows to their credit, were hired to write Red's scripts.

And overseeing the whole operation for CBS was Nat Perrin, a former writer for the Marx Brothers who had just become an executive at CBS. Perrin was installed as executive producer, charged with the awesome responsibility of coming up with a workable new format.

After carefully considering the matter, and looking over some old tapes of the previous season's programs, Perrin's remedy was to give the show a subject-matter each week. It wouldn't have a story per se, but it would have a theme or background: baseball, college, football, politics, Christmas, crime, marriage— in fact, any subject at all that lent itself to being kidded in Red's monologue and sketches and that would be topical enough to get some instant audience recognition.

The first show of the season—presumably because it was World Series time—was about "baseball," and featured guest stars Leo Durocher, Earl Wilson, and a new black singer named Diahann Carroll. The two high spots in the program were Diahann Carroll's singing and a sketch featuring Red as a rookie pitcher demonstrating his mound art to Leo Durocher, who had signed him without seeing him. But according to the majority of the critics, even the low spots were good. Wrote *The Hollywood Reporter* on September 23, 1954:

> Tuesday's debut of the new Skelton Show was a perfect demonstration of the fact that when the writers give the redhead a break he is one of the funniest men in the business.

The ratings didn't reflect the improvement, and subsequent shows of the season didn't live up to the promise of the opener. Part of this was due to the old bug-a-boo: material. It would take more than a team of two writers to keep Red supplied for a whole season: a dozen would be more like it. And part of the show's problems, according to Perrin, was the fault of Red himself and his unbusinesslike attitude during rehearsals. "Red paid no attention to the director or the script," says Perrin. "Most of the time he just gagged around for the benefit of the ten or fifteen people who'd be sitting around the rehearsal hall watching and kibitzing."

"Worse than that," adds Hal Goodman, "Red kept bringing in his old material from his Edna Skelton radio days and sticking it in the script behind our backs, and then pretending during the actual performance while we were on the air that he was ad libbing the stuff. All kinds of so-called 'mistakes'—stagehands forgetting props, characters forgetting lines or getting their tongues twisted—everyone in the audience had either seen or heard before, and knew weren't spontaneous muffs and therefore weren't about to laugh at. In fact, they were being turned off by how 'obvious' he was. Moreover, we could never get to the crazy guy to tell him why the scripts weren't working. How can you write for a comic when you can't even get to talk to him?''

On top of that, Doug Whitney wasn't up to the job of producing or handling Red. So after a couple of months, he was let go, says Nat Perrin, ''and I hired Cecil Barker to replace him. Barker was a talented guy, but more than that, he was a pretty heavy boozer himself, so I figured he and Red were made for each other.''

That was the kind of thinking that it took to make a Marx Brothers' writer. But unorthodox as the approach seemed to be, it had good results. Barker and Red got along as only two reformed alcoholics could. Barker would stay on as the show's producer for the next six years.

His presence didn't help the ratings much—at least not right away. By early spring of 1955, the show was in eighty-sixth place in the ratings, and Pharmaceuticals, Inc. decided to look for a star who could get them a wider market to sell their Geritol and Serutan, even though they weren't paying the full rate.

Before season's end, Hal Goodman and Larry Klein decided to quit, too, complaining to their agent, Bob Braun of the William Morris office, that Skelton was just ''too damn crazy to work for.'' Because the Morris office, headed by Lilliputian-sized Abe Lastfogel, handled the entire Skelton show package, Braun regarded Goodman and Klein as a couple of turncoats in a class not much higher than Benedict Arnold. ''At least have the decency to wait for Red to fire you, like everyone else,'' said Braun. When they refused, Braun threatened to keep them from getting any further work on William Morris packages.

''You try anything like that,'' retaliated Goodman, ''and I'll go under your head to Abe Lastfogel.''

When Lastfogel, who has absolutely no sense of humor

about his size, heard about Goodman's crack, he issued a dictum that Goodman would forever be barred from entering the hallowed doors of the William Morris Agency.

Lew Meltzer and Joe Bigelow, a couple of veteran movie writers, replaced Goodman and Klein and finished out the wobbly season without suffering too much trauma. But at the end of the season, they, too, were fired.

By then Red was disenchanted with Jack Donahue as the show's director and informed CBS that he wanted Seymour Berns back. "He'd heard how well I had done without him, and it really bugged him," says Berns, who, in the intervening year had not only directed Chrysler's *Shower of Stars* but also a number of filmed TV comedy dramas. One of these, in fact, *Public Pigeon Number One,* had starred Red Skelton in the title role, and it was probably the biggest success Red had enjoyed in a number of years.

"I didn't really want to go back working for Red steadily," says Berns, "but Skelton had CBS make me the kind of an offer I just couldn't refuse no matter how much of a kook Red was."

So Berns finally said "Yes," and he would end up staying with Red for a total of thirteen seasons, a feat which certainly deserves mention in *The Guinness Book of World Records.*

Together Seymour Berns and Cecil Barker turned the show into a winner. Of course, they couldn't have done it without first-class writing help, the bulk of which they got from Sherwood Schwartz, their new head writer—a man who had some very definite ideas on how he saw the format of the show.

To the public, Sherwood Schwartz is perhaps best known as the creator of two hit TV series—*Gilligan's Island* and *The Brady Bunch.* But among his writing peers, Schwartz will always be remembered by what Hal Kanter once said about him while introducing him at a testimonial dinner. "Sherwood Schwartz," said Kanter. "He sounds like Robin Hood's rabbi."

In the mid-fifties, Robin Hood's rabbi had just come off a season with *The Joan Davis Show,* and because of the tales he'd heard from other writers who had preceded him, he was no more anxious to accept a job with Red than Seymour Berns had been.

"I finally took it," recalls Schwartz, "but with one proviso—

that I never had to see or be with Red or otherwise have anything to do with him."

Inasmuch as Red, by that time, no longer wished to see any of his writers, either, this presented no problem to the management, and Schwartz was signed and given carte blanche to hire any other writers he needed to assist him.

The day that Schwartz took the job was a turning point in the show's fortunes. Of all the people who had worked for Red until then, Schwartz was the first to recognize a most important axiom of the TV comedy business—the less realistic a comic is, the bigger his jokes have to be. "If you're not being at least a little true to life, your script has to blast a laugh out of the audience every few seconds because their emotions are not involved," wrote no less an expert on comedy than Steve Allen in his fine book, *The Funny Men*, in 1956. "But if the audience is intensely interested in *what happens* to your characters, they will laugh amiably at almost any little joke you sprinkle the story line with."

If they know the character well enough, it doesn't even take a joke per se to amuse them. In the right story situation, it can be just a straight line that evokes the biggest yak. And sometimes it can be done with no line at all, as Jack Benny demonstrated time and again.

But Red Skelton had no character as himself, which was one of the reasons his monologue was always the least successful part of his act; and the majority of his characters, though funny, were less than true to life.

Moreover, one tired of seeing Red parade his entire stable of characters out every week.

Schwartz felt that the answer to Red's troubles was "to turn the show into a 'story' show built around just *one* of Red's characters each week." That way a Freddy the Freeloader or Cauliflower McPugg or the "mean widdle boy" would only turn up on the tube once every four or five weeks, with the result that the audience wouldn't tire of them. Hopefully, they might even look forward to seeing them again, which would give the audience a reason to tune in.

To help implement his new format, Schwartz added Jesse Goldstein, Mort Green, and Dave O'Brien to his writing staff.

Another good omen for the Skelton show besides the hiring of Sherwood Schwartz was that two very important sponsors—Johnson's Wax and Pet Milk—unaccountably decided to pick up the entire tab for the 1955–56 season. It was "unaccountable" because the ratings were still low, and most sponsors are more interested in ratings than in giving the public good entertainment.

But whatever motivated them, the Johnson Wax–Pet Milk sponsorship gave Red some much needed confidence and security. "I know they're not going to fire me on a whim like has happened to other comics," Red once said. "I know they don't worry about the ratings, so I don't worry about them, either."

According to Red, they also didn't interfere with the running of his show. Red blamed his past failures on "too much interference."

Ironically, the reviews of the opening Skelton show of the season did not augur any great new success, or give even the slightest hint that Red Skelton would be holding forth on that same network, at the same hour, every week of the season from then until 1969—long after all his current opposition had faded away.

The opening show of the 1955 season, which originated from New York, had been tailored by the writers to accommodate Jackie Gleason as Red's guest. Not bad thinking since Gleason had been Number Three in the ratings the previous season, and this was an opportunity to pick up some new viewers. But at the last minute, Gleason's sponsor—Buick Automobiles—said "no dice" to their star appearing as a guest on anybody else's show prior to his own season's opener on the coming Saturday night. So Gleason was postponed until the following week and was replaced by Ed Sullivan—hardly an adequate substitute, especially since there was no time to write a new script for Sullivan and he had to play the role intended for Gleason. The switch played havoc with the comedy, and as a result both *Variety* and *The Hollywood Reporter* bombed Skelton's lead-off program on September 29, 1955.

Variety:
No comic has been tried in more formats than Red Skelton. None apparently has clicked and neither will this one. Things just didn't go his way on the opener and there will have to be considerable improvement if the comedian is to make his presence felt in the ratings. He was at the mercy of weak material and had to get his laughs from hard falls.

The Hollywood Reporter:
If Red Skelton would stop laughing at his own material, this show would be much better. As it is, Red returned for the season with last year's asides, pratfalls, and mugging still being framed in the same manner.

From those two reviews, it's a wonder that Robin Hood's rabbi and his Merry Men at the typewriters were around for the second show.

Luckily for them and everyone else involved, the public did not share the critics' tastes. Judging by the show's upward climb in the ratings, Red's audience certainly didn't mind that he laughed at his own jokes, took too many pratfalls, overdid his mugging, and stepped out of character frequently to make funny "asides."

According to Steve Allen, "they actually seemed to be rooting for Red as he came smiling onto their TV screens week after week."

There could be no other explanation for the fact that by the following spring, the *Red Skelton Show* was solidly established among the first ten in the weekly Nielsens, and was Number One for Tuesday evening in the "overnight" Trendex ratings.

It is, of course, a well-established fact that success begets success. But nowhere does this axiom hold true quite so much as it does in show business.

Suddenly, Red was in big demand again, and he was making the most of it.

Early in 1956, Mike Todd invited Red to play a cameo role in his newest blockbuster film—*Around The World in Eighty Days*—along with a host of other important stars.

In May, Red was hired to star in a feature film called *Public Pigeon Number One*, which was adapted by Harry Tugend from the television drama. Because the TV version had received such accolades, Universal Pictures decided to join forces with CBS and remake it for theatrical distribution, with Red getting 35 percent of the profits.

Late in 1956, Bo Roos brought Red an offer from *Playhouse 90* to play the part of "Buddy McCoy," a punchdrunk ex-pug in a drama called *The Big Slide*. This was heavy drama—not exactly Red's specialty—but remembering what a change-of-pace role in *From Here to Eternity* did for Frank Sinatra's career, Red decided to follow in the singer's footsteps, and accepted the challenge.

He did not regret it. In fact, he gave such a stunning performance as Buddy McCoy that later in the year he received a nomination for "Best Performance by an Actor" at the Ninth Annual Emmy Awards.

Red didn't win the Emmy. Jack Palance walked off with top honors for his stirring performance in *Requiem For a Heavyweight*. But considering the stature of the other contenders—Fredric March, Sal Mineo, and Lloyd Bridges—just getting the nomination was ample reward for the Vincennes redhead who once was fired from a tent show repertory company because every time he walked on the stage in a straight role he got guffaws.

18

$\mathbf{R}$unning concurrently with Red's struggles to attain his former popularity on television were his personal tribulations with Georgia. His life with her since they had last reconciled following his hernia operation in 1952 continued to be an endless series of stormy confrontations, usually punctuated by Red moving out of the Sarbonne house and into an expensive hotel suite or apartment around town, from which he would issue statements to the press about how impossible Georgia was to live with and how he was never going to go back to her. And this time he *meant* it. More often than not, the story of their split would barely reach the public prints before Red was back banging on

Georgia's front door, begging to be allowed in and promising to be a good boy.

The most persistently recurring theme in Red's public utterances about Georgia was that he felt she was jealous of his success and was either treating him indifferently, or else she disturbed him so much at home with her constant nagging that he was unable to write.

From Georgia's point of view, however, "jealousy of his success" had little to do with her displeasure; it was more basic than that: a plain and simple case of neglect. Because of Red's total absorption in his career he just wasn't paying as much attention to her and the children as she would have preferred.

If he wasn't at CBS doing his show, or somewhere off in the hinterlands making a personal appearance at a state fair, Red would usually be sequestered in his bungalow study on his Sarbonne estate. There he'd stay up for perhaps half the night working on scripts, developing new impersonations, writing "short stories," and attempting to self-educate himself by reading books that Gene Fowler had recommended to him.

In the beginning of his relationship with the former newspaperman turned biographer, Red had regarded Fowler strictly as a drinking companion. And for that Red couldn't have selected a better man. After being a bosom companion of W. C. Fields, John Barrymore, and other celebrated Hollywood drunks for years, Fowler was no slouch with the bottle himself, and, if necessary, was not even averse to climbing a tree in order to keep from drinking alone.

After their friendship thickened, however, and Red came to regard Fowler as the father he never had, he started to admire the man for his erudition as well as his ability to match him drink for drink. To emulate Fowler, who was a prodigious reader, Red started to show interest in books. He first tackled his son Richard's twenty-four-volume set of the *Book of Knowledge*. From there he worked his way up to Van Loon's *Story of Mankind* and simplified biographies of historical figures such as Washington and Lincoln.

He also read small snatches of Thackeray and Dickens, and

after somebody told him that first editions were a good investment as well as an enhancement to the looks of one's library, he started collecting first editions of the classics. Before he was through he had, among other first editions on his library shelves, eight Dickens novels in their original magazine form.

As a result of Fowler's literary influence, Red also started to try his hand at writing short stories. Inasmuch as the short story is probably the most difficult writing form to master, it's not surprising that none of Red's short stories has ever been published.

Over the years, however, Red turned out over a thousand of these nocturnal creations, most running from ten to fifteen pages in length. He never even tried to have them published, but he thought enough of them to have them copyrighted and bound in red morocco with gold titles. He says that he plans to leave them to his family as a legacy that will be worth "maybe ten or fifteen bucks" when he goes. "Maybe somebody will get a surprise when they read them," he adds with a chuckle.

When Red did go to bed, he didn't sleep much. Three or four hours' rest was the most he ever got. He spent the remainder of the night jumping in and out of bed to jot down ideas for new routines, or else roaming restlessly around the estate, waiting for dawn to break.

Spending the evening alone, while Red was trying to emulate Balzac, was not Georgia's idea of a rip-roaring good time. What she yearned for was a stimulating social life of the kind she'd known before she'd married Red. Like a good many models and showgirls who had migrated to Hollywood during the exciting live-for-the-moment days of World War II, Georgia had once been a frequent habitué of the Swanee Inn, a little joint on South La Brea Avenue that featured "all-black" entertainment and attracted most of the real Hollywood "swingers" of that period. Nat King Cole got his start there, singing for $100 a week. It was while hanging around the Swanee Inn as an "available" single girl that Georgia originally got hooked on drinking, pills, and some of the other residual benefits indigenous to such an environment.

Inasmuch as Red was a star, and stars are associated with glamorous existences, Georgia no doubt felt that her marriage would be just a continuation of the cafe-society life she had led when she was a beautiful, single girl. But as she discovered, that was not to be her lot at all. After being married to Red for eight years by 1953, and bearing him two children, she found that her social life had been cut down to practically nothing. Not just because Red was becoming more and more of a recluse as time went on, but because he had so few actual friends. This was partly Red's doing. Despite his public declarations to the contrary, he actually didn't like or trust many people. Dave and Betty Rose, and Gene Fowler, until the latter died in 1960, were his absolute favorites, and he would have them to the house to dinner as often as they would come. But there were few others with whom he felt comfortable.

Despite Red's reclusive tendencies, Georgia tried, from time to time during their marriage, to become a successful hostess on a grand scale. To this end she started courting socialite Cobina Wright, who was a friend of the Queen Mother Nazli of Egypt, when King Farouk was still on the throne.

One night, the Skeltons threw a fancy party for the Queen Mother at their Bel Air estate. It was so fancy that few people in the entertainment business were invited. The guest list was made up of the *crème de la crème* of Beverly Hills and Bel Air society: people like Ed Pauley, the multi-millionaire oil man.

In keeping with her royal position, the Queen Mother held court in the Skelton's living room. Georgia would curtsy whenever she introduced a guest to the Queen Mother.

Eventually it came time to introduce Georgia's husband Red. "Your Majesty," began Georgia, "may I present my husband Richard Skelton."

It was one of the few times anyone had ever heard Red addressed by his given name.

Red was not impressed. "Queenie," he said, "do you know your son is Farouking Egypt?"

That put an end to Georgia's plans to become a social lioness, on the Perl Mesta scale.

Sometimes, out of sheer loneliness, Red would invite his

producer, director, or whoever else he happened to be working with (except his writers) to have dinner with him and Georgia.

Rarely were these invitations to his staff premeditated. Usually they'd be given on the spur of the moment at the end of a working day at his house, when a meeting had just broken up. "Suddenly he'd want you to stay to dinner," recalls Seymour Berns, "and before you could say 'no' or think up an excuse, he'd be running to tell the cook to get the steaks out of the freezer." Basically he was a very lonely man, so if you didn't want to get stuck eating with him and Georgia, because you'd rather be with your own family, it would be wise to have your secretary phone you around four o'clock, with some phony reason why you had to leave—such as your dog was run over or your house was on fire."

Red could be an amusing host, however, according to Ben Brady, who, with his wife Estelle, were occasional guests at the Skelton residence before Brady got fired. "He could be extremely funny if he wanted to," recalls Brady. "In a room he kept you constantly in stitches, and he couldn't do anything without being a clown. Not for what he said so much as what he did. He'd walk across the room to pick up a phone and you'd die laughing. Maybe he'd walk like a girl, or maybe he'd trip over some imaginary object and take a forward pratfall."

The Skeltons' marriage, however, probably could have survived a dull social life if other aspects of it hadn't been deeply troubled.

For one thing, Red was extremely jealous of Georgia—some believe for good reason.

During the few times Red insisted that she come down to CBS and stand in the wings while he was doing his broadcast, it wasn't because he needed her moral support, as he publicly proclaimed. "It was because he was afraid to leave her alone," asserts Seymour Berns.

Throughout their marriage, Red suspected Georgia of having affairs with just about every man with whom she ever came in contact—from his business managers to Gerald, a muscular young man who worked at the Skeltons' house for years, and then was mysteriously fired.

According to Seymour Berns—and just about everyone else who knew the Skeltons well enough to be called insiders—it was no mystery why Gerald eventually left. Red came home from the studio one day and caught Gerald and Georgia in bed together.

"I know it's true," says Berns, "because Red personally told me the story of coming home and catching them in the act. Bo Roos told me the same story. He knew about it because Red made him do the firing of Gerald."

Red hated confrontations, and though he had been cuckolded by his servant, he didn't have the heart to fire Gerald himself, and so made Roos do it for him.

As any husband would be, Red was shattered to discover that Georgia was cheating on him. But probably the only reason he didn't decide to call an end to the marriage then and there was because he knew that he wasn't exactly a paragon of husbandly fidelity himself.

Red was never the indefatigable girl chaser so many of his show business brethren are. "He liked pretty girls, as most guys do," declares one of his former writers, "but in my opinion, if he had his choice of getting laid or getting a laugh, I think he'd opt for the latter."

Nevertheless, when opportunity presented itself for some extra-marital sex, without detection, there is ample evidence to show that Red took advantage of it. And for a major star like Red, there were plenty of opportunities around Hollywood with young, aspiring actresses.

A story about Red that has been making the rounds of Hollywood's gossip grapevine for years involved him and one of the town's great beauties, who at the time of the incident was a young contract actress at MGM.

It happened during the filming of *Southern Yankee*. While the company was on a battlefield location, waiting for the special effects men to set off the charges for a battle scene, Red became bored and restless, and invited the young actress to his trailer dressing room.

As was her custom, the young lady was soon on her knees in front of Skelton, doing her own version of *Deep Throat*.

Just at the moment of climax, the special effects crew on the battlefield outside accidentally set off a dynamite charge, rocking Red's portable dressing room. Clothes racks fell over. Pictures dropped from the walls. Glasses tumbled to the floor from the bar. In short, the effect was one of an A-bomb explosion.

Smiling with satisfaction, Red patted the actress on the head and said, "Good girl."

Judging by the foregoing—and other tales of Red's profligacy—it is fairly clear the he must share some of the responsibility for their marriage eventually going on the rocks.

Gentleman that he was, however, Red never gave anything so serious as infidelity or suspected infidelity to the press as a reason for his frequent battles and separations from Georgia. He always blamed their rifts on something much more mundane.

When Red next separated officially from Georgia, late in 1953, a few weeks after he returned from the trip to New York where he found God, he told the press, "Every time I try to write gags, Georgia starts an argument. I can't work at home. She makes it her business not to let me succeed."

On this occasion, Red moved into a posh suite at the Beverly Hills Hotel, and came out of it only to drive to CBS in his Rolls Royce. Otherwise, he remained in seclusion, and probably would have been content with hotel life forever if it weren't nearing Christmas and Georgia wasn't making it so difficult for him to see his children.

Georgia knew that the one chink in Red's armor was his love for Richard and Valentina. Consequently, whenever Red left her, she used the children as a lever to force him to give in and beg to come back. Red was especially vulnerable during the holiday season, when the mere sight of a store window full of Christmas cheer, of a happy family out on the street doing their shopping together, brought tears of penitence to his eyes.

So after only a few weeks of residence in the Beverly Hills Hotel, Red packed his bags and returned to his hilltop fortress again. This time he told the press, "I love my kids. I'm in love with my wife. All I want to do is see my children. I don't want my wife to lock the door against me."

Red might have been trying to gain sympathy from the press, but there wasn't any doubt that he really loved Richard and Valentina, and that he missed them badly when he was away from home.

How could he help but love them? Valentina, at the age of six, was growing into a beautiful little red-haired girl like her mother, and Richard, also sporting freckles and a carrot top, bore an uncanny resemblance to his father. From the way Red beamed at him when he was showing Richard off to his friends or posing for photographers, it was obvious that the boy meant something very special to him.

And the children adored having Red Skelton for a father, too. Not only because he could be such a clown around the house and bought them expensive toys, but because it was fun having a celebrity in the family to boast about to other schoolchildren. In a way, it made celebrities out of them, too.

As Eddie Cantor used to do when he talked about "Ida and the five kids" on the air, Red always included jokes about Valentina and Richard on his television program. The kids ate it up, and would wait eagerly in front of their set at home every Tuesday evening for Daddy to mention their names.

At any rate, Red was home and playing Santa Claus in front of the fireplace by Christmas of 1953. From all appearances he was finally fully resigned to living out his life with Georgia—at least until Richard and Valentina grew up.

But only a month later, on January 30, 1954, Red and Georgia separated again. This time the split seemed as if it might be permanent, for Red didn't just move into a hotel; he took a top floor apartment in the Wilshire Palms apartments, which he still owned. "This is it," Red announced to a press who'd heard him cry "wolf" so many times before they could hardly keep a straight face. "I've taken all I'm supposed to take. I'm ruining my life. Georgia says I'm ruining hers."

Meanwhile, a few blocks away at the Bel Air Hotel, Georgia was playing hostess at a champagne and caviar party she was throwing to celebrate "Red's leaving." Invited to this unusual Last Supper were about two dozen of the Skeltons' friends, acquaintances, and business associates, including Ben Brady and his wife. It was a deadly affair, according to those who attended; but the slightly tipsy Georgia wouldn't let it break up until the wee hours. "It was like having a wake without a corpse," recalls one of the guests.

However, judging by the way Georgia carried on about that "S.O.B. Red" that night, the marriage was definitely dead, corpse or no corpse.

But a few weeks later Red surprised everyone by going back to Georgia. Surprised everyone but Georgia, that is. Through her lawyers, Georgia had communicated with Red that under absolutely no circumstances would she ever give him a divorce. It was against her religion. So he might as well resign himself to that fact of Catholic life and come home. Friends of theirs said that Red was quite morose and unhappy about this turn of events, and Georgia knew it. But Georgia's pride insisted that she hold onto Red, whether or not there was any love there.

There was very little public battling between the two after Red returned to Georgia that time—at least for quite a few years. In fact, the two seemed to go out of their way to show the public and the press a very happy couple, at peace with each other.

Nevertheless, even when the marriage was sailing along smoothly, Red was constantly alluding to Georgia's sexual promiscuity in his everyday conversation, or otherwise saying things that were sure to embarrass or hurt her in front of their friends.

One time, in the sixties, Red invited Seymour Berns and Charlie Isaacs, the show's head writer at the time, to his home in Palm Springs for a luncheon meeting with him and Georgia about the script. While Red was showing Seymour Berns around the house, Georgia, who was into astrology, came into the den where Charlie Isaacs was waiting, and asked him for his birthdate.

"September 17," replied Isaacs.

"Oh, you're a Virgo, just like me!" exclaimed Georgia, whereupon she threw her arms around Isaacs and hugged him affectionately.

At that moment, Red returned to the room with Berns.

"Guess what, honey?" Georgia said to Red. "Charlie's a Virgo, just like me. He was born September 17, too."

"September 17," exclaimed Red derisively. "Does that mean I have to sleep with him, too?"

On another occasion, Red and Georgia were guests at a fancy

party thrown by John Wayne at the Beverly Hills Hotel. Red and Georgia were standing with Humphrey Bogart when an exquisite foreign actress, with whom Tyrone Power was having an affair, passed in front of them, swinging her hips provocatively.

All the men looked at her, and Red asked, smacking his lips, "Who's that?"

"I don't know her name," replied Bogart, "but Ty Power says she's the best cocksucker in town."

Whereupon Red patted Georgia on the head fondly, and said to Bogart, "Aw, now you've gone and hurt Georgia's feelings."

"Oh, Red, you're disgraceful," were all the words the embarrassed Georgia could muster.

Shortly after Christmas of 1956, Richard, who had been eight years old on his last birthday, came down with a mysterious fever. At first Richard's governess thought it was a touch of the flu, or the result of "too much Christmas." But when the fever lingered on and the normally active Richard became weak and listless, his pediatrician admitted him to the UCLA Medical Center for "routine tests."

A few days later, on January 4, 1957, a UCLA specialist in rare blood diseases sat Red and Georgia down in his office and solemnly informed them that Richard had leukemia, and that his life expectancy was "from five months to a year."

Red and Georgia were in shock. *Leukemia! Five months to*

live! This was something that happened to other people, in other households, not to you personally.

Was he sure of his diagnosis? Couldn't there have been a mistake at the lab? Or, possibly in Richard's case it wasn't incurable?

The doctor shook his head sadly, and explained that Richard had been struck with a particularly virulent kind of leukemia; it came on with no warning, and ran its deadly course rapidly. There was nothing anybody could do.

Suddenly all the problems that had made married life so unbearable for Red and Georgia were swept away by the enormity of this tragedy that they must now face and share together. Richard was dying. *Dying!* Their only boy was dying. They couldn't believe it; they couldn't change it, either. But they could share it by forgetting their own grievances and doing everything within their power to make Richard's last months on earth as pleasant as possible under the circumstances.

But there were grim decisions to make. Was Richard to go home, or remain in the hospital? Was he to be told the truth, or was his fate to be kept a secret from him?

The doctors at UCLA advised the Skeltons that their son should, as soon as he'd completed his initial round of examinations and medications at the hospital, return home and continue to lead the same normal life he'd known before his illness—until he was no longer able to, that is. That date could possibly be postponed if Richard took his medication regularly, reported back to the hospital for periodic check-ups, and got plenty of rest. It was important that none of these things be ignored.

And if they expected Richard's cooperation, they would, of course, have to inform him that he was ill. Not deathly ill, but enough so that it was important to do as the doctor ordered.

None of this was very comforting, and Red and Georgia were still in shock when they drove home from UCLA in the gloomy, chilly January twilight.

"Red called me up the same night he found the kid had leukemia," recalls Seymour Berns. "To give you an idea of the loneliness of the man, I'm the one he called. Anyway, he phoned, and my wife Annie and I went up to the house and sat around with him and Georgia in their huge living room, and tried to tell them not to give up—that there was always hope, always the possibility of a miracle. Georgia just sat there numbly, weeping and drinking, and Red was staring off into space."

When Richard returned home from the hospital a few days later, Red—doing his utmost to put on a "happy face"—informed him that he had a disease called leukemia and said that it was extremely serious, but that if he did exactly as the doctors told him, everything would be all right. He even read to him from a book about the disease, and insisted that Richard listen carefully. Red didn't want Richard to feel that secrets were being kept from him, but he also didn't want to frighten him, for it was important to keep him in good spirits.

"You've got to eat lots of meat and vegetables and get lots of rest," said Red, playing the most heartbreaking scene of his career, "and take your medicine without goofing off, and then you'll be okay. Is that a deal?"

"Okay, Buddy," replied Richard after thinking it over carefully for a few moments, "you've got yourself a deal."

For the first few months of his illness, Richard was able to lead a fairly normal life. He did everything the doctors and his parents wanted him to, although sometimes it was tough for him to have to come indoors to rest or take medicine when all his friends were out playing baseball or riding bicycles. But he didn't complain, even during those intervals when he had to be readmitted periodically to the hospital for more tests and an occasional blood transfusion. It was boring to have to remain in a hospital, where the only exercise and fun he got was a fast ride up and down the corridor in a wheelchair. But he always maintained his good spirits. He joked with the doctors and nurses, assured them that he knew more about what was wrong with him than they did, and to prove it he'd throw long medical terms around like a professor.

When he first was afflicted with his illness, Richard wasn't in any particular pain or discomfort. There were times, however, when despite the best medical attention money could buy, Richard wasn't feeling as well as others. Richard would never admit it to his father, but Red could always tell when his son wasn't up to par, for he'd become irritable and withdrawn. At these times, Red tried to be cheerful, and would clown for his benefit. Usually it would work, and Richard would snap out of his depressed mood quickly. It was harder for Red to keep his own spirits up.

When Richard's illness was first diagnosed, Red's immediate inclination was to cancel his television show and spend every waking moment with Richard, trying to entertain him. But he soon came to realize that that wouldn't have been the fair thing to do to the many people who depended on his show for a living. Besides, he had been advised by Richard's doctors that, for the boy's sake, it wouldn't be wise to depart too far from his normal life pattern. If he did, Richard might become suspicious that his illness was fatal, which would only hasten his death. So in the true show-must-go-on spirit, Red kept on doing his television program every week, and only cancelled out-of-town engagements, such as Vegas, that would take him away from Richard's side for long periods.

But it wasn't easy being funny under the circumstances. If rehearsals were difficult for him to take seriously before, they were impossible now. "I've never seen a man go through such agony," recalls Willie Dahl, who was stage manager for the Skelton television show. "He used to stare into space during rehearsals and say, 'What the hell am I doing here?' "

During the actual performance, if he saw a boy Richard's age in the audience, he'd break up.

Red also stopped making jokes about his kids on the air, as he had previously been in the habit of doing. He couldn't even bring himself to mention their names on the show any more—or off the show, for that matter. So touchy had Red become on this subject that his writers and the rest of the people on his staff tried to avoid any reference to Richard and Valentina in just normal conversation. And they had to fine-tooth comb the script before submitting it to make sure there was no mention of names that sounded like Richard or jokes or situations that might possibly remind Red of his son or illness.

This continued for several weeks after Richard's sickness was diagnosed. Then, one night when Red came home after a show and tiptoed into Richard's bedroom to give him a good-night kiss on the forehead while he was asleep, he found Richard waiting up for him.

"Hey, Buddy, how come you don't tell jokes about me and Valentina on the show any more?" asked Richard, with a disturbed frown on his face.

Red suddenly realized that this was one of those normal routines of Richard's life which had been so vital to the boy's sense of security, from which he should never have deviated.

Of course, now that Richard had brought it up, it was perfectly obvious to Red that the boy would wonder why his father had suddenly stopped joking about him—and even talking about him—on the air, breaking a ritual that had gone on for as long as he could remember.

Red made the boy feel better by assuring him that the elimination of their little private jokes hadn't been done intentionally. The jokes had merely been the victims of some necessary cutting due to an unusually long script.

Red made amends on the show the following Tuesday evening by throwing in a few more gags about Richard and Valentina than he normally would have. As he joked about them, he felt an instant chill descend on the studio. People on the staff and in the audience were suddenly looking at Red as if he were an unfeeling, heartless monster. Whatever could he be thinking of, making jokes about a boy stricken with leukemia?

Yet he couldn't defend himself publicly and say why he was doing it, because if he did, it would surely get in the newspapers that the boy had a fatal disease, which was the one thing he was hoping Richard would never discover.

Red kept his mouth shut in the face of unjustified criticism. And what made him able to stand up to it was the knowledge that he had done the right thing for his son, who, according to his governess, had sat cross-legged in front of the television set that night, with a broad smile on his face at the mention of his name, feeling nothing had changed nor was about to change.

Another problem the Skeltons had to face was Valentina. Because of all the attention given to Richard, she felt left out and neglected. Several times she even tried to run away from home. To counter this, Red and Georgia did everything to make her feel important and useful. One of the things they did was give her the responsibility of helping Richard answer all the letters he received. Since news of his illness had reached the public prints, letters of sympathy had been arriving at the house by the carload. Red's secretary answered the letters that came to him personally. But Richard was allowed to open and answer the mail addressed to him. This continued until Red and Georgia discovered that people, while trying to be genuinely sympathetic and kind, were often tactlessly blunt. One woman, whose own son had died at an early age, had had the temerity—some call it stupidity—to give Richard the name of her son and hope that the two might "get together and become friends after you get to Heaven."

After that, the Skeltons screened all the incoming letters first to make certain that there was none among them to upset Richard.

In the spring, Richard seemed a little stronger and peppier, giving his parents the false hope that he might be winning the battle against leukemia. But the doctors explained that this wasn't so. Richard's disease was merely in a "remission stage," they said. It was a time when the cancerous blood cells, partially due to so much concentrated medication, lay dormant.

It was then that Red was struck with an inspiration. He decided to pack into those final months that Richard had remaining as much of the miraculous, the beautiful, and the fascinating in the world as the average person might not even encounter in a lifetime.

Since the show was on "spring hiatus" for two weeks, Red and Georgia seized the opportunity to take Richard and Valentina on a trip to the East Coast to show them some of the historic landmarks they'd never seen before, and which, in all probability, Richard would never see again—places like Concord, Lexington, Mount Vernon, the White House, and the Statue of Liberty, where they went up into the lady's hand.

As the Skelton family progressed across the country, they found a miracle not to be found in the guide books—the miracle of friendship and sympathy from complete strangers. Richard was inundated with gifts from people he'd never met before—

souvenirs, press cards, waiters' buttons, police badges, keys to cities, and all sorts of odds and ends offered on impulse.

In New York, among other things, Red arranged for the family to drive a train through the yard at Grand Central with the four of them sitting in the cab with the engineer, who let Richard handle the controls briefly; they ran an elevator up to the tower floor of the Empire State Building; and they went on a special tour of the subways.

Naturally, the tour attracted a great deal of publicity, good and bad. "The idea of the trip," said Red in an interview with the press, "is to show the kids all the wonderful things there are in the world. I want them—especially Richard—to learn and see everything there is to see. For the rest, we are in God's hands."

Returning to the West Coast, Red told the press, "The little fellow got such enjoyment out of that trip—and no ill effects— that as soon as school is out, and I'm finished with my show for the season, we're going to show him the rest of the world."

After examining Richard, his specialists assured Red and Georgia that the boy's leukemia would probably remain in the "remission" stage through the summer, so the trip overseas would probably do him no harm, provided they stopped long enough in the major European cities for him to have regular check-ups en route. The specialists in those cities would be notified in advance to expect Richard and advised what to do for him.

As if Red weren't having enough troubles, in May of that year, *Lootville,* a novel by Benedict and Nancy Freedman, was published. The main character in *Lootville* just happened to be about a red-haired television comedian who bore an uncanny resemblance to Red Skelton, even to the point of his collecting guns and having an alcoholic, slightly nymphomaniacal wife.

Some member of Red's staff, claiming not to have known what the novel was about, except that it was written by one of Red's former gag writers, gave a copy of *Lootville* to Red. After reading the book, Red was so upset and embarrassed by its publication that, even if he hadn't been planning to take Richard to Europe prior to that, nothing could have kept him from going abroad.

Red just had to get away from the town that was treating him so shabbily. So on July 9, he, Georgia, Valentina, and Richard set out for Europe on what was to be one of the saddest odysseys of the century. On their itinerary were Denmark, Italy, Switzerland, Great Britain, and France.

Red and Georgia, knowing the media, had realized that they would never be able to keep the journey a secret. But there were a lot more reporters and photographers following them around than they had ever expected. It seems that everyone was interested and touched by the thought of a young boy battling a serious disease, a boy who was being shown the beauty and wonders of the world by a father who was a famous clown.

As the people of the various countries they visited studied newspaper photos of Richard's brave, boyish face smiling in a famous restaurant with his comedian father, or gazing at the Vatican or racing through the Tivoli Gardens or peering up at the Eiffel Tower, it must have flashed through their minds that he might never see these things again. But Red, who refused to recognize the reality of the situation, didn't feel that way; or if he did, he didn't show it publicly. And Richard didn't, either. Red was sure that science was working on a cure for leukemia and that the researchers would come up with it in time to save Richard.

When the Skeltons stepped out of the jet liner at Heathrow Airport in London, they were immediately surrounded by members of the Fourth Estate. Red, whose nerves were always on edge after any flight, tried to answer as many questions for the reporters as possible. But Richard was exhausted after the long flight, and Red, anxious to get him away from the crowd and into their suite at the Savoy, made his excuses to the press and tried to steer the family toward a waiting cab. The press was accommodating in this instance. However, one reporter, who identified himself as being a representative of the *Daily Sketch,* forced his way through to Red and demanded a private interview. Red told him pleasantly that he was giving no private interviews, that this was not a publicity excursion, but a pleasure trip for his ailing son.

Immediately after they checked into the Savoy, the manager

informed Red that about forty newspapermen and photographers from all over the world were in the lobby and wanted a "press conference." At first Red was reluctant, emphasizing as he had earlier at the airport, that this was not a publicity junket but a pleasure trip for his son. The manager advised Red to hold the conference, anyway. He explained that it was an old London tradition for a visiting celebrity to invite the press in, serve them sandwiches and drinks, and answer their questions. Otherwise, it might create hard feelings, with reprisals in the press. So Red agreed.

For the most part, the reporters were a pleasant enough group of men and women, who, after Red had spoken briefly— and perfunctorily—about the nature of Richard's illness and the purpose of the trip, seemed to be satisfied with that and soon moved on to subjects relating to Red's show business career.

When there were just a few reporters left, and no sandwiches or liquor, the writer from the *Daily Sketch* who had approached Red at the airport began grilling him again about the medical aspects of Richard's illness, and right in front of Richard. Red told the writer that he was not equipped with the technical knowledge, nor did he have the desire to give him this information, and therefore had no more to say on the subject.

The newspaperman shrugged philosophically, and left. Red thought no more about it and he and Georgia began poring over travel folders to plan what they were going to see in London. The following morning, the *London Daily Sketch* ripped into the Skelton clan with the venom of a vindictive cobra.

"This jamboree was sickening," began the story. "Think of it: a dying boy sitting unnoticed in a corner while everyone else was whooping it up."

The story went on to imply that the trip was nothing more than a crass publicity stunt, and it bolstered this theory by mentioning that Red's press agent was standing at the door handing out pamphlets of the comedian's life story, thereby capitalizing on the illness of his son.

The latter was utterly false. Milt Weiss, Red's publicity man, did not accompany them on the trip, nor did any other press agent. And no matter what else one may think of Red, if you knew him at all, you could never ascribe that kind of a crass motive to his trip.

Red tried to make light of the *Sketch*'s story in another statement to the press. "That last statement is utterly ridiculous," he said. "If there were any pamphlets on my life story (which there are not) even *Confidential* would not be able to print them, so what would my own press agent be doing with them?"

But inside he was shocked, angry, and hurt by this cruel and unwarranted attack. His first impulse was to march down to the paper and punch the reporter in the nose. But Georgia finally calmed him down to the point where he settled for sending the *Daily Sketch* reporter a telegram saying simply: "Sorry that you are sick, both physically and mentally."

Worse than the many false accusations in the press was the fact that Richard, as a result of all this publicity, became aware for the first time that he wasn't expected to recover.

This was more of a shock to Red than it was to Richard. Red called off the rest of the trip, except for a brief detour to Rome for an audience with Pope Pius XII which Father Carney had arranged. The audience was completely private, and afterward Red described it as "the most moving thing I have ever done in my life."

According to Red, the Pope assured him and Georgia, "If life is taken away from one person in a family, they are never separated, because they remain united in eternal life."

Three days later, Red announced to the press that the trip was proving too much for Richard and that the Skeltons were coming home.

Before leaving for the States, Red was told of a Padre Pio, who was headquartered in a nearby monastery, who had a reputation locally of being able to accomplish "miracles" when it came to healing the incurable. In their desperation, Red and Georgia sought Padre Pio's help. For an hour, Red and Georgia lay prostrate at the Shrine of Our Lady of Fatima, while Padre Pio said prayers for Richard.

The prayers, however heartfelt, were not successful. Nothing short of God Himself could cure their son. Defeated, and tired beyond human endurance, the Skeltons returned to Los Angeles.

An Associated Press photograph of Red and Richard, both wearing Swiss Tyrolean caps and smiling broadly as they deplaned at the Los Angeles International Airport, gave no hint of the tragedy about to take place. In fact, if the picture could be trusted, Richard never looked healthier, nor Red happier.

But on the following day, Richard was readmitted to the UCLA Medical Center. For the next few months he was constantly in and out of the hospital. The disease was no longer in a "remission stage." It was now just a matter of months, and waiting.

Watching Richard die, while putting on such a brave front, was the bleakest period of Red and Georgia's lives. As death drew nearer over the fall and winter, the tensions in their marriage tightened to the snapping point.

Red's only escape was in doing his television show. For the hour or so he was on the air or doing a preview or a rehearsal, he was able to forget the tragedy of his personal life.

Ratings no longer mattered. Forgetting was all that was important. But Georgia had no such escape. "And sometimes," according to Seymour Berns, "Georgia would come down to the studio and right before Red was to do his show, she'd rush up to him and say, 'I just came from the hospital. Richard's worse today.' Red would be so upset he could hardly go on. I think Georgia subconsciously wanted to destroy him."

But if Georgia wanted to destroy him, her actions certainly didn't reflect that on the night of December 31, 1957, when Red was suddenly stricken with a severe asthmatic attack while the two of them were at their home in Bel Air. When Red started to choke to death from the attack, Georgia tried to phone their family doctor. But when he couldn't be reached, she had the presence of mind to phone the Fire Department, which rushed up to the Sarbonne estate with an emergency crew and saved Red from what would have been certain death. (Those were the days before sending for the paramedics was a standard procedure in those kinds of emergencies.)

Though Red's life was saved, the asthma attack brought on what Red's personal physician referred to as a "heart seizure," and he had to be hospitalized at St. John's for the next several weeks.

Barely a month later, and still pale from the ordeal, Red was out of St. John's and back rehearsing for his TV show.

On January 21, it was Georgia's turn. She was admitted to St. John's, suffering again from "exhaustion."

On February 10, Red was rushed again to the hospital. This time his doctor said he was suffering from "nervous collapse and lung congestion." His asthma was acting up again. Asked to explain what exactly was wrong with the comedian, Red's doctor told the press, "Supposing there were ten steps to death. Red's taken nine of them."

But Red was stronger than anyone suspected, and he had to survive, if only for Richard's sake. And, of course, he did.

But the months, days, and hours became nightmares for Red and Georgia. They could only wait for the inevitable.

According to friends, they'd sit in a corner and have crying jags. But never was a tear shown in Richard's presence. Red, a classic example of the sad and lonely clown, did everything he could to make Richard smile again.

In April, Richard took a turn for the worse, and was readmitted to the UCLA Hospital. Fearing from what the doctors told him that the end was near, Red cancelled a three-week booking to play the Hotel Riviera in Las Vegas that month just to remain at the boy's bedside as much as possible.

It was a torturesome period for both Red and Georgia. Richard had to undergo daily blood transfusions. By May his veins had been punctured so many times that his hands, wrists, and forearms were black and blue. As a result there were few places left to insert a needle, and an incision had to be made in his leg in order for the transfusions—now sometimes as many as three daily—to continue.

Shortly before Mother's Day, Red was visiting the hospital room without Georgia, when Richard said, "I don't think they'll let me out of here with this cut on my leg, Daddy. So will you get Mommy that red blanket she wanted for Mother's Day, and charge it to me?"

Red had to leave the room suddenly as the tears welled up in his eyes, and he collapsed into a chair in the corridor.

On May 10, at about six in the evening, Red and Georgia received a call from Richard's doctor who said that they should come over to the hospital quickly. He was afraid that death was near.

They brought Valentina, and the three spent Richard's last two hours alone with him.

When they arrived in the room, Richard seemed to sense that this was the end. He smiled weakly, and asked each of them to give him a kiss.

Red and Georgia kissed him tenderly on his pale forehead, but Valentina, perhaps awed by the prospect of seeing someone die, lingered timidly in the background.

Impatient, Richard waited for her kiss, then suddenly exclaimed weakly, "Hurry up, Valentina, I haven't got all day!"

It was true. He died a few minutes later, at 8:40 P.M. According to Red, "The little fella knew it all right. But he didn't show it. He didn't cry."

But Red did. And because he was too overcome with grief to do his show, he took a hiatus from television that week, and Milton Berle, Jo Stafford, Donald O'Connor, and Sidney Miller filled in for him.

Funeral services were held three days after Richard's death, at Forest Lawn's Church of the Recessional. Red and Georgia were so shaken that neither of them could stand without assistance.

Red, Georgia, and Valentina remained in a separate room, apart from the chapel auditorium where 120 friends and business associates of the Skeltons sat. Another 500 persons remained outside the building, hoping to catch a glimpse of the celebrities in attendance.

The Reverend Dr. James Stewart of the Beverly Vista Community Church—the same reverend who had married Red and Georgia—officiated at the services, while actor William Lundigan, a friend of Red's, performed a brief but touching eulogy.

"What praise can awaken a sleeping child or explain the meaning of God's will?" asked Mr. Lundigan. "The boy was manly, very human and life-loving, yet there was a saintly quality about him. Richard did not complain through the long months of his illness. A president and a Pope were his friends. Hundreds who never saw him were his friends. He was a special child who touched many lives."

By the time Lundigan had concluded, there wasn't a dry eye in the house. Red wept and listened numbly to the services, all the while clasping in his hand a crucifix of Richard's that had been blessed by the Pope.

Richard was buried in a private crypt in the Forest Lawn Mausoleum Sanctuary of Prayer where Red also had purchased space for himself and Georgia when their time came. Buried in the vault with Richard were his rosary and the same crucifix Red had been clutching during the funeral services, and which Red put in his hand just before the casket was closed.

Nobody who was at Forest Lawn that day would ever forget the picture of the grief-stricken Red and Georgia leaving the Mausoleum, wrapped in each other's arms for support, and crying like babies, as they were helped toward a waiting limousine. For the moment, at least, death had brought them together.

"That night," recalls Seymour Berns, "Annie and I, Dave and Betty Rose, and Cecil Barker went up to the house on the hill to see Red and Georgia. We were the only ones there. . . all evening.

"Red and Georgia weren't in the living room when we arrived. They came down a few minutes later, with bloodshot eyes and circles under them. Georgia had been drinking, but Red was sober.

"Then Georgia went out, and came in a few minutes later carrying a beautiful plant. 'Guess who sent this?' she said to Red. But Red said sullenly he didn't feel like guessing. 'Then I'll tell you,' Georgia said, with almost a smile on her face. 'Gerald sent it. Wasn't that nice of Gerald?' Red blew his stack at the mention of Gerald, and they had a fight in front of the five of us that you wouldn't believe. This was the night of the kid's funeral. That's the kind of people they were. We went home early."

Richard's death had a sobering effect on Red Skelton. *Literally.* One of the first things Red did after little Richard had been laid to rest in the family mausoleum was to make a promise to himself that he'd never again touch a drop of hard liquor.

The agonizing months that he and Georgia had spent watching their only son's life fading irrevocably away had given him a certain homespun philosophy of life and death that helped him get through the days and nights without cracking up and the fortitude to stick to his resolve.

"Richard made me understand about pain and to feel for people who were suffering; also to enjoy the happiness around us," Red told a friend months later. "People say 'Merry Christmas' during one week of the year. I go around saying, 'Merry Day.' For years I've lived to learn—now I'm learning to live."

Part of that experience was learning to see life through eyes that weren't bloodshot.

According to Joe Ross, the well-known show business attorney who took over the management of Red's affairs in 1961, his client had a secondary motivation in going on the wagon. "His asthma was so bad by then that he'd break out into an asthma attack if he even thought about taking a drink," says Ross.

Whatever the reason, he did swear off the hard stuff.

He could still drink beer without bringing on an asthma attack. And at times he consumed enough of it to give him a weight problem, which he learned to handle himself by sitting out in the sun in a yellow rain slicker buttoned high around his neck, looking like a buddha while sweating off the excess poundage. But nobody ever saw him take a drink of hard liquor again, nor can anybody recall seeing him drunk or even slightly intoxicated in public.

Which is more than could be said of Georgia, who continued to be a "closet" alcoholic until the day of her suicide. In fact, by the early sixties, Georgia was also heavily into pills, according to a business acquaintance of Red's who spent a good deal of time with the Skeltons during their last years together.

Part of Georgia's problem was that she couldn't get her son's death out of her mind. Red at least had his work to take his thoughts off Richard during the day, but Georgia, with no occupation except being a wife and mother, was to have haunting memories of him for the rest of her life.

Of course, Red's attitude toward the dead boy didn't make it any easier for Georgia to forget the tragedy.

For some reason Red wouldn't allow anything in Richard's room to be changed or moved after the funeral. Red insisted that his clothes, books, souvenirs, a Bible given to him by the Pope, mailbags filled with thousands of letters sent to him during his fatal illness, and enough toys and sporting equipment to fill F.A.O. Schwarz—including a completely assembled set of electric trains—all remain exactly as they were on the day Richard died.

Red even erected a little shrine to the boy, containing his photograph and several of Richard's most cherished mementos, in a glass display case outside his bedroom.

According to Georgia, the shrine had a depressing effect on everybody who came to the house, herself included, and she was always trying to persuade Red to get rid of it. But Red found some kind of solace in being reminded of Richard, and insisted on keeping all of his things on display for the next five years. Frequently he would even sit down by himself in Richard's room and talk to the dead boy as if he were still there.

Strange? Well, not to Red. He said it made him feel very close to Richard, which in turn enabled him to maintain his equilibrium and carry on with his career during the months immediately ahead. "Everybody has tragedy and learns to live with it," explained Red in trying to rationalize how he could maintain his sense of humor and continue with his clowning career following the boy's death. "If the little guy were sitting here, I'd be telling the same jokes, living my life the same way. I believe we were all put on this earth for a purpose. His was to show me the meaning of life through death—and I was put here to make people laugh. That's good enough for me."

Such was Red's frame of mind when Bo Roos brought him an offer to play the Riviera Hotel in Las Vegas for $20,000 a week later in the summer of 1958.

Despite his philosophy of life and death, Red had qualms about making an appearance in a nightclub so soon after Richard's death. He was afraid the public might dislike him for it. But after all of his friends and managers convinced him that it would be therapeutic for him and Georgia to get out of town and see some new faces and a change of scenery, Red reversed himself and okayed the deal.

As it happened, the trip to Vegas was anything but therapeutic, although his show was a tremendous hit there.

How could it be anything else, after all that publicity attendant to his pilgrimage through Europe with a dying boy? "Good night and God Bless," delivered with a tear at the end of his act, had more meaning now than ever. And the fans applauded his courage as well as his comedy.

But life continued to plague him, even in the fun-filled town of Las Vegas.

A few days after the opening, Georgia had to be rushed from the Skeltons' eighth floor suite in the Riviera Hotel to a room across town in the Sunrise Hospital. There a spokesman for the hospital told reporters that she was suffering from "a nervous breakdown," a reasonable enough explanation considering what she'd been through in the past year and a half.

It was upsetting, but Red had been through many similar episodes before, so his ability to carry on with two shows a night for the remainder of the engagement was not seriously affected. But what nearly caused him to come unglued—and in the process, nearly commit murder to boot—was a brouhaha between him and Bo Roos that broke out in Red's suite shortly after Roos arrived in Vegas to see his client's show.

Roos had not attended the opening, but had come down to Vegas sometime during the second week, bringing with him a check made out to Red from the insurance company with whom the comic had a $25,000-policy on Richard's life.

But the check Roos handed Red was only in the amount of $8,000, and when Red wanted to know what had happened to the other $17,000, Roos confessed that it was gone. He said he had taken a loan out on the policy.

"For what?" Red demanded. "Don't we have an income of nearly $55,000 a week?"

Roos explained that the reason for the loan was that most of Red's money was tied up in investments and that he was short of cash to take care of his immediate expenses.

Red exploded, for this more or less confirmed rumors that he'd been hearing from some of Roos's other dissatisfied clients (namely, Humphrey Bogart, Fred MacMurray, and John Wayne) who'd already left, or were in the process of leaving, Bo Roos's management.

According to their complaints, Roos had a nifty trick of borrowing money on his clients' life insurance policies, and putting the money in short-term, high-interest paying investments such as commercial "paper." When the money came due, he'd return the principal to the client's policy and bank the interest earned in his own account. Usually the client never knew the difference.

But Richard's untimely death prevented Roos from repaying the loan before Skelton could find out about it.

"So you steal from children, too?" shouted Red. And with that, he temporarily lost control, grabbed Roos around the throat and started to strangle him and push him out the eighth-floor window.

If the struggle had gone on for just a few seconds longer, it would have been "Good night and God Bless" for Bo Roos, too. Despite years of dissipation and high living, Red was still a bull of a man; when aroused he could be tougher than Cauliflower McPugg. Fortunately, two people in Skelton's entourage heard the melee, broke into his suite, and pulled Red's strong hands off his manager's throat before he could push him the rest of the way out the window.

If it wasn't the literal end for Bo Roos, it was his swan song as Red's business manager.

Bo Roos's management certainly had been beneficial to Red's financial well-being in many ways during their association; nevertheless, Red had become increasingly disillusioned with the man as well as with some of his questionable business practices—even before learning about the shortage in Richard's life insurance policy.

Among other things, Red had learned that Roos had once been secretly on the payroll of a company with whom he was supposedly negotiating the best deal he could for his red-haired client, and that Roos cheated his clients even on small matters, such as buying a mink coat.

"For example," explains a prominent Beverly Hills furrier who had many dealings with Roos, "the client or his wife would come into my shop—or someone else's—and pick out the mink coat he wanted. Roos would then take care of paying for it. If the coat sold for five grand retail, Roos would tell his client it cost ten grand, and with the extra five he'd buy a coat for his wife. The client never knew the difference."

Although Red was to have two more business managers between Roos and the time he swore off them entirely, there is no doubt to whom he is referring in the following dissertation he made some years later on the general subject of business managers:

"I'm sure you've read about how I'm supposed to be distrustful and suspicious, because people have taken me to the cleaners," said Red. "Well, the truth is that they have, not because I'm suspicious but because I'm trusting, maybe too trusting. A few years ago after forty years in this business, I woke up one morning, and found I was broke. Not completely broke. I'll never be that, because I've got a God-given talent to entertain and make people laugh, and I guess I can always make a living. But the people I'd associated with, who were supposedly looking after my affairs, you just wouldn't believe it what they did to me.

"I'll tell you what business managers do—not all of them, but some of them in the Hollywood group. Whenever a business manager walks up to you and says, 'You've had a great year, a sensational year, but we can't pay the tax yet,' I'll tell you what they've done. I knew a guy who used to manage about nine stars and pay their income tax, and of course he had power of attorney. He would have 'em sign checks for the tax, which came to about two million dollars. Then he'd ask the government for an extension, maybe for six months, maybe for a year. He'd deposit the $2 million in various banks, collect the interest for himself, then eventually pay the government.

"In addition to this he takes 10 percent for management fees and 10 percent for accountancy fees. And he gets a cut on all the purchases. I knew this all along—that I was being taken. But if you're an entertainer, you entertain; you don't have too much time to check the books. When eventually you do, the guy who's checking for you, he gets bought off. He comes to you and says, 'A lot of this stuff doesn't add up, but let's not fire your man yet, let's wait a while.' So you wait until he takes his cut.

"I think I've lost close to $10 million by not managing my own affairs.

"And what these business managers did to my personal life! They make trouble. They confuse you. They divide your family. Like they used to come to me and say, 'You've got to stop spending so much money.' And I'd say, 'Who's spending?—not me.' They'd say, 'Of course, not you. It's Georgia, she's spending dough like it was water.' Then they'd go to Georgia and say, 'Listen, you've got to keep dressed in the highest style. After all, you're Mrs. Red Skelton. You're out in the public eye.' And then they'd spread divorce stories. They believe in divide and conquer."

While it's highly unlikely that anyone—even a business manager—could exacerbate the situation between Red and Georgia any more than they were able to do for themselves, Red nevertheless had ample cause to want to be rid of Bo Roos.

However, it wasn't until 1959, when a severe stroke forced Bo Roos to retire, that Red was completely able to sever his business ties with the Beverly Management Company. Shortly after that Roos succumbed. At about the same time Red also dissolved his long partnership with Freeman Keyes.

Just what caused this relationship to go sour Keyes refuses to disclose, even though he is alive, and well, and living in Chicago, and incidentally, running the same small ad agency, the Russell M. Seeds Company. (Skelton himself, in keeping with his practice of rarely naming names even of people who've done him terrible wrong, refuses to discuss him, either. In fact, in the dozens of articles that have been written about Skelton—and with his cooperation—over the past thirty years, there is not even a hint that a man by the name of Freeman Keyes, who, after all, did have a considerable influence on his career, ever existed.)

Refusing to acknowledge the existence of someone was Red's way of mentally "burying" people to whom he once was close but no longer wished to have a relationship. It was the same treatment he gave Edna, and he was to carry this form of mental burial to even greater and more bizarre extremes later in his life.

Thanks to Georgia, Red wasn't without a business manager for long. During one of their stays in Las Vegas, Georgia introduced Red to Chuck Luftig, a bail bondsman with whom she had become friendly while hanging around the casino of the Riviera Hotel one night while waiting for Red to finish his act.

Luftig, according to those who remember him, was about ten years younger than Red, tall, good-looking, and a flashy dresser.

He was also single, and had the kind of personality that appealed to unhappy women who were looking for a little action.

Little else was known about him except that apparently he was successful in the bail bonding business, that he had sold out, and was currently looking around for a new enterprise in which to become involved on the West Coast. But he had a great gift of financial gab, as well as for the kind of charming cocktail bar small talk that makes a lonely woman feel important. Georgia was attracted to him from the start, and not just because he knew the difference between a debenture and a municipal bond.

As a result, Luftig had no difficulty in winning Georgia's confidence and persuading her that he was just the man to take over her and Red's business affairs. Georgia, because she liked having Luftig around, immediately began a campaign to persuade Red to hire the handsome bail bondsman as their business manager.

It didn't take much persuading. First of all, Red was always, despite his other differences with Georgia, surprisingly receptive to any suggestions she made in the way of business ventures. And second, he liked Luftig as an individual (he didn't learn of any romance between Luftig and Georgia until much later), and still being a babe in the woods when it came to business matters, could easily be swayed by anything the smooth-talking Luftig told him, especially if it was seconded by Georgia.

As a result, Chuck Luftig took over where Bo Roos left off. Georgia was so grateful that she persuaded Red to give Luftig a gift of a brand new Rolls Royce a few days after he went to work for them.

Shortly after that, Red became involved in a business deal that drove him to the brink of bankruptcy. This took talent, considering that Red's income at the time was close to $1 million a year and that he owned a considerable amount of valuable income property, along with other high-paying investments.

The deal that nearly wiped him out involved Red's purchase of the old Charlie Chaplin Film Studios on La Brea Avenue just south of Sunset Boulevard in Hollywood.

For some years prior to the purchase Red had entertained

thoughts of owning his own studio, just as Desi and Lucy owned Desilu Studios, and taping his show from there, away from the watchful eyes and prying eyes of CBS executives, whom he still didn't trust. He also had an urge to branch out and produce other things beside the Skelton show, and he wanted to do them in color. Most TV programs, including his own, were still being done in black and white in those days.

Red's ideas more or less coincided with Chuck Luftig's own personal ambition. He, too, wanted to become an entrepreneur, and run a film studio. So when it came to Luftig's attention that the Chaplin Studios could be bought for something in the general price range of $1.5 million, he, with an assist from Georgia, suggested to Red that he buy it.

Charlie Chaplin, of course, no longer owned the studio, and hadn't since he had moved to Switzerland prior to World War II. The studio was owned by a bank which was leasing it (for a sum just large enough to pay the taxes) to a small film company called American International Pictures, headed by Sam Arkoff. However, AIP was using the lot mainly for office space, because it wasn't much good for anything else. Only one sound stage was usable, provided some foolhardy person wanted to spend the money to renovate it completely. The rest of the sound stages and dressing rooms were in a state of total disrepair. Any slightly realistic person would have easily been able to see that the ten acres on which the studio stood would have been more valuable empty. This was confirmed by several CBS executives whom Red brought in to look the place over and give him an opinion as to the practicability of using the studio as a place to tape his own TV shows. Everybody, including CBS Vice-President Howard Meighan, thought Red was insane to want to buy the studio. So as not to seem arbitrary about it, however, and possibly insult CBS's Number One comic, Meighan hired a company that specialized in efficiency expertise to look over the Chaplin Studio and make a survey on the feasibility of turning it into a paying operation.

"After their findings were in," recalls Seymour Berns, "Meighan brought the results to Red and told him, 'Red, there's no way in the world that this God damn studio idea of yours is going to work.' But Red didn't believe him, or the survey. He said to me, 'CBS is just afraid of the competition from me.' And he went ahead and bought the studio."

Whatever drawbacks the Chaplin Studio had, they could not outweigh what to Red, at least, was its major asset: that it had once belonged to the Master pantomimist of all time, Red's boyhood idol, Charlie Chaplin. As far as Red was concerned, the aura of Chaplin still hung over every decrepit, cobweb-filled sound stage and dressing room. And once Red became its owner, he would be able to sit in the very same office He used, and at the very same desk He ruled from, and control his own destiny much in the way He did. To Red that was reason enough to buy the studio.

So ignoring the best professional advice available, Red formed a company with Chuck Luftig called Reddio–Video Enterprises and purchased the Chaplin Studios for $1.5 million—all cash—most of which he raised by divesting himself of the better part of his real estate holdings in Los Angeles, including his share of the Wilshire Palms apartments. The only piece of property he hung onto was his estate in Bel Air.

"Red was pretty short of cash after he bought the studio," recalls an associate. "Not just because of the initial outlay, but because of the hundreds of thousands of dollars he had to pour into the place just to keep it going. Neither he nor Luftig, who was supposed to manage the operation but who in reality was just a figurehead, knew the first thing about how to run a studio."

One of Red's largest expenditures after acquiring ownership was to renovate completely the only usable sound stage on the lot. This included a new roof, new catwalks, a new electrical system to conform to the fire laws, and finally the installation of an air-conditioning unit that alone cost close to $100,000.

Red figured that he'd soon get his money back from his investment, plus considerable profit, by taping his own show from the renovated sound stage and charging CBS rent for its use. Moreover, when it wasn't being used for the Skelton show, he planned to rent the space to outsiders.

And in theory it made sense—but only to Red and Luftig. CBS saw no reason at all to move the *Red Skelton Show* away from the finely equipped Studio 33 in Television City on Fairfax and Beverly Boulevard to some jerry-built sound stage on the antiquated Chaplin lot, just so Skelton could amortize his ill-considered purchase. Not only would it be an unnecessary expense to CBS, but it would be terribly inconvenient to move the show's home base away from Television City where its production staff had everything at their fingertips, from the finest technicians to the latest in equipment, plus a marvelously inventive prop department (a necessity on the Skelton show), a well-staffed publicity department, a commissary, stenographic services, and easy access to some of the best delicatessens on the West Coast.

Red was not interested in any of CBS's rationale. He wanted to tape from his own studio, and if they would not allow him to, he said, he would walk off the show.

In the end, CBS agreed to a compromise: they would allow Red to tape six shows out of thirty-nine a year from his own studios. Red accepted this face-saver, and returned to work until mid-December, when he was hospitalized again. This time his old hernia was giving him trouble again, so he had to be readmitted to Cedars of Lebanon for corrective surgery, forcing the cancellation of his TV show featuring Diana Dors, the English sexpot, in the guest spot. Wan but combative, Red was back in harness two weeks later, complaining to Seymour Berns that he was so fed up with doctors and medical bills that "Georgia and I have made a pact. If we get sick again, no more doctors. Fuck 'em, we'll die."

The way things were going at the Chaplin Studio, that could have been wishful thinking. Even though CBS was allowing him to do six shows a year from there, it was hardly enough to get Red off the financial hook. He might have been able to live with the situation, however, if his initial plan of renting his studio facilities to outside production companies had been successful. It wasn't, and for a very simple reason.

There were much more up-to-date facilities for independent production around Hollywood than what Red had to offer at the Chaplin Studio. Consequently, there was no great demand for stage space, no matter how attractive he made the rental fees. Even Sam Arkoff, President of AIP, who'd been renting the studio prior to Red's ownership, had said upon announcement of the sale, "I'm relieved to have a reason to get off this lot."

"In addition," recalls Seymour Berns, "Red had this thing about color TV. He thought that was the medium of the future. And in retrospect, he was right. The trouble was, color was extremely expensive in those days—not like it is now—and most indie production companies couldn't afford it. We weren't even shooting in color. But that didn't make any difference to Red. If some guy wanted to lease space from Red and he wasn't planning to shoot in color, Red would turn the business down."

Besides spurning potential customers, Red poured a small fortune into the designing and building of a fleet of vans—approximately the size of large Greyhound buses—which he planned to use for video-taping in color away from the studio. These vans, personally designed by Red, contained the latest in color videotape and sound equipment, at a cost of about $150,000 a vehicle. In today's dollars, the cost would be over a millon per vehicle.

It was Red's scheme to dispatch the vans to various sections of Los Angeles, and possibly even the rest of the world, for the purpose of shooting color commercials in their actual locale. This would add to their realism as well as eliminate the expense of building sets. He also believed that his studio could turn a nifty profit by going out into the field and shooting, unsolicited, background material, storing it in a videotape library, and renting the footage to whatever production company had a need for it.

At the start of his venture into production, Red, with his usual childlike enthusiasm, explained his plans to a reporter:

"I've got a busy year ahead of me. I've got a new business manager and partner, you know. Chuck Luftig. We're putting together three mobile color tape units, ten trucks to each unit. We're going to do some commercials in Europe, and may cover the Olympics in Rome for CBS."

It was typical of Red to honestly believe that CBS would assign his company to covering something as important as the Olympic Games, when he was aware that they didn't even have enough confidence in him to encourage the taping of his own show from a place as close to them as La Brea Avenue.

Naturally nothing came of his Quixotic dream. On most days Red's costly six-wheeled behemoths wandered no farther away from the Chaplin Studio than the curb on La Brea Avenue outside the studio gates, where they were forced to park, because there wasn't room for them on the studio lot. To the rubbernecks in the sightseeing buses that passed by, the Skelton Studio looked more like the Greyhound bus depot.

By the 1961–62 television season the only production company using the studio at all was Red Skelton—for taping his own show. Fortunately for Red, CBS had backed down and was allowing Red to tape all his shows from the Chaplin lot by this time, despite the inconvenience and the expense.

Thanks to high ratings, Red was in a position by the beginning of the sixties to dictate to CBS, rather than the other way around. Not only were his ratings on or near the top most of the time, but the Skelton show had received a nomination for "Best Comedy Series" at the 1958–59 Emmy Awards, and in 1961 its writing staff won the Emmy for "Best Comedy Writing" in television.

"A funny thing happened before that year's awards," recalls Sherwood Schwartz, who was still head writer for Skelton in 1961. "When the nominations were first announced, the Academy didn't nominate Red, even though his name was on the crawl as one of the writers every week. And they were right not to nominate him. After all, he really wasn't a writer. He just insisted that his name be on the crawl every week, so who of us was going to stand up to the star and say it shouldn't be? But now that the Nominating Committee had seen through that ruse and didn't nominate him, he phoned up the Academy and threatened to sue them if his name wasn't included among the nominees. So naturally they ended up having to nominate Red, and when we won the Award for "Best Comedy Writing," Red got an Emmy, too, which he still boasts about whenever he's being interviewed in order to validate what a great writer he is."

In addition to his high ratings, CBS had still another reason for cow-towing to Red. His contract would run out in 1962, and CBS was anxious to re-sign him for another three years.

Meanwhile, Red was steadily going broke trying to make the Chaplin Studio a paying proposition.

Nothing Red tried could change his luck, including getting rid of Chuck Luftig as his studio manager and replacing him with other more knowledgeable men in the studio management field. Ed Hilly took over the helm for a year; after him came Phil Feldman; and finally Bob Cinetor, who now has an important job at Universal.

But no amount of skillful handling could get Skelton's sick white elephant off its knees to perform profitably. Moreover, no one even wanted to buy it from Red, except at an enormous loss to him, which he, in his stubbornness, wouldn't consider. Then, just when bankruptcy appeared certain for one of Hollywood's biggest money-makers, a strange series of events transpired, beginning with a fight with the management of the Riviera Hotel in Las Vegas that led Red, in a convoluted way, to a man who was to extricate him from his financial woes forever.

The dispute at the Riviera occurred when the manager of the hotel upbraided Red, after the early dinner show, for staying on the stage too long.

"But the audience was having a good time," explained Red. "I didn't want to stop." Red was always very generous about giving audiences a little extra.

"They're not here to enjoy themselves," snarled the hotel operator, glowering at Red. "They're here to lose their money. The more time they spend watching shows, the less time they have for gambling. Now I'm telling you, Red, you gotta get off sooner, if you know what's good for you."

Red, who was responsible for breaking attendance records at the Riviera every time he came to town, was livid at being treated so unappreciatively. He took his revenge at the midnight show by staying on the stage only ten minutes, and then retiring to his suite. Disappointed, the audience demanded their money back, and the hotel manager demanded that Red return to the stage and finish the show. But Red screamed at him to "get lost" through the hotel room door, and concluded by shouting that he'd never play the Riviera again.

By the following morning, all of the Las Vegas insiders had heard of the incident, including Jack Entratter, president of the Sands Hotel, and an ardent admirer of Red Skelton's comedy.

Red was just sitting down to breakfast in his hotel suite when Entratter and his assistant, Al Freeman, called on him and presented him with a proposition to play the Sands for $25,000 a week, for as many weeks a year as he cared to play the free-swinging desert resort. What's more, they promised, there would be no limitations on the amount of time Red stayed on the stage.

Over strenuous objections from the Riviera's management, which threatened to sue but never did, Red bolted and signed an exclusive long-term contract with the Sands Hotel in 1960 for $25,000 a week.

One of the many fringe benefits Red insisted on as part of his deal was that the hotel furnish his suite with his very own slot machine, in which he could drop quarters to his heart's content. At the end of Red's engagement, all the money that had been stolen by the one-armed bandit would be returned to him.

A close friendship developed between Red and Jack Entratter that resulted, after a year and a half, with the latter supplanting Chuck Luftig as Red's business brains.

Although it was the main consideration, Red didn't fire Luftig for purely business reasons.

One day in 1961, according to a friend, Red came home from CBS unusually early because he was ill, and saw Luftig and Georgia out by the swimming pool, acting chummier than a business relationship called for.

Red didn't voice his disapproval at the time. He waited until he was in Washington, D.C. a few weeks later on a personal appearance tour, and sent Chuck Luftig a wire telling him he was off the payroll. Red was too softhearted a guy to fire him in person.

Luftig's departure was no hardship on Georgia. She liked Jack Entratter, too. In fact, it was she who now talked Red into letting Entratter become his business manager. Because of his duties running the Sands, which required his presence in Las Vegas most of the year, Entratter couldn't devote full time to all areas of business management, so he agreed to be merely a "consultant" to Red on show business deals, for 5 percent of Red's income, and turned the bulk of the work over to Joe Ross, of Pacht and Ross, one of Hollywood's top show business law firms.

A suave, dignified man of about fifty at the time, with enough temperamental clients, including Jerry Lewis, to give him more headaches than any one human needed, Ross at first was reluctant to take on another show business kook. But because Jack Entratter was also a client, not to mention his closest friend, Ross agreed to do him a favor and service Red, too, for 5 percent of his income. Between the two, Red wound up paying them 10 percent, or what an agent normally gets.

Ross's services would have been worth it at three times the price.

"When I joined Red in 1961, I'd never seen such a foul-up in my life," recalls Ross, a modest man, but one who nevertheless tells it like it is. "He had bought the Chaplin Studio, which I called the Black Hole of Calcutta because of the way he was pouring money into it. His little whim about sitting at Chaplin's desk was costing him about $10,000 a week. He couldn't get any-body else to use the place, not even for filming commercials. It was a rat's nest, and he was spending all his time worrying about repairs, paying bills, and checking on things like light bulbs. He trusted nobody then—and with good reason. He had been taken, but royally. People had bought themselves ranches with his money."

According to Ross, the first thing he did after taking over Red's affairs was to try to get rid of the Chaplin Studio. Under other circumstances, the probability of finding a buyer would have been nil, but since Red's contract with the network was about to run out, Ross came up with the brilliant idea of having CBS take it off his client's hands as part of the deal to get him to re-sign.

Jim Aubrey, CBS's new president, wasn't exactly overjoyed at the prospect of getting stuck with the Chaplin Studio in order to have Red clowning on his network every Tuesday night. But what choice did he have? He couldn't afford to lose Red, so he had to think of a way of living with Ross's deal.

"One day," recalls Seymour Berns, "Aubrey called Cecil

Barker and me into his office and said, 'Listen, we're talking about signing Red again—his contract's running out—and we have to take that God damn studio as part of the deal. And the only way we'll get out financially is to make the show an hour, and keep it on the air for a few years. Do you guys think you can do an hour show with him?' "

A successful hour show generally generates more revenue than two half-hour shows, because its production costs are not twice as much as a thirty-minute show, while at the same time twice as many commercials can be squeezed in, and at a higher billing rate.

"Sure, we can do an hour show," Berns and Barker assured Aubrey. In fact, they added, they thought Skelton might even be better in the longer format because he wouldn't be under the pressure of having to watch the clock, and would be able to relax and improvise more.

Hearing that, Aubrey went ahead and made a new deal with Skelton, which included the purchase of the Chaplin Studio.*

"I got them to buy the studio for $5.5 million," reveals Ross. "As far as Red was concerned, he was in the clear financially for the first time in years."

With Red's fiscal worries eliminated, Ross set about trying to remove some of his new client's other problems. Says Ross, "I told Red he *had* to get out of the Bel Air house, where he and Georgia sat brooding over Richard all the time. Why, they actually commemorated the day he died every year by not speaking for an entire twenty-four hours. My advice led to their buying the Palm Springs house in 1962. They wouldn't give up the Bel Air house altogether, but a few weeks after they moved out into the desert, a miracle occurred. Suddenly he and Georgia were spending a lot of time together because there was no place else for Red to go, and they were learning to do a lot of constructive, creative things together. It was wonderful to see two people come out of the twilight zone."

---

* Eventually CBS sold the Chaplin Studio to Herb Alpert of the Tijuana Brass, who refurbished it completely and turned it into a successful recording company, which it still is today.

21

In the previous November, a brush fire had swept through the Santa Monica Mountains for three days, destroying nearly $1 billion worth of luxury homes and property in Bel Air and Brentwood. Red and Georgia's house on Sarbonne Road was in the path of the holocaust and seemed destined for certain destruction—not only because there seemed no likelihood of the strong Santa Ana winds that were feeding the flames changing course, but also because there wasn't sufficient water pressure on the crest of the mountain where they lived to man the fire hoses.

When things looked bleakest, Red suddenly had the presence of mind to summon a crew of workmen from his studio (which he still owned) who arrived with a powerful water pump just as the huge flames were licking at the periphery of the brush-surrounded estate. With Red supervising, the studio crew was able to tap the 35,000 gallons of water in the swimming pool and hose down the roof and the combustible shrubbery, saving the house from destruction.

That scare, coupled with Red and Georgia's desire to get away from the gloomy surroundings of the Bel Air house, filled with so many tragic memories of Richard's death, prompted the Skeltons' decision to start looking for a home in Palm Springs in 1962.

Ironically, it was a wish to be nearer to Richard rather than to escape his memory, that caused Red and Georgia to become interested in the house they bought in the desert, and which Red still owns but does not live in today. His daughter Valentina occupies it.

The strange and eerie incident that led the Skeltons to their new house occurred in the spring following the Bel Air fire, while Red and Georgia were spending some time in the desert as the house guests of Jack Entratter. Like their attorney Joe Ross, Entratter was urging them to buy a house in Cathedral City, near his. Entratter had a home there, on one of the fairways of the fashionable Tamarisk Country Club, where Frank Sinatra, the Marx Brothers, Bob Hope, and a great many other show business luminaries hacked out their daily divots while presumably relaxing in the sunshine. Entratter spent most of their visit taking the Skeltons for long walks through the desert resort and along the Tamarisk fairways, pointing out houses that were up for sale. But nothing appealed to Red and Georgia until one day the three of them strolled out onto the sixteenth fairway and stood talking in front of a beautiful, one-story house that was built in a U-shape around a swimming pool.

As Red and Georgia looked toward the place, they both simultaneously thought they saw the ghost of Richard playing and laughing on the grass in front of the house.

Convinced that the wraith of their deceased son was some kind of a divine signal from the Great Real Estate Salesman in the Sky, Red said he had to have that house. He said he felt that

Richard was trying to tell his parents that he would always be there, though "invisible to most," and that he wanted them close by.

Entratter told Red to forget about that particular house; he knew the owner, a widow named Mrs. Edgar Richards, and she was very happy there, and didn't wish to sell.

"How much do you think she'll take?" persisted Red.

"Well, it probably cost $50,000 to build, and lots around here originally went for $5,000 apiece."

Red mulled over the figures for a moment, then climbed into his Rolls Royce with Georgia, and drove to a Palm Springs branch of the bank he did business with in Los Angeles. There he withdrew $150,000 in cash and stuffed it into an attaché case he always carried with him. Following that, he and Little Red drove back to Thompson Road, which was in the Tamarisk development, and rang the widow's doorbell.

Mrs. Hughes came to the door, and after learning what the Skeltons had on their minds, informed them that she wasn't interested in selling. However, as a favor to Red, whom she recognized, she would be honored, she said, to allow them to look through her house and even have a cup of coffee with her.

Red took a cursory tour of the premises. The house, decorated in pastel desert shades, with sliding glass picture windows opening out into the pool area and golf course, had every luxury needed to make life in the desert comfortable, including air-conditioning and separate "his" and "hers" wings.

Following his and Georgia's inspection tour, Red returned to the large, cheerful, sunshine-filled living room, opened up his attaché case, and spread $150,000 in crisp, new bills of rather large denominations on the coffee table in front of Mrs. Hughes. As the elderly widow stared bug-eyed at such a display, Red told her she could have the entire bundle right then, with no quibbling, if she would just change her mind about selling.

Mrs. Hughes couldn't resist and she and Red entered into a formal sales agreement immediately. Well, almost immediately. First she insisted that Red drive her to her own bank while an official there verified that the $150,000 was real.

Once he and Georgia took possession of the house on

Thompson Road, Red, with his customary childlike enthusiasm for new projects, started making spectacular improvements. He began by buying the vacant lots on each side of the house. Then, over a span of the next couple of years, he added two more bathrooms, enlarged the living room, and built on another round bedroom (there was already a round bedroom in the opposite wing, which Georgia had commandeered for her own).

During several trips to Japan in the late fifties and early sixties, Red and Georgia had fallen in love with the Japanese people, their culture, and their mysticism. As a result, after buying the Thompson Road house, Red built a Japanese garden on one of the extra lots he acquired. This included a Japanese tea house, where he liked to hole up and create, meditate, or sleep. However, no real Japanese would consider it a very authentic tea house, for it contained a steam room, a library filled with the first editions and leatherbound copies of Red's short stories, a piano, a bed, recording equipment, a number of TV sets, and the first Sony video playback machine. "Red's tea house looked more like the playhouse of a crazy inventor—only with a Japanese motif," recalls a friend who visited him there often.

On the third lot Red designed a perfect replica of a formal Italian garden. This was filled with statuary and fountains Red had picked up in Florence on one of his many trips to Italy. According to experts, his collection of statuary would be a welcome addition to any museum specializing in Italian and Roman artifacts.

It was in this unusual setting that Red and Georgia at last found some well-deserved peace with each other, and contentment—at least for a few years.

Joe Ross was right about the salutary effects the new environment would have on his clients. Three months after they moved to Palm Springs, Red returned to their Bel Air house by himself, and cleared all the clothes and toys out of Richard's bedroom, and donated them to charity. "From that moment on, Red was a different guy on the show," recalls Willie Dahl. According to Dahl, who had known Red for twenty years, he had "never seen such a radical change for the better in any man."

* * *

However, Red didn't get rid of the Bel Air house for another six years, despite his and Georgia's eagerness to start a new life in Palm Springs. To Red, owning two houses was not a luxury, but a necessity. After all, he wasn't retiring; he still needed a place in which to reside in town at least two nights a week while he was preparing, rehearsing, and taping his new TV program.

Now that the show was going to sixty minutes in the fall of 1962, scripts could not be just slapped together. More thought was required in their preparation. Also, more dedication from Red if he hoped to attain the perfection for which he was always striving, but rarely achieving on the air.

With the hour format, with its new-old look of a Jackie Gleason extravaganza, it was more important than ever to Red to have a success. Not only was it important for his own vanity, but also to teach a lesson to those people who were so eager to kick him when he was down in 1952 and 1953. He needed to prove himself to those who still thought his show was no good and that he didn't deserve to be as high in the ratings as he was. One of CBS's highest executives, Hubbell Robinson, was among the group who wished Red would fail.

For many years, Red had been having a feud with Robinson when he was chief of programming. Robinson hated what he called Red's "cheap ad libs" that were not really ad libs at all, and the way he always broke up at his own jokes on the air. He felt it very unprofessional behavior for an experienced comedian, and from the time Red joined the network he was always after him to stop it. After he was replaced as president in charge of television by Jim Aubrey, Robinson defected to NBC, where he took over producing, and also emceeing, in Ed Sullivan fashion, a new extravaganza called *The Show of Shows,* which was opposite Skelton on Tuesday nights. Robinson was hopeful that his "touch of class" would quickly run Skelton's ratings down to the bottom of the list and eventually take Red off the air. But just the opposite happened. *Show of Shows* bombed, to Red's great delight. After failing on NBC, Robinson rejoined CBS, and in 1963, at a dinner for CBS's top executive, Dr. Frank Stanton, he actually ate crow publicly by admitting to Red, "You see, Red, 'if you can't lick 'em, join 'em.' "

It was a moment of great vindication for Red.

Another reason Red wanted to succeed in the hour format was that he stood to make millions from his new CBS deal, which Joe Ross had so expertly put together. Under its terms, Red was no longer just an employee of the network, but he was in partnership with CBS with his own newly-formed company, which, for some reason, he chose to name Van Bernard Productions. The Bernard seems to be derivative of his middle name, if "Bernard" is indeed his middle name, which most people doubt. "I'm sure he pulled that middle name, Bernard, out of thin air one day," said his late friend, Marty Rackin. This is seconded by Guy della Cioppa, a former CBS vice-president of radio, whom Red eventually selected to run Van Bernard Productions and act as his executive producer.

"When we formed our production company, Red said we should call it Van Bernard Productions," reports della Cioppa. "I have no idea where the 'Van' came from, and I'm positive Bernard isn't his middle name. But he always thinks of himself as two people. The offstage Skelton is Red. The fellow who performs onstage he always refers to in the third person as 'Victor Van Bernard.' "

According to the terms of the new contract, CBS was also required to subsidize Van Bernard Productions in the producing of any new projects created by the Skelton company.

CBS allotted the new hour-long Skelton show $212,000 a week for its production budget (exclusive of air time). Out of that sum, Van Bernard drew $50,000 per show to pay the salaries of Red and his production staff.

An important addition to Red's staff was Guy della Cioppa, whom he hired in May of 1962.

A dapper, dark-haired, moustachioed man of fifty, Guy della Cioppa was the ideal man for the job. Not only did he know every aspect of broadcasting, but his soft-spoken manner and even temper were the right ingredients for getting along, over the long haul, with someone as volatile as Red.

Guy della Cioppa spent the spring and summer of 1962 organizing Van Bernard Productions and helping Red prepare the format for the new hour show, along with Seymour Berns and

Cecil Barker, and, of course, the writers. Skelton kept the same writing staff—Dave O'Brien, Artie Phillips, Al Schwartz, Marty Ragaway, and Hugh Wedlock. But there was a change in head writers. Sherwood Schwartz had to be replaced by Ed Simmons (later producer of *The Carol Burnett Show*), because he was leaving to write and produce his own creation. Red considered this tantamount to treason, and was extremely angry that one of his best writers was leaving to better his own career. Sensing Red's ire even before he gave him his notice, Sherwood told his brother Al, "You'd better quit when I do, Al, because if you don't, Skelton's liable to fire you."

"Why should he fire me?" asked Al. "I didn't do anything."

"Just listen to me," pleaded Sherwood. "I know what I'm talking about. I know the guy."

Ignoring his brother's advice, Al stayed on—for about a week, at which point Seymour Berns called him into his office and said, "Sorry to tell you this, Al, but you're through. Red wants you off the show."

"What's the matter?" asked Al. "Isn't my work satisfactory?"

"That has nothing to do with it," said Berns, somewhat embarrassed. "Red just came to me and said, 'Seymour, get rid of that other fucking Schwartz.' And when I asked him why, Red said, 'Because I don't want anybody named Schwartz on my show any more.'"

Being a Skelton writer was not the most secure feeling in the world, despite the prestige it carried with it.

The financial remuneration, however, was always better than on most shows. No member of the Skelton writing staff ever made less than $2,500 a week, and some even received as high as $4,000. You can take a lot of abuse for that kind of money.

Red also gave good presents to his staff. At Christmastime his writers would receive Sony tape recorders, portable TV sets, and even solid gold pencils and yardsticks.

But the one thing they couldn't get from Red was appreciation for their contribution to the show's success.

"I once saw Red take out his wad, peel off a $1,000-bill, and give it to a stranger who claimed he had just had an operation and was broke," recalls an ex-Skelton writer. "He was always being taken by fakers like that. But the people he focused his main suspicion on were his writers. He usually had eight top men grinding out material for him at all times. He couldn't do his show without them, and yet he acted as if we were picking his pockets. He even tried to pretend to himself that we weren't there and that he didn't need any of us. He hardly ever talked to us, and he dealt with us through an intermediary—usually Seymour Berns or maybe Guy della Cioppa."

Artie Phillips, another top gag man who slaved for Skelton, recalls a very revealing example of just how little attention Skelton paid to his writers. After working for Red for five years, Phillips and his wife wound up at the same banquet table with his boss one night at an Emmy affair. When the couple sat down, Red looked at them with uncertainty mixed with suspicion, then turned to Seymour Berns and asked in a loud voice, "Who the hell is that guy?"

"Red truly believed he didn't need any of us," states Marty Ragaway. "He believed that what we gave him was merely a blueprint for him to take off from. And he really resented having anybody know that he needed us. I remember once I had to go to his dressing room at CBS to deliver some new pages to him for the show we were rehearsing. Now going there was a mistake to begin with. The writers usually tried to stay away from him— because it could only get you in trouble. Only this time it was worse because sitting with him was a newspaperwoman who was interviewing him for an article. Anyway, I burst in, and someone else who was there—probably Seymour—introduced me to her as one of Red's writers. She looked at me, and suddenly exclaimed, 'Oh, are you one of the fellows who makes up all those marvelous funny things that Mr. Skelton says and does?' I was scared shitless to answer that. It was pure death to say 'Yes' with Skelton sitting right there. I said to myself, 'Oh, God, what am I going to tell her?' Then it came to me in a flash and I quickly said, 'No, our function is to provide the canvas for Mr. Skelton to paint on.' Skelton looked at me, terribly pleased and said, 'You know, that's the first time I ever heard anyone come up with the function of what a writer really does.' "

After Red got his own company, and the show went to an hour in October of 1962, and subsequently was a tremendous success, Red's attitude toward his writers grew worse.

At script reading sessions and rehearsals there was never any way of predicting how Red would react to the new material, but his moods were mercurial enough to keep his staff quaking with apprehension for several days before.

While Richard Nixon was running for President against JFK, one week the Skelton writers wrote a beginning to the show that kidded Nixon. After Seymour Berns read it, he gathered the writers and told them to write a new beginning. Didn't they realize that Red was a Republican and a large contributor to the Nixon campaign? "He'll never do this anti-Nixon stuff you wrote."

So they went away to try to think of a new opening. While they were struggling to come up with something, Berns returned and said, "Okay, boys, you can forget the new beginning. Red read the first one you wrote, and he thinks it's very funny. He wants to do it just as it is."

"What about the Nixon stuff?" asked one of the writers.

Berns shrugged. "Red said, 'Screw Nixon.' As long as the stuff's funny, he'll do it."

Nobody could figure Red's moods.

"We had a list of things a mile long Red didn't want to do," says Berns. "This list of 'no-nos' became a joke. We kept it on the bulletin board on the writers' wall. It was terribly irrational. He'd say, for example, 'I don't want to do any more Milton Berle jokes. Berle's a Russian spy.' Something insane like that that didn't make sense. I'm just using Berle as an example. It could just as well have been Hope or Groucho or even the head of General Motors. Anyway, suddenly Berle's name would go up on the list on the bulletin board. We had a list of 'don'ts'—you can't believe how long it was.

"Anyway, one day I'm sitting up in the office, just before dress rehearsal, which we did in front of an audience, when somebody calls me up from the studio and says, 'You'd better get down here right away. Red's going home to Palm Springs.' 'What do you mean—Red's going home?' 'Red's going home.' 'Well, what happened?' 'I don't know. He's just going home.'

"So I ran downstairs and out to the CBS parking lot, to head him off, and there he was, sitting in his Rolls Royce, about to drive off. So I stepped in front of his car. . . . I figured if I was going to go, I might as well go with 'R.R.' on my chest . . . and he stopped the car. Then I walked around to the driver's side and said, 'What's the matter?' He wouldn't answer so I repeated it. Finally, after about five minutes of him sitting silently behind the wheel, he said, 'You know I told the writers I didn't want to do any Milton Berle jokes.' So I said, 'Well, cut the joke.' And he said, 'Okay,' and went back to work.

"But if I hadn't run out there, the crazy guy would have driven all the way back to Palm Springs and left us with a studio filled with people.

"It was always that way with his list of 'don'ts.' Instead of stopping the reading right then when he heard it and simply saying he didn't want to do it, like any rational human being, he'd want to throw the whole script out. And maybe the writers, too."

According to Marty Ragaway, it took more than writing talent to be able to last with Skelton. "You had to be constantly outwitting him. For instance, he had a lot of standard, sure-fire bits that he'd developed over the years that we liked to have him use in a sketch occasionally. Catching his finger in a refrigerator door, for example, or getting hit in the head by a door that opens just as he goes to reach for the door knob himself. But if we needed to use one, we didn't dare write it into the script. Because he'd say, 'How do you like those bastards? I'm paying them a fortune every week and they're giving me back my own material.'

"So we'd write up to the spot where we'd like him to, say, get his finger caught in the refrigerator door. We'd just write the sketch without that happening. Then at rehearsal, he'd ask, 'How come we don't have something funny here?' And then he'd suddenly say to the director, 'Hey, I know what I'll do. How about getting my finger caught in the refrigerator door?' And he'd put it in himself, and then it would be okay to do it. But it was a constant battle between us and him."

In the middle sixties, Red had Mickey Rooney as a guest on his show, at the insistence of the CBS brass. The reason for their insistence was that CBS had made a pilot with Rooney that didn't sell, so as an excuse to amortize it they wanted to use part of it as a filmed insert on the Skelton show, with Mickey Rooney guesting in person. The pilot had been written by John Fenton Murray, former partner of Benedict Freedman, who had written the novel *Lootville* that Red felt was a *roman à clef* about him.

Because he was the author of the Rooney pilot, Murray's name went on the script along with the regular Skelton writers. Red didn't notice this until he came to rehearsal and looked at the script for the first time. For reasons unknown to anyone else, Red hit the ceiling when he saw Johnny Murray's name on the script. "I'm going home," he shouted. "I will not do a show that John Fenton Murray had anything to do with. I hate the bastard."

Cecil Barker, who was producing the show, cajoled Red into staying around through the dress rehearsal by reminding him that people had come all the way in from as far away as West Covina to see his show. Certainly he didn't want to disappoint all those loyal fans? So he stayed, but walked through the rehearsal, then went home angry and barely talking to anybody.

When Red arrived to do the show the following day, he was happy as a lark, which nobody could understand. To keep him happy, Barker and Berns secretly went around reminding everybody not to mention a thing about the day before, thinking Red had forgotten about it. Suddenly a cameraman who hadn't been tipped off, saw Skelton and said, "Gee, Red, you sure were in a lousy mood yesterday."

Everybody's hearts went into their mouths. But instead of the explosion they expected, Skelton smiled and said, "That reminds me. When I got home last night, Georgia reminded me that it wasn't John Fenton Murray I hate—it's Ben Freedman."

Most writers are an independent lot, however, and will usually take only so much from their crazy comic employers before deciding to strike back. Red's writers were no exceptions.

Red once made an appearance on *The Tonight Show* when Jack Paar was still its host. During the interview, Paar asked him where he got the material that allowed him to be so funny year after year. "All my jokes are put in my head by the voice of God," replied Red without batting an eye.

Red's writers, already bristling because Red would often give a prop man special mention to his audiences while never saying anything complimentary about the men who prepared his scripts, were furious. After gathering their courage, they asked him how he could have given God all the credit. Red, however, was not about to make a retraction. "You're just sore because I gave God top billing," he told them. This was one time when Red's writing staff would not be denied revenge.

On the following Friday, when the script was due, the writing staff handed Red fifty blank pages clipped together like a script. Attached to the pages was a brief note:

Dear Red:
 Please have God fill in the empty pages. Thanks.
        Your Writers

22

Whether it was the hand of God, or Red's talented writing crew, or a combination of both, plus the comedy genius of the show's star that was responsible, there is no arguing with the fact that the *Red Skelton Show,* in its hour format, at its new time (8:30 to 9:30 P.M. Tuesday nights) was an unqualified and spectacular hit from the moment it was sent out over the ether on the night of September 25. All the reviews were enthusiastically pro-Skelton, with everyone agreeing that the new hour-long format was just what Red needed in order to take full advantage of his kind of visual comedy. "From opening to closing gag, Red Skelton's new one-hour show was a hilarious treat," wrote *The Hollywood Reporter* on Thursday, September 27, 1962.

Although Red had two strong guest stars—Harpo Marx and Mahalia Jackson—on the opening show, it was Red who dominated the hour.

That the critics were not out of touch with the masses was verified by the results of the first national Nielsen ratings of the season, as reported in a story in a December issue of *Daily Variety:*

> "The Beverly Hillbillies" is still riding the crest of the Nielsen national report for the two weeks ending Nov. 25, with a comfortable margin at 33.7, accounting for 16,783 homes, or roughly 35 million watchers. Red Skelton's hour show bounded into second place, with 31.4, followed by "Candid Camera" at 30.1.

At the end of the season, during which Red was in the first five of the Nielsen reports most of the time, the Skelton show was nominated by the TV Academy for "Outstanding Achievement in the Field of Variety." Red was nosed out in the final balloting by *The Andy Williams Show.* Nevertheless, Red was having an outstanding season in front of the video cameras, which was a source of great personal satisfaction to a performer who was counted out by most people in the entertainment world in 1953.

Since those bleak days he had traveled a long and bumpy road. To his credit, he had not given up, and had overcome more personal problems than most people have to face in a lifetime or maybe two. He also was more dedicated to his art, and worked harder than most, which possibly was the real secret behind his climb to the top again.

Although Red enjoyed his existence after he and Georgia moved their home base to Palm Springs, the schedule he was forced to maintain in order to put a live TV show on the air thirty-five weeks a year did not permit him to lead the leisurely life of a retired country gentleman that a man of his wealth and age deserved. In television you could not—even if you were one of the greats—rest on last week's ratings or last season's Emmy awards and nominations if you expected to remain at the head of the pack.

Moreover, in Red's case, he did not wish to rest—and certainly not retire. "That's what he lived for every week—forty-five minutes of love from a live audience," believed Cecil Barker. "He's happy as a recluse in Palm Springs, but without coming in for his ration of love every Tuesday, I think he would die. This is his plasma. The core of all his problems is that he never knows when he'll come in some week and suddenly there'll be no more love, no more plasma."

Red's weekly battle for more love, more plasma, usually began on Tuesday night, immediately after he finished delivering his "God Bless" benediction to the studio audience and retired to his dressing room, which was cluttered with cameras, tape recorders, Japanese artifacts, TV awards, photos of Georgia and Valentina, and photos of himself with his arms around various celebrities. There, while he was cleaning off the makeup, toweling off the perspiration that flowed so profusely from his entire body during the taping session, and dressing for the drive back to Palm Springs, Red would discuss next week's show plus the one he had just completed with his producers and director.

"How'd you think it went?" Red would ask his producer, Guy della Cioppa.

"Fine, Red. Just great."

"I thought it could have been better," he would say.

"Red had to be constantly reassured that he'd done a good show," recalls Don Ferris, his accompanist and arranger since his first days in radio. "He'd get four standing ovations at Vegas, and then he'd come into his dressing room and say, 'Was the show all right?' "

Following a short discussion about what could have been done better, Red would be handed a copy of next Tuesday's script which usually ran about sixty pages. This would contain the two main sketches and his famed "Silent Spot," but not his opening monologue. Red's monologue, which would have a topical flavor, was never written until the last possible minute—usually right before the first dress rehearsal on Monday—in order to take advantage of the latest news breaks that might lend themselves to topical jokes in the monologue. Why the monologue had to be saved until the last minute when the shows were taped three weeks in advance of their air dates, however, is something no one can actually explain. It's just something Red insisted on, so that's how it was done.

With script in hand, and polo coat draped David-Belasco–style over his shoulders, Red would exchange words of farewell and final bits of advice for next week's show, with his production staff, then stride out to his gray Rolls in the CBS parking lot and drive the 130 miles back to Cathedral City, usually by himself. Georgia never came up to town to watch Red perform, except on rare occasions.

Arriving home, Red would watch the show he taped three weeks ago, and which would be on the air that night. He had videotape recorders at home in Palm Springs, and Georgia would have taped it from one of their TV sets as it came over the air from eight-thirty to nine-thirty. She also would have taped the competing shows on NBC and ABC, as Red liked to watch himself and the competition at the same time.

"Wednesday would be 'Unhappy Day' for Red," recalls della Cioppa. "He'd be exhausted, physically and emotionally, from doing his show. He'd never even glance at the script we gave him until as late as Saturday or Sunday nights, when he came back to town for our first rehearsal early Monday morning.

"We'd leave him alone all day Wednesday. If there were problems with the script, or new pages that had been rewritten, we'd send them to him by special messenger on Thursday. If there were problems relating to the new stuff—possibly the cancellation at the last minute of a guest star—we'd go to see him on Friday. That would be the day we'd transact any business that had to be done either in relation to the coming show or something involving Van Bernard Productions. On Sunday, he'd come back to Los Angeles, and the grind would start all over again on Monday morning. But on Wednesday through Saturday in Palm Springs, he'd do his writing, composing, photography, gardening—all the activities that had, for a time at least, replaced the destructive things in his life."

In his Palm Springs abode, Red spent most of his time in the Japanese side of the garden, either in the tea house ruminating and creating, or outside working at his favorite hobby—cultivating bonsai plants. Since becoming enamored of Japanese culture, Red would spend hours by himself, trimming the roots and branches of young local pines to stunt their growth, and twisting wire around their branches so that they would grow in unusual and grotesque Oriental shapes. Often Red would ride around the grounds in a little red tractor, which he used for hauling trees, dirt, and stones to the Japanese garden.

When Red wasn't absorbed in the art of bonsai, he would usually be inside the tea house, writing short stories—sometimes as many as four a day—jokes for next week's monologue, and daily "love letters" to Georgia. Except for a time when he was in the hospital in 1958, Red claimed not to have missed a day of writing Little Red a letter since they were married. It was such a ritual with him, in fact, that he started his day off at 5 A.M. by going straight to the tea house and dashing off an epistle assuring Georgia of his undying love for her. A letter to her might be as long as ten pages, and filled with samples of his Edgar Guestian poetry and perhaps some of his pencil drawings, too.

Usually his letters to Georgia would be signed with some comedy nom de plume, such as "Lord Baron Von Humpty Doc."

After dashing off his daily love letter to Georgia, Red would sit down at the piano and begin what was another of his daily rituals—composing music. Red, of course, had had no musical education, and according to della Cioppa, he couldn't "even beat simple two-four time." But he could pick out with one finger the notes of a simple melody that perhaps had come to him in a moment of leisure—usually in the middle of the night. This he would record on tape and turn over to Don Ferris to put into lead sheets. If any of these tunes sounded particularly promising, Ferris would make full arrangements of them, and Red would have them copyrighted.

By his own count, Red claims to have composed five tunes a day, seven days a week, for a total of 20,000 songs over the years. Many of these are marches, which are played by school bands around the country.

Red may have been exaggerating slightly about the total

number of compositions he's created, but it is a fact that some of his marches have been arranged for concert bands and published by legitimate publishing houses. For example, "The Kadiddle-hopper March," and "Red's White and Blue March" were both published by the Sam Fox Publishing Company, which also published many of John Phillip Sousa's classics. The same company also puts out, at $1.50 a copy, *The Red Skelton Piano Book,* simple compositions for the piano bearing such patriotic titles as: "American Through and Through," "Freedom and Glory," "Main Street March," and "Praise the Flag," among others.

All of these compositions show Red Skelton as the sole composer, but, in fact, he probably couldn't have written them without the assistance of Don Ferris, his talented arranger.

One of the reasons for Red's obsession with composing music was that he was desperately trying to change the image he felt most people had of him.

Even during the sixties, when his television show was on top and he was the recognized king of the comics, he felt that most people in the business thought of him as just a "baggy-pants burlesque comic" who, through some lucky fluke, made it to the top.

"Most people think I'm just a cheap vaudeville clown," he used to complain sorrowfully to his producer, Guy della Cioppa. "I get no respect from anybody."

In Red's mind, the only way he could get this "respect" was to make a name for himself in one of the arts associated with "class," such as writing short stories, painting, and composing music.

By the time Red had finished composing his morning quota of five songs, Georgia would be awake and waiting for him to bring her his morning love letter.

Along the way back to the main house, Red would be joined by his pets—a huge red macaw, which would sail down from a tree branch and follow him into the house, along with a black pigeon, a white cockatoo, and five poodles. The animals and birds and Red would then congregate on the foot of Georgia's bed while she read his morning's offering. (Georgia once told a newspaperman that she had more than "seventy bound-in-leather volumes of Red's love letters in my possession. But they are much more than love letters, really. They're a chronicle, a philosophical examination, if you will, of our lives together.")

After reading her husband's love letter, Georgia, in turn, would open up the Bible and read a prayer to Red and his menagerie. "It would be a different prayer every morning," said Red. "That's how we started our day together."

Following Georgia's prayer reading, she and Red and the animals would all have breakfast together out by the pool. Then Red would either go to work in his Japanese garden, or set up his easel and canvas and spend the rest of the day painting.

Of all of Red's avocational artistic outlets, the one at which he is probably the most gifted is painting.

Although he didn't become serious about his career as an artist until after he and Georgia moved to Palm Springs, Red says that he first started dabbling around with paints back in 1943, after he walked into the Acosta Gallery in Beverly Hills and saw an oil that he thought he'd like to own.

"How much is it?" Red asked the dealer.

Not recognizing Red—his face wasn't very well-known in those days—and assuming he was some kind of a rube, the dealer said, "Five thousand wouldn't take that."

"And I'm one of the five thousand," retorted Red, making a fast exit.

Figuring he could do just as well himself with a little practice, Red went out and bought a seventy-five-cent canvas, some paints and a couple of brushes, brought them home, and after getting a few pointers from Georgia, started painting pictures of his favorite subject—circus clowns.

Since that day, Red has turned out over 600 oil paintings, by his own count. Most of these are portraits of clowns which, considering that Red is a self-taught artist, have a very professional look to them. Through the intervening years, Red has also experimented with still-lifes, landscapes, Japanese brush drawings (a style he became interested in during a trip to the Orient), and watercolors of birds and animals, which he has used to illustrate a children's book, *Gertrude and Heathcliff* (published by Scribners in 1971), about his two seagull characters.

The watercolors in *Gertrude and Heathcliff* are quite imaginative and deftly done, and show Red to be extremely talented at illustrating a child's book where stark simplicity, plus a sense of humor, are requirements.

But of what he considers his major works—his oils—it is his clown portraits that are the most successful. Red has never been able to master perspective, and consequently his landscapes and still-lifes come off somewhat flat and amateurish looking. It isn't necessary to know perspective or to be familiar with anatomy in order to paint an acceptable clown.

Moreover, there appears to be a market for original oil paintings of clowns with Red Skelton's name affixed to them, or prints thereof, and has been ever since it came to the public's attention that he could paint.

In the beginning, Red took up painting mostly as a means of relaxation, with no thought in mind of commercializing on his talent, large or small. He just painted away—sometimes turning out as many as five clowns a day. Then he would have them expensively framed and hung somewhere in his house. Among his celebrity friends around Tamarisk Country Club, such as Harpo Marx and Frank Sinatra, Red soon established a reputation of being quite facile with a paintbrush and canvas. But the general public wasn't aware of Red's paintings until Jack Entratter put on an exhibition of them in conjunction with one of Red's appearances at the Sands in the mid-sixties. This attracted national and worldwide attention as a result of a stunt Red devised to promote his first art show.

Twenty-five of Red's most representative works in clown portraiture covered one entire wall of the corridor outside the entrance to the room in the Sands where Red was doing two shows nightly. However, one of the portraits, which hung about fifteen feet up the wall, was not a painting at all; it was actually Red Skelton's real face, under a straw hat and made up as a clown, peering sadly out at the public through an opening in the wall the size and shape of the picture frame surrounding it. The rest of Red was standing on a ladder behind the wall.

Even though the fledgling Rembrandt took his painting seriously, he was still a clown at heart and couldn't help going for laughs at his first exhibition.

Corny as the stunt was, it called worldwide attention to Red Skelton as an artist who specialized in clowns.

The event was covered by the media, and *Look* magazine photographed it—along with Red's puss looking out of its cut-out—and ran a double-page center spread, in color, in one of its issues, plus a story praising Red's talent as a painter.

Overnight Red acquired a reputation of being a fine artist. The art stores around the country that cater to tourists started featuring Red's oils, along with inexpensive reproductions of the same. Even "clown" placemats have been sold successfully to many Skelton admirers.

Although a $10,000-price tag on some of Red's original oils is not unheard of, the majority of Red's fans are not people who can afford to pay such fancy prices. They are satisfied to own a small reproduction, or a placemat, which they can acquire for just a few bucks.

And Red is satisfied to have made even that small mark on the art world.

During the early sixties, when Red was busy turning out music and clown portraits, the life he and Georgia led in Palm Springs was a peaceful one, almost verging on the mystical. Red had everything he needed or wanted to make him happy right there on the grounds of the Thompson Road house without having to leave. And from Tuesday until Sunday he rarely ever did venture beyond the confines of his fences. He and Georgia never attended parties or nightclubs any more. They rarely went out to dinner, for they had a very good cook at home, and they saw few people outside of their immediate family and Red's business associates, who occasionally drove up from town to have lunch with him and to discuss some matter pertaining to his career.

Georgia's parents, Mr. and Mrs. Mack Davis, who were getting on in years, moved to Palm Springs shortly after their daughter did, and into a small house Red was generous enough to buy them. Red also bought a house in the Palm Springs area for his mother, whom he still saw regularly until she died of cancer, in a Brentwood nursing home, in 1967.

Unlike most of the other celebrities who lived in the Tamarisk area, Red rarely hobnobbed with any of the big names, or participated in any of their charity affairs, such as the Bob Hope Desert Golf Classic. He was, however, a large contributor of money, and on several occasions donated some of his clown paintings to charity auctions, where they brought a good price.

Although he was a natural athlete, and well-coordinated enough to do his own stunts on his show, Red shunned all organized sports. He never played golf or tennis, and the swimming he did still consisted of dunking himself in the shallow end of the pool, and then drying off in the sun while he played and talked with his animals and birds and occasionally Georgia. In the late sixties, however, Red did make a concession to Georgia and he joined the Tamarisk Country Club—not for the golf but because the dining facilities there were the best in the area, and Georgia, who was becoming a little "stir-crazy" by then, thought it might be good for the two of them to get out of their cocoon and see some different faces once in a while.

After the Skeltons first moved to Palm Springs, Valentina lived with them and attended a school in the area. Red was extremely good to Valentina, and bought her everything she wanted, including her own horse, which she boarded at a local stable. Valentina was a good and enthusiastic equestrienne until the horse threw her one day, and she landed on her head on a cement road and suffered a concussion that nearly killed her. Having the resiliency of youth, plus the best doctors her father's money could buy, Valentina eventually recovered. But the scare cooled her enthusiasm for riding, and she soon gave up horses altogether and took up "boys" instead.

On Sunday afternoon a thoroughly rested Red Skelton would kiss Georgia good-bye, get in his Rolls, and head back to town for rehearsals, which would begin early Monday morning in Studio 33 in CBS's Television City.

"When they first moved to Palm Springs, Georgia would come up about twice a month to watch the show," recalls Guy della Cioppa. "But she soon cut that down to once a month, and after a while she never came around the studio."

During the two nights Red spent in town for rehearsals—Sunday and Monday—he would sleep in the Sarbonne house, which he still kept open, and at considerable expense, all year long, with a full-time housekeeper, a French woman named Clementine Trelease, who had been in his and Georgia's employ for a number of years now, running it and doing whatever cooking was necessary, and her husband Jim, who did the chauffeuring and butlering.

It would have been cheaper to sell the Sarbonne estate and check into a hotel for the two nights a week Red used the place. And he probably would have done just that were it not for the fact that by the mid-sixties Valentina had had her fill of her father's monastic existence in Palm Springs and had moved back into the Sarbonne house. Ostensibly this was so she could attend Santa Monica City College. But actually it was because she had developed into a beautiful, red-haired teenager by now, who was as restless as her father once had been. Consequently, her happiness required more of a social life than she could find among the sand dunes, gopher holes, and retirement condos of Cathedral City. She craved the company of people her own age.

As a result, Valentina resided in the Sarbonne house, which was just a ten-minute drive from the Sunset Strip discos, where she could find all the action she could handle. But on Sunday and Monday nights, when her father was in the city, she generally was available to eat dinner with him.

Although the chances were good that Red still hadn't read or even glanced at next week's script yet, even though he'd had it in his possession since the previous Tuesday, Red would be so eager to get on with rehearsals Monday morning that he would often arrive at Television City as early as 7 A.M., dressed as though he were attending a board meeting of IBM, in a wide-lapeled business suit, with pleated trousers, complete with shirt, tie, and gold cuff links. There wouldn't be another car in the parking area as Red, with hand on the steering wheel and the other gripping a small Sony into which he'd been dictating monologue ideas since leaving the house, pulled his Rolls into his private space marked "Red Skelton." Then, with his coat draped cape style over his six-foot-two, 230-pound frame to protect his asthma-plagued body from the morning chill, Red would alight from his car and stride across the macadam-covered parking lot and down a short flight of cement steps to a door marked "Artists Entrance."

Inside the Artists Entrance Red would stop to exchange a few jokes with the cop seated behind the desk who was guarding the premises. Something like, "Hi, Joe. You know we had a girls' basketball team in the studio last week? Called themselves the Redheads. You know what a redhead is? A latrine on a Russian warship."

The cop would laugh, and Red would start down the corridor into the interior of the cavernous deserted building.

Before he'd taken many steps, the guard would call out to him, "Hey, do you know your studio is still locked, Mr. Skelton?"

"No, but I know the dirty lyrics to Winchester Cathedral."

After getting another laugh or two, Red would head for the rehearsal hall. There, for the next hour and a half, until the huge CBS complex came awake with office workers, technicians, and creative people, and the members of his own personal staff drifted in, Red would sit at a piano, picking out sad, simple tunes and recording them on his Sony for Don Ferris to later put into publishable form.

The pace would pick up considerably after Seymour Berns and Cecil Barker arrived between eight-thirty and nine o'clock and began getting things ready for the first reading of the script. The reading generally began around ten, with Berns, Barker, the cast regulars, Dave Rose, Dave O'Brien, and whatever guest star happened to be on the show that week sitting around a large table while Red and the actors stumbled through their lines for the first time.

No one ever expected a first reading to be up to performance level, and it never was, mainly because Seymour Berns couldn't get Red to settle down until the first dress rehearsal before an audience Monday night. Until then, the script was out the window, while Red ignored the written word and threw in his own ad libs.

GUEST STAR: I'm a neophyte.

RED AD LIB: I understand you fellows are allowed to eat meat on Friday now?

So why have a first reading at all, or for that matter any rehearsals, with a fellow like Red?

Well, it was done primarily to get the cast and guest stars acquainted, to give the prop man a chance to learn what props would be needed, and to give the assistant director a chance to get a rough timing of the show.

Red didn't have many guest stars on his programs, especially those of the superstar variety. He was still afraid that they would detract from his importance. In addition, they usually asked for a good deal of money, and that would have to come out of the budget allowed Van Bernard Productions by CBS, which would mean less profit for Skelton at the end of the season. As a result, the Skelton show had few guest stars, and the ones it did have were usually in the second echelon from the top—people like Tennessee Ernie Ford, Richard Chamberlin, Mickey Rooney, Martha Raye, Marilyn Maxwell, and Diana Dors. Talented people, yes, but not stars of the first magnitude.

After the first reading, Red would retire to his dressing room where, while he was waiting for Seymour Berns to start putting the sketches on "their feet," he would either dictate a new monologue to his secretary, using old material culled from his joke file, or else he would dash off a couple of short stories.

The rehearsal itself would generally get under way around twelve-fifteen. Since this was the lunch hour for most of the CBS personnel, the studio would start filling up with secretaries anxious to have a couple of laughs during their noontime break. The star of the show didn't disappoint them. While the rest of the cast, crew, and technicians were scurrying around preparing for a complete run-through, Red would sit down on the apron of the stage and start telling the secretaries dirty stories.

If as occasionally happened, a nun or a priest walked into the rehearsal hall, Red might cut off one of his risqué stories in the middle, with an apology to the secretaries like, "I'm sorry, girls, I guess we're going to have to have a clean rehearsal today." The girls would react to this with loud groans.

When the rehearsal finally did get under way, it would be a complete shambles. Props wouldn't work. Actors would stumble around, knowing neither their lines nor their moves. Some of the scenery would still be unfinished, and many of the props would be missing.

Props played a large and expensive part of every Skelton show, and because Red was so dependent on them for many of his gags, causing the prop department to be unusually resourceful, CBS reaped the residual benefit of having the best-equipped prop department of any of the networks. There was nothing the CBS prop geniuses weren't called upon by the Skelton writers to devise—from break-away doors, walls, and vases to a fireman's pole upon which Red could slide *up* instead of down. The fireman's pole gag alone cost the Skelton budget $3,400, and that was back in the sixties. But as far as Red was concerned, if the gag was good enough, damn the expense—full speed ahead!

Most of the props and scenery never worked properly during rehearsals, throwing a scare into cast and crew. Red, meanwhile, continued to fool around, thus compounding the problem. While the crew, the other members of the cast, and the producer were wondering how this mess would ever be in good enough shape to tape the following night, Red would be playing to the secretaries in the audience, straying from the written word, ad libbing jokes that had most of the women in the cast blushing and the producer hoping Red wouldn't attempt them on the air. But Red couldn't be cured of this: he was simply getting himself in the mood for the three-fifteen rehearsal, which, over the years, became known to insiders in the business as "The Red Skelton Dirty Hour."

The Dirty Hour, in which Red pulled every dirty gag or stunt he'd ever learned since his burlesque days, was probably funnier than anything he ever did on the air or before a paying audience. It didn't start out to be the Dirty Hour; in the beginning it was just another rehearsal before the final preview, but it somehow evolved into the Dirty Hour.

"We let him do it because we really had to let him get it out of his system before we let the audience in," recalls Seymour Berns. "It was like letting a little kid go to his room and throw things around. While Red was doing a 'snatch' joke, we'd be in the control room trying to figure out what would go in that spot that would be clean."

Anyone who's ever witnessed a Dirty Hour rehearsal would never again believe Red's oft-repeated claim that he is basically a "clean comic." And there certainly must be plenty of witnesses, since Red did his Dirty Hour every Monday and Tuesday afternoon for close to ten years.

Of course Red's regular audiences, the ones regarding him as a solid citizen who loved Mother and Apple Pie and the American flag and who said "God Bless" at the finish of his show, never were privileged to see Red's Dirty Hour. The studio was sealed off from everybody but CBS personnel. But among CBS insiders the Dirty Hour had such a reputation for being hilarious and chock full of delicious ribaldry that it often disrupted the work schedule at CBS on Monday and Tuesday afternoons, because so many people left their desks to sneak down to Studio 33 to witness the irrepressible Red at his wickedest.

"When *Playhouse 90* was still around," recalls Willie Dahl, "they used to schedule their rehearsals so their whole cast and crew could come to our Dirty Hour and unwind."

If it had a therapeutic effect on some, it had the opposite effect on the CBS brass. So little work was finally being done around CBS on most Monday and Tuesday afternoons that executive orders forbidding workers to leave their desks between the hours of three and four had to be posted on office bulletin boards.

But people still slipped away to see the likes of—for example—Martha Raye making a grand entrance that caught everyone's attention. She had a hand on each one of her breasts and was thrusting them upwards. The effect was that of a child playing with a big mound of silly putty. She next stepped over to the bar and ordered a beer, only to find that the bartender had slipped her the real thing. Hearing that it was real beer, Skelton rushed over as quickly as he could, guzzled down the entire mug, and let out a big burp at which Miss Raye quipped, "Why don't you switch ends and save your teeth?" This broke Red up—and for real.

However, now he owed her one and he was quick to retaliate. When Miss Raye blew into her sweatshirt to indicate how hot the weather was, Red pointed into the air and exclaimed, "Look, a bat flew out!" The score was now even but by the time they had talked about closet queens and breast transplants, Miss Raye had a small lead. Red didn't let her keep it for long, however. Separating her breasts with his hands and peering into her ample cleavage, Red looked back at the audience and said, "My God, there are two of them."

Another exchange of dirty ad libs took place during an alleged love scene between the two.

MARTHA: Gee, you're swell.
RED: Gee, you're swell.
MARTHA: I think you're swell.
RED: You're so swell.
MARTHA: You'd better stop talking and do something before all the swelling goes down.

On the week when the guest was Patrice Munsel—who did not offer a serious challenge to Red as far as ad libbing goes—Skelton was entirely on his own. He stepped into a telephone booth and the dialogue went something like this.

"Hello, operator, gimmie Trafalgar 60006." After a slight pause: "You heard me, you filthy bitch. Trafalgar 60006. Spell it? What's wrong with you? What do they teach you in college?" Pause. "Besides rioting?" (Pause) "Humping? Oh, well. Look here, operator, I want to talk to my sweetheart from the country. She's a country girl, sweet and pure. Only had the clap once." (Pause) "Hello, sweetheart. It's me, lover boy. What are you thinking of, dear, the cord is getting hard. . . ."

In the same show, Red played a sketch in which he portrayed a stupid doctor who treats Robin Hood's men in Sherwood Forest. Red walked in wearing antlers and was addressed by one of the men.

MAN: Why do you wear antlers?
RED: To fool the deer.

MAN: You can't fool the deer with that.

RED: Then how come I got one of them knocked up?

At another point, one of Robin Hood's men came in with a five-foot spear in his stomach. Red examined the spear and then remarked, "If that's not a spear, I know a girl who'll marry you." Then he innocently looked up at the camera and told the audience that he might have to change that line during the actual taping.

When asked by one of the men in the forest how he became a merry man, Red replied, "You see, I met this dirty old man with a candy when I was a little boy."

Finally, in the closing sketch, Marian wanted to marry Red for saving her life. Red moved away from her, embraced a cast-iron deer, and said that he was already spoken for.

Still embracing the rump of the deer, he again faced the camera with a bewildered look on his face and added, "I understand back East they do this with women."

But that's a rather classy joke compared to the bit he liked to pull on glamorous female guest stars. Taking a pratfall near a girl's feet, he'd look up her skirt, then pull his head away and exclaim loudly, "My God, Marilyn, you're wearing pants."

By the mid-sixties, reports of Red's Dirty Hour were beginning to be heard outside Television City. To make sure the reports weren't exaggerated, the *UCLA Daily Bruin* sneaked a reporter into one of Red's Dirty Hour rehearsals to cover it for its readers. The reporter wrote a detailed account, which appeared in the *Daily Bruin* one day under the banner headline:

IS RED SKELTON A DIRTY OLD MAN?

The story left absolutely nothing to the reader's imagination, reporting every ribald word and nuance exactly as Red performed them on the stage, and the account so embarrassed Red and CBS that for a time there was talk of suing the college newspaper.

But as Guy della Cioppa wrote to John Howard, head of CBS Public Relations at the time, "A complaint to the *Daily Bruin* will do no good at all since the story is true."

The only thing that could be done was to protect themselves

in the future by making sure there would be "tighter security." Everyone entering Studio 33 during Red's Dirty Hours would be carefully screened.

If the purpose of the Dirty Hour was to "relieve Red's tension" before the preview, it failed miserably.

By 6 P.M., when Studio 33 began to fill up with tourists clutching tickets, Red, dressed in his tuxedo for his opening monologue, would be as jittery and pensive as if he were facing an opening night audience in New York's legitimate theater. All the carefree buffoonery of the Dirty Hour was gone. Red helped relieve the tension by jigging nervously in the wings to Dave Rose's music as he waited anxiously to be introduced.

When he'd finally run out onto the stage, he'd be taut and self-conscious, for he was not at his best as Red Skelton in a tux—he much preferred hiding behind the mask of one of his outrageous characters—but as the roar of the audience welled up, an instantaneous transformation would take place.

The applause seemed to infuse Red's entire body and he would do an extra twenty minutes of monologue for the studio audience before the actual show began. The audience wasn't aware of it, of course, but it was the same routine, more or less, that he had done for twenty years as a warm-up. His warm-up wasn't without a liberal sprinkling of risqué lines. Sample: "I was a real dickens the way I used to chase girls when I was young. Now I *still* chase girls, but I've forgotten why." He'd then look at the audience with a naughty-little-boy expression and add, "Better laugh now. You won't hear these jokes on television." But for the most part he kept his warm-up clean, because otherwise it would be too hard for his television show to follow.

After the preview, which he'd top off with his usual "Good night and God Bless," Red would head back to the hill to have dinner with Valentina, while Berns and Barker would get together with Ed Simmons or whoever else was the head writer, and spend the next couple of hours in a smoke-filled room making whatever cuts or changes in the script that the reaction of the preview audience seemed to indicate were necessary.

The script would then be sent out to mimeo, so there would be clean pages for tomorrow's rehearsals and taping.

Early Tuesday morning the grind would begin all over again. Red, as usual, would be the first to arrive, and would spend his time at the piano picking out more new tunes. Rehearsals would begin around ten and continue until three, with Red becoming more nervous and temperamental as the day progressed and the hour of taping grew near. It wasn't just Red's basic paranoia that caused difficulty. Frequently there would be real problems in the script that didn't become noticeable until rehearsal and that required last-minute fixing—usually by Red himself. One week, for example, Red felt that a dream sequence in the "Silent Spot" wasn't coming off the way it was intended. In this sketch Red was supposed to play a man who ate a nauseating potpourri of food before going to bed and then had a nightmare about it. When it didn't seem to be playing, Red stopped the sketch halfway into it and walked forward to the stage apron.

"Do you realize this is a dream sequence?" he asked a secretary sitting in the first row. When the girl said, "No," Red turned to Berns and Barker and said, "You see, that's what's wrong." Red frequently got his opinions about the show from secretaries, tradesmen, elevator men and even golfers who walked by his house in Palm Springs on Tamarisk's seventeenth hole.

Red believed that the audience ought to be told it was a dream sequence before it started. Berns and Barker resisted on the basis that it was "obvious."

Red stuck to his convictions. "Comedy is fantasy to begin with," he said, "so when you put in a dream, it's a dream within a dream, and the audience gets confused. We had the same problem with a dream sequence at MGM when we made *Du Barry Was a Lady*."

Berns's mild resistance collapsed, a conference was called with the writers, and a "subtle" way was sought to label the nightmare sketch a "dream." Red's own idea was finally accepted, and it wasn't so subtle, but it was effective: open the sketch with a large closeup of a book entitled *How to Avoid Nightmares*.

Red's instinct was right; the sketch played funnier when the audience knew what it was about. Rehearsals proceeded into the afternoon. There would be another Dirty Hour at three o'clock, followed by a brief respite, and then it would be six o'clock and time for the actual taping.

Again Red would be fraught with nervousness as he climbed into his tux and Studio 33 filled up and the place acquired the air of pre-curtain tension in a Broadway theater. As Red waited in the wings, the show's makeup man would wipe the sweat from Red's glistening face. Frequently before his opening cue, Red would have to make a mad dash to a nearby john to throw up everything that was in his stomach. The nausea would generally disappear once the curtain was up; Red could forget himself in the characters he was playing, and the audience would begin to respond. The weariness and the pain would suddenly be gone from his face, and he wouldn't miss a single one of the ad libs he had been devising for the past two days. In addition, there would be new ad libs and new improvisations he hadn't even tried before.

Sometimes the new things worked, and sometimes they didn't; but often his ad libs gave the show an unpolished look, which critics, insiders, and his staff hated. But the general public didn't seem to object at all, if they even noticed.

As mentioned earlier, Red would have welcomed the approval of his show business peers. But what mattered most to him was the audience. As long as the ratings held, and the audience loved him, and he could hear their wild clapping and whistling as he stood bowing and smiling and wiping the perspiration from his brow at the end of a taping, that was all he really cared about. That was his plasma, and that was what he knew he lived for—and that only—as he climbed into his Rolls and drove the 130 miles back to Palm Springs again on Tuesday night, with next week's script on the seat beside him.

By the end of the TV season, in the spring of 1965, Cecil Barker and Ed Simmons decided that the time had come, as it must to all men, to cease working for Red Skelton. Their nerves couldn't take the strain any longer. So after the final program of the season they tendered their resignations as producer and head writer respectively.

Important as their contribution to the show had been, however, Barker and Simmons' exodus didn't have any noticeable effect on the future welfare of the show. After thirteen years on the air, the *Red Skelton Show* was steaming merrily along under its own impetus, and nothing—certainly not the loss of a couple of crew members—was going to slow it down.

Barker was immediately replaced by Seymour Berns, who gave up his directorial chair to produce the show, and Bob Schiller and Bob Weiskopf signed on as head writers. Berns then hired Bill Hobin, who'd been the director of *The Show of Shows*, to replace himself.

With Berns producing, Hobin directing, and Schiller and Weiskopf head-writing, the Skelton show continued its climb to the top of the Nielsens, and Red became the nation's Number One eccentric.

"I'm nuts and I know it," he used to tell people who criticized his strange ways, "but as long as I make them laugh they ain't gonna lock me up."

That he could make them laugh there wasn't any doubt. He was the nation's favorite television comedian, and he was no flash-in-the-pan. After a shaky beginning he had managed to outlast every other television comedian on TV except Bob Hope and Hope no longer did a weekly show.

In addition, Red was a hit at Vegas whenever he appeared there. And he commanded from $25,000 to $50,000 a night playing state fairs, where he drew as many as 30,000 people a night.

So popular was the Hoosier state's most famous son in the mid-sixties that a two-span bridge across the Wabash River was named the Red Skelton Bridge, in a ceremony personally attended by Red, Guy della Cioppa, and Charlie Pomerantz, a publicity man. In addition, a school in Vincennes was named "Red Skelton High School." In return for these honors, Red set up in his home town the Red Skelton Foundation, a nonprofit organization that awards scholarships to worthy students.

By the mid-sixties Red's "Good night and God Bless" had become as well-known in the United States as Bing Crosby and the Pledge of Allegiance. And thanks to Red's almost fanatical patriotism to the country that had given him the chance to rise from patent medicine salesman to millionaire, the Pledge of Allegiance was actually enjoying a resurgence in America. A devout Republican, Red believed in America, right or wrong. Never was this more evident than during the wave of anti-American feeling that was sweeping the U.S. at the height of its Vietnam involvement. Red's reaction to the antiwar demonstrations was to recite the Pledge of Allegiance on his television show one night in January of 1969, with addenda supplied by him interpreting its exact meaning.

Red concluded his recitation of the Pledge of Allegiance by saying, "Since I was a small boy, two states have been added to our country and two words have been added to the Pledge of Allegiance—'under God.'

"Wouldn't it be a pity if someone said, 'That's a prayer' and that would be eliminated from schools, too?"

After the broadcast, CBS and the *Red Skelton Show* were inundated with letters from fans asking for copies of the Pledge of Allegiance as Red recited it on his program. There was such interest in it, in fact, that Red had it copyrighted in his name; then he recorded it for Columbia Records, with CBS and Van Bernard splitting the production costs. They gave 30,000 pressings of the records away to the public at a considerable loss, but the publicity was well worth it.

Later, Red had thousands of copies of his Pledge of Allegiance struck off on parchment paper, and he personally sold them to the public on his various trips to state fairs and other centers in the Midwest where he was so popular. According to his traveling companions, Red would sit in the lobby of his hotel between performances and peddle his personally autographed Pledge of Allegiance for a dollar a copy.

None of this wealth and power that was accruing to him in the sixties did anything to allay Red's worsening paranoia which, if anything, grew worse the more successful and world-famous Red became.

Ever since he had made it big in show business, Red had always feared that some mysterious group of predators, whom he referred to as "they," were out to separate him from his possessions. A few had succeeded. A couple of times, for instance, he had been the victim of minor burglaries. In Las Vegas once, while he was walking along a badly lighted garden path between the casino and his hotel suite, he was held up by a man who stuck a gun in his ribs and demanded everything he had. Red only had a couple of hundred dollars on him at the time, but he gladly handed it to his assailant. But as the man looked at Red, he recognized him and changed his mind about robbing him. "I wouldn't rob you, Mr. Skelton." And he started to hand the money back. Playing Alfonse and Gaston, Red then returned the money to the burglar, saying, "You must need it, young man, or you wouldn't have gone to all this trouble."

The man took the money, but only on the condition that Red would give him his address, so that he could return it when and if he could ever afford to. "Would you believe it?" says Red. "A couple of years later, I opened up an envelope that came in the mail and there was my money. It makes you have faith."

Notwithstanding, Red didn't have much faith in humanity.

He was constantly afraid of being robbed. In Palm Springs, for example, he paid for round-the-clock private police protection. As a further deterrent, he also kept four Rolls Royces parked in his driveway in front of the house at all times, because he was thoroughly convinced that after seeing the cars parked there, potential burglars would think he was home, even when he wasn't, and be afraid to enter the place.

In addition, Red and Georgia both slept with .38 caliber revolvers within reaching distance of their beds, whether they were at home or on the road traveling.

To give himself a feeling of security, Red carried from $5,000 to $10,000 in cash on his person at almost all times. He jokingly referred to it as his "get-away money," but was deadly serious about the sense of well-being it gave him to have a wallet bulging with thousand-dollar bills.

"Before Joe Ross took over, Red used to carry as much as $50,000 in cash around with him at all times," recalls Seymour Berns. "But Ross put a stop to that after Red left $17,000 in cash he had just received for playing a county fair in a barf bag on an airliner. Red didn't remember he had put the money there until he was off the plane, and the plane had taken off. Red never did recover the money. After that, Ross made him carry travelers checks, but not in the amounts you and I would. He'd have from ten to fifty grand worth of travelers checks with him everywhere he went in his attaché case."

After the Cuban missile crisis, Red was afraid that a time

might come after a real atomic attack when all the money in the world would be useless to fill his and his family's stomachs. To prepare for this Armageddon, he evidently took to stockpiling food, according to what producer Irwin (*The Towering Inferno*) Allen discovered one day. Allen reports that one time in the sixties he and his good friend, the late Groucho Marx, went into a grocery store in Cathedral City to buy some fresh fruit. To their surprise they found there was nothing left in the store to buy. All its shelves and bins were empty.

"Going out of business?" Allen asked the proprietor.

"No, sir," said the proprietor, a rural, country store-keeper-type.

"What's happened to your stock?"

"I'll tell you. Little while ago ... that redheaded comedian fella ... Red Skelton, I think his name is ... backed a truck up to the front of my store and bought out my whole place lock, stock, and barrel and took it home with him. Said he wants to be ready in case of an attack."

Red may have found peace and harmony and contentment in Palm Springs as he claimed, but he did not bring any of that with him when he returned to Los Angeles.

One day Red blew up at Seymour Berns in the middle of a rehearsal, threw down his script, stopped the proceedings, and then picked up a phone and called his banker.

"Meet me at Pier 4, at Wilmington, on Thursday morning at eleven, and bring a suitcase filled with $132,000 in cash. I'm quitting the show."

He then stormed out of the studio and vanished completely as if he had taken off into space in a flying saucer. He didn't go home to Sarbonne, nor back to Georgia in Palm Springs. "We even checked the hotels he normally stayed in when he was leaving Georgia," states Berns, "and he wasn't in any of them."

Since he walked out in the middle of a show, a rerun had to be substituted in the Skelton spot on Tuesday night.

But they couldn't get by with reruns indefinitely.

"Well, what are we going to do?" asked Barker. "How are we ever going to find him?"

"I'll tell you how we're going to find him," said Berns. "We're going to Pier 4 and wait for him."

So Berns, Schiller, and Weiskopf took themselves down to Pier 4 in Long Beach, where a Pacific and Orient liner was preparing to sail for Japan, and waited for their man to show up. It seemed a long shot that Red would actually carry out his threat, but fifteen minutes later, Red walked across the pier to the gangplank, carrying an attaché case bulging with cash.

"It took us an hour to talk him out of leaving the country," recalls Berns. "And then we had to promise we'd let him keep his cash and that we wouldn't tell Joe Ross or Jack Entratter about it."

Another time he stuffed his attaché case with $100,000 in cash, and walked around with it, telling everybody, "Nobody's going to take this away from me."

By the summer of 1966, Red's marriage was again in serious trouble.

Georgia's drinking and her addiction to pills continued to be the one trouble spot that Red couldn't cope with. She was on booze or pills or both most of the time. Like most alcoholics, she refused to recognize her problem, and as a result nobody could do anything to stop her.

Understandably concerned, Red did his utmost to keep Georgia reasonably sober, but again like most alcoholics, she had many devious ways of fooling him.

For example, on a personal appearance trip to Houston once, Georgia used to pay a bellboy to bring up gin in a water carafe so that Red wouldn't know she was drinking alcohol. After downing the gin, she would wash her mouth with Listerine so that Red wouldn't catch on.

Another time—while he was still living in Bel Air—Red invited della Cioppa and Jack Entratter up to his house on Sarbonne to have lunch. When the two men arrived there, Georgia wasn't around, and "Red was grumpy and growly," says della Cioppa.

"What's the matter?" Entratter asked him.

"It's Georgia," replied Red sadly. "Her drinking. She's getting worse and worse all the time."

At that particular moment, explained Red, she was upstairs, dead drunk, in her bedroom. Entratter investigated, and found Georgia unconscious on her bed, surrounded by liquor bottles and boxes of pills.

Entratter dumped the pills down the toilet and the remaining liquor in the sink, and then he came back and the three of them had lunch.

When Johnson's Wax was one of the sponsors of Red's show, a group of bigwigs from their company came to Hollywood from Racine, and hosted a luncheon at the Bel Air Hotel for Red and Georgia, Red's staff from the show, and a few network people.

Red had warned Georgia to stay off the booze, and she promised. But, of course, an alcoholic's promise is even more meaningless than a politician's in an election year. Georgia, unbeknownst to Red, slipped one of the waiters at the luncheon a twenty-dollar bill to keep filling her water glass with gin while ostensibly pouring water from a pitcher.

By the time the luncheon was over, Georgia had passed out in her chair, and had to be carried out to the car with all the Johnson's Wax people looking on.

When Georgia was drinking heavily, of course, any domestic squabble was apt to be blown way out of proportion.

For twenty years, Red and Georgia kept a large white parrot named Gauguin for a pet. Red was so in love with "Gogie" that he used to carry him on stage and hold him in his arms while he did the closing spot on his TV show. In Palm Springs, Red used to insist that Gogie sleep in the guest shower, because he didn't want him to be exposed to the cold night desert air outside.

One day Red came home and found Gogie lying dead in the shower—apparently of old age. Georgia hadn't lifted a finger to remove him, which infuriated Red. When he asked Georgia how it happened, she said she didn't know. In fact, she was completely indifferent to the poor bird's demise.

Red exploded at her attitude, and accused Georgia of deliberately killing Gogie. As a result, the two didn't talk for days and, in fact, had one of the worst fights of their marriage.

In addition to being unable to cope with Georgia's drinking

problems, Red was still obsessed with the notion that she was having affairs with just about everybody within their social and business orbit. He believed, for instance, that Jack Entratter was one of Georgia's lovers, but he never caught them at it or was able to substantiate his allegations, so Entratter continued to be his friend and business manager until something else besides Georgia caused an estrangement between the two men.

In July of 1966, Red was playing the Sands Hotel in Vegas. Because it was around the time of his birthday (July 18, 1966) Georgia decided to come along, too, as did Valentina and her boyfriend from college, Art Coleman.

Guy della Cioppa, Seymour Berns, Schiller, and Weiskopf had also accompanied Red to Vegas that week, for twin purposes: to help their boss celebrate his birthday, and to confer with him about the TV script for the first show of the coming season.

Red did his early Sands show on July 20, to several standing ovations. Between shows, Schiller and Weiskopf dropped into Red's dressing room to tell him how much they had enjoyed his performance. While they were there, Georgia came in, wearing a very décolleté gown.

"Red didn't like the dress," recalls Schiller, "and he bawled the hell out of her for wearing it. He really was furious, like only Red can be."

None too stable after several drinks, Georgia burst into tears and fled the room.

At midnight, Red was doing his second show of the evening when Valentina and her boyfriend, who were fixing themselves something to eat in the kitchen of the Skelton suite, heard moans coming from Georgia's room. Rushing in, they discovered Georgia in a near-unconscious state on the bed, with a wound from a .38 caliber bullet in her breast and the gun on the floor beside the bed. Valentina sent for the hotel doctor, who removed the bullet, and called for an ambulance to take her to the Sunrise Hospital.

Red was just coming off the stage when Guy della Cioppa informed him that Georgia had "accidentally" shot herself and had been taken to the Sunrise Hospital by ambulance.

Red broke into tears upon hearing the news, and of course

rushed right over to Sunrise Hospital to be at Georgia's side during her ordeal.

At the hospital Red was told by the attending doctor that Georgia had been lucky. The bullet hadn't penetrated her rib cage, with the result that the wound was superficial, and she would recover.

According to Georgia's version of the "accident" that she gave to both Red and the investigating police when she recovered consciousness, she had been asleep in her hotel room when she thought she heard a burglar. She reached for her gun, but it slipped from her hand and dropped to the floor. The impact caused the bullet in the chamber to fire accidentally, wounding her in the breast.

Georgia's account wasn't terribly believable. To anyone familiar with guns, it was apparent from the trajectory of the bullet and also the fact that a .38 caliber Smith and Wesson barrel type revolver can't be fired unless the trigger is pulled, that Georgia couldn't have shot herself accidentally.

Obviously, she had tried to take her own life. Either that or she had bungled the job on purpose just to make Red feel guilty.

However, since Georgia insisted that her version of the shooting was the truth—and there were no facts to prove otherwise—the incident went down officially in the police records as an "accidental shooting," and that was how it was reported in the press the next morning.

The near-tragedy did not dampen Red's enthusiasm to keep and bear arms. It also didn't stop him from making jokes alluding to the fact that Georgia couldn't be trusted farther than you could throw Kate Smith.

Two and a half years after the accident—in the spring of 1969—Red and his entourage, which included Georgia, Guy della Cioppa, Seymour Berns, and Charlie Isaacs, traveled to Boston, where he was slated to appear as a "guest" conductor with Arthur Fiedler's Boston Pops Orchestra. On the program, Red was to lead the orchestra in a comedy version of *The Poet and the Peasant*. One of Red's gags during the number called for him to pick up a pistol loaded with blanks, and fire it into the air, to punctuate a beat.

But while Red was rehearsing this particular bit with full orchestra the morning before the concert, he realized that his prop man had failed to supply him with a gun.

Since no member of the Boston Pops carried a pistol, the rehearsal came to a halt while the gun problem could be solved. Finally, Red remembered that he and Georgia had a pistol in their hotel room, so he asked the manager of the concert hall to dispatch a messenger to the Ritz-Carlton to fetch it. The manager said he would go, and started to leave. Just as he was walking out the door, Red shouted to him in front of the full orchestra. "When you get to the room be sure to knock first. Georgia may have a customer."

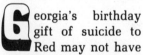

eorgia's birthday gift of suicide to Red may not have succeeded, but it was a portent of things to come.

During his sixth decade that elusive thing called happiness continued to slip through Red's fingers like a live, wet trout. But then why should this time of his life be any different from any other period? No matter how well he was doing otherwise, tragedy or some kind of travail or turmoil always seemed to be stalking him around the next corner.

From 1966 to 1971, Red managed to get rid of everyone who ever meant anything to him—from his producer of thirteen years to his wife of twenty-six.

The wholesale firings started with Jack Entratter, to whom Red was paying 5 percent of his income for business advice.

"Red began to feel that Entratter was no longer his friend," says Guy della Cioppa, "when he realized that Entratter was only paying him $25,000 a week to play the Sands while most of the other big name entertainers who played there were getting fifty and sixty grand a week. But Georgia liked Entratter, so she kept persuading Red to stay with him, anyway. But then Georgia turned on Entratter for some reason, at which point Red made up his mind to fire him.

"So Red wrote a letter to Entratter, firing him, and telling him he wasn't going to pay him any more percentage of his income, and sent a copy to Joe Ross. Entratter then got mad and said he was going to sue Red. Red said he had no case because they had no written contract, and took his case to Joe Ross and said, 'Joe, I want you to represent me in this lawsuit.' But Joe Ross felt it was unethical to represent Red against Entratter since it was Entratter who had introduced him and Red in the first place. He felt it would be a conflict of interest. So Red fired Joe Ross, after all he had done for him, and hired Irell-Manella, on Lucille Ball's recommendation. But Red only lasted with them for a few months. They *fired* Red because he was too big a problem."

Eventually, Entratter called off the lawsuit, and he and Red came to a somewhat amicable parting of the ways. By then, Red had not only lost Irell-Manella and Joe Ross, but he had gone through several other law firms as well.

In April of 1967, the Skelton show climbed to Number One in the Nielsens. It also received another nomination from the Television Academy for "Outstanding Show in the Field of Variety."

One week later, Bob Schiller and Bob Weiskopf, who'd been head writers on the show since 1965, received word through their agent that Red was firing them.

Curious as to Red's reason for axing them, inasmuch as the show was doing so well, the writing team asked Seymour Berns for an explanation. Berns looked at them rather sheepishly, and said, "He told me that writers get cocky and lazy if you keep them on too long."

At the end of the following season, Seymour Berns also got the ax. "I was in New York, vacationing," recalls Berns. "The Skelton show was Number Three in the ratings at the time, when I got a call from the coast from della Cioppa. He said, 'Red doesn't want you back next year,' and that was it."

So after thirteen years, Seymour Berns was out.

Red replaced him with Bill Hobin, who became both producer and director. Hobin, in turn, hired Charlie Isaacs, another excellent comedy writer and a veteran of more than twenty years of the television and radio wars, to fill Schiller and Weiskopf's shoes.

"Right after I left, Red also fired Milton Weiss, his publicity man," recalls Berns. "Weiss had been with him twenty years, and was probably more loyal to Red than any human being who ever worked for him. Yet Red didn't even bother phoning Milty. He simply sent him a letter telling him he was through, with no other explanation."

According to those who've known Red the longest, there is no logical explanation as to why he ends relationships with people. "He simply trusted no one," recalls an acquaintance, "and once he stopped trusting, he viewed them as enemies who had to be taken care of."

If, for example, Red believed that someone had deliberately done him wrong, double-crossed him in a business deal, perhaps, or possibly just written something of a negative nature about him of which he didn't approve in a magazine article or newspaper column, Red had his own unique way of dealing with that person.

The first time Red felt he'd been wronged, he would get into a Japanese ceremonial robe, then take Georgia and Valentina out to a little shrine in his Japanese garden. There the three of them would get down on their knees before the shrine, bow their heads in prayer, and try to think three good things about the person Red felt had offended him.

If this ceremony had no positive effect on the person Red felt had harmed him, and if this person continued to affront him, Red would return to the shrine with Georgia and Valentina, and go through a different kind of exorcism. In this ceremony, he would "mentally bury the offender," he told a member of his writing staff.

"He always used to say to me," recalls Guy della Cioppa, " 'the minute anybody hurts me or my family, I consider them dead, and I never think of them again.' "

In 1969 someone entered Red Skelton's life who Georgia wouldn't have minded burying, figuratively at least. Her name was Lothian Toland, and she was the thirty-two-year-old daughter of the late Gregg Toland, one of Hollywood's most talented cinematographers (*Best Years Of Our Lives, Little Foxes*) and winner of a number of Oscars.

Ironically, it was because of Georgia's insistence that Red become more active socially in Palm Springs that he met the girl who eventually stole him away from Georgia. After joining Tamarisk Country Club, Red and Georgia usually ate lunch there on Sundays and occasionally even attended club parties. Through Frank Sinatra, who was also a member, the Skeltons met Frederick "Fritz" Loewe, partner of Alan J. Lerner and composer of such musicals as *My Fair Lady, Brigadoon, On A Clear Day*, and *Gigi*.

Loewe, who also lived in the desert community, and the Skeltons enjoyed each other's company, and soon were making a regular habit of exchanging dinner invitations. Loewe's most constant companion on these occasions was Lothian Toland.

Lothian Toland was presumably working for Fritz Loewe as his secretary, but in reality she was his girlfriend, or "nymphet," as Georgia was wont to refer to her bitterly after the relationship developed into one of those messy triangles. Whatever her title, Loewe always brought Lothian along as his date whenever he socialized with the Skeltons.

Lothian was approximately twenty years younger than Red, with a tall, reed-like figure, and a long, rather plain face framed with straight dark hair. To those who'd seen both women, Lothian's angular looks bore a certain resemblance to the first Mrs. Skelton. But whatever her appeal, she adored Red—in fact, idolized him—and it wasn't very long after their first encounter that they were having clandestine meetings that soon evolved into a full-fledged affair.

Because it's not easy to fool a wife, especially in a small town like Cathedral City, Georgia was well aware of the affair almost from its inception. According to what she told one of the producers of the Skelton Show, "You wouldn't believe how that girl went after Red." Georgia said that the moment she would have to leave the house to run an errand, Lothian would show up at Skeltons' front door "to visit."

Georgia suspected that Lothian shacked up with Red whenever she [Georgia] was sick and had to go to the hospital. Because Georgia was in and out of the hospital frequently, due to bouts with the bottle and other illnesses, during the last few years of her life, Lothian and Red had ample opportunity to be in bed together. Usually, it was Red's king-sized bed in the Japanese tea house.

However, when Georgia found out for sure that Red and Lothian had been in bed together in the tea house, she became so furious that she had the bed removed when Red was not around and replaced it with a narrow, uncomfortable cot that even a monk wouldn't have been happy on.

Because the tea house was offering less and less opportunity for the two lovers to be alone now that Georgia was onto their little game, Red eventually took to spending the night with Lothian, in her small condominium apartment, on a hill overlooking Cathedral City.

"It got to be a terribly sad story ... a really weird ménage à trois," related this same informant. "After spending the night with Lothian, Red would come back to the tea house in the morning. There he'd work on his painting or his writing. I don't know if he was still writing daily love letters to Georgia. I doubt it. Then he'd go through the mail or do whatever else he did in the tea house. Then he'd have lunch with Georgia, spend the rest of the afternoon puttering around the garden or working in the tea house, and then he'd go away and spend the night with Lothian.

"The only reason Georgia permitted this situation to exist was because she was trying to get Red to come back. She had some strange psychological attraction to him. She wanted him no matter how bad they were for each other."

During the waning months of their marriage, Georgia went to pathetic lengths to win Red back.

Once, for example, she invited one of her boyfriends to move into the Thompson Road house with her. But she wasn't actually interested in the man; she merely wanted to make Red jealous. However, when her boyfriend discovered why he was there, he became angry and moved out in the middle of the night. This was a blow Georgia couldn't get over, particularly since it was the night before the anniversary of Richard's death, a time when she always felt the most blue. Consequently, she phoned Red up at Lothian's house and said, "Red, are you coming back to me as you promised or not?"

"I'm busy," snapped Red. "I can't talk with you now," and he hung up.

This resulted in Georgia going on a three-day spree with the bottle, and winding up having to be taken to the Desert Hospital in an ambulance.

By January of 1971, when Red played the Las Vegas Hilton, he wasn't making any effort to conceal his affair with Lothian. Lothian made the trip with him, and the two shared a suite in the Las Vegas Hilton.

Although by now there were all kinds of rumors making the public prints to the effect that the Skelton marriage was about to crumble, and that a girl named "Lothian" was the primary cause, Red and Georgia still clung tenaciously together—at least officially. Apparently Red was suffering from an attack of the guilts and just couldn't bring himself to the point of actually asking Georgia for a divorce and leaving her alone.

There were two very understandable reasons for Red's reluctance to leave her, although he loved Lothian. He was aware that Georgia was quite mentally ill and might not be able to cope with the separation. And without Red, Georgia would have no one, not even Valentina. Their daughter had moved out of the house in 1969, shortly after reaching her twenty-second birthday, to marry Carlos J. Alonso, a waiter in a Sunset Strip nightclub who was seven years her senior. Neither Red nor Georgia had approved the match, so relations were strained between them and their daughter, and they rarely saw her, even after Valentina made them grandparents in August of 1970, by giving birth to a girl, whom she named Sabrina.

Although the marriage was nearly over, Red and Georgia made one last stab at playing the happily married couple in May of 1971, in order to grant the last wish of a little boy from Des Moines, Iowa, who was dying of cancer of the brain. Knowing he had only a few weeks to live, Billy Long had expressed two hopes to his parents: he wanted to see Disneyland and meet Red Skelton before he died.

Being a sentimentalist as well as having gone through a similar tragedy, Red, for one wonderful day in May, played the perfect clown and the devoted husband on the grounds of their Tamarisk estate. Just as he'd done with Richard, Red made Billy laugh until it almost hurt. Then, when it came time for Billy and his parents to leave, Red put his arm around Georgia and handed her his handkerchief to wipe her tears. Red was crying, too, as the Longs pulled out of their driveway, with Billy bravely waving good-bye to them.

It was the last time Red and Georgia were ever seen together.

In August of 1971, Red officially separated from his wife of twenty-six years, and moved into a house in the foothill community of Anza, that he had bought for Lothian.

When Georgia still wouldn't file for a divorce, Red filed his own petition in a courthouse in nearby Indio, California, citing "irreconcilable differences which have caused a breakdown in our marriage."

Details of the financial settlement were not disclosed, but under California law Georgia was entitled to at least half of everything Red had earned during their marriage, which by his own admission, was considerable. Red rarely boasted about his money, but once in a conversation with Don Ferris and Ferris's wife, which took place in a Mexican restaurant in Palm Springs, Mrs. Ferris remarked to Red, "I imagine you must be a multi-millionaire by now, aren't you, Red?"

"My dear," replied Red, "if I just sold Van Bernard Productions I'd have $15 million."

That was a slight exaggeration. According to Guy della Cioppa, Red realized "$2.5 million in cold cash" from his half of his partnership when CBS and Van Bernard Productions split up after his show went off the air.

The $2.5 million was over and above Red's weekly salary of approximately $40,000 a week, and was money largely accrued from assorted show business ventures Van Bernard had sponsored or helped create over the years—such as Irwin Allen's *Lost In Space* television series, Jonathan Winters' summer show, and random music publishing ventures.

Because he still used it for an office, Red kept the tea house section of the Thompson Road house, which was on a separate lot, for himself, but gave Georgia the main house as part of their divorce settlement.

At the time of the divorce Red no longer owned the house on Sarbonne Road in Bel Air. He had sold it in 1968 to Barry Gordy, who owned Motown Records, for $600,000.

Financially, Red was well-fixed and would never have to worry about money again. He still had business worries, however, because by 1969 his television show was faced with the bleak prospect of cancellation by the network. After a record breaking, seventeen-year run on the air.

Cancellation was imminent in spite of the fact that Red's program was consistently in the top five of the Nielsens, and as late as April of 1967 was rated the Number One show in the land.

Part of the problem was that in spite of the fact that Red had a large audience, it did not attract the kind of viewers to whom Bob Wood, who supplanted Mike Dann in 1969 as president of the network, wanted to appeal. According to CBS's demographic survey, Red Skelton appealed either to the "very young or the very old." And while there were millions in those age groups, that was not the audience that bought products, except perhaps Geritol and Alka-Seltzer. Unfortunately for Red, the accent in America as the war in Vietnam wound down was on youth, and that was the audience Bob Wood was out to capture: the young adults, the people in their twenties and thirties. According to the survey, the young adults were not tuning into the Skelton show.

To them, his comedy was as old hat as most of the hats his characters wore on the air; he hadn't adjusted to the rapidly changing social times. They were into more "hip" comedians—Woody Allen, Mel Brooks, Mort Sahl, Godfrey Cambridge, and Bill Cosby.

In addition to the demographics, there still existed the same faction at CBS, from Paley on down to some executives in the lower echelons, who weren't wild about having the network represented by what they considered a "low-down" comic.

Besides an admitted prejudice by the network executives against Red's bucolic humor, the Skelton show was becoming much too costly, in their opinion, to warrant its remaining on the air. It's above-the-line expenses were costing the network at least $200,000 a week.

Red's latest contract with the network expired in February of 1970. "We kept renegotiating for a new one," recalls Guy della Cioppa, "but Mike Dann was having a fight with Bob Wood, the new president at the time, over general policy. Wood wanted to get rid of all the old tried and true shows—*Ed Sullivan, Red Skelton, The Beverly Hillbillies, Green Acres.* Mike Dann felt the opposite. But in the end Wood won the struggle. They never came back to us with a firm offer."

They didn't even bother to inform Red officially that he was out. Red first heard it from Georgia, who had been tipped off by della Cioppa. As the show's executive producer, della Cioppa also hadn't been officially informed; he just suspected it from the rumors he heard around CBS, plus the fact that when CBS's fall schedule was announced, the Skelton program was not on it.

When the cancellation of the Skelton show finally was made official in the spring of 1970, CBS board chairman, William Paley, sent Red a drawing, inscribed "with deep respect and gratitude."

By then it was almost too late into the next season for Red to get on another network, should any other network want him.

"However," recalls della Cioppa, "we took a chance, picked up the phone, and called NBC before they announced their fall schedule, just to let them know our availability. They had already penciled in some kind of a sitcom from Screen Gems for eight o'clock Monday night. But they figured Skelton might go well there; it was against *Gunsmoke,* and they needed something strong. So we signed to do a half-hour show for the 1970–71 season, with NBC giving Van Bernard Productions a budget of $100,-000 a program to pay all the 'above-the-line' expenses, including salaries for Red and the rest of his production and writing staff. Guy della Cioppa stayed on as executive producer; Perry Cross was the line producer." Terry Kyne directed the show, and Mort Greene and Artie Phillips were the mainstays of the writing staff.

But despite their hard work and considerable talent, the show seemed destined to fail.

Perhaps Bob Wood was right. Red Skelton had run his race on TV, and was getting a little winded. If that were the case, he was entitled to be out of breath, for it had been a marathon race, lasting twenty years, and that was a long time for a man sixty years old to still be running.

Red was terribly disillusioned about his abrupt cancellation by CBS, however, and during the first few weeks on NBC seemed determined to show Wood and Paley that they were wrong. Red and Guy della Cioppa even tried to capture a new *young* audience by booking some of the new, hot rock musical groups on the program. But "rock" apparently wasn't the answer. And once it became clear to Red that he was running far behind in the battle of the ratings, he gave up and began to lose interest. He didn't return to the bottle again—his stomach couldn't take anything stronger than beer—but he wasn't devoting the kind of time to the show that was necessary to make it a success.

"He'd give us only one day a week," recalls della Cioppa. "He'd arrive at NBC in Burbank Monday morning—the same day of the show. We would try to do a preview at four o'clock. And we'd do the actual show at seven-thirty that night. Unlike the old days, he did the preview and the show in the same day, and then he'd drive back home. But sometimes he never even gave us one day. Sometimes he'd walk out and go home. Once we lost five shooting days—that is, five shows during the season that we didn't shoot. He and Georgia were having a dreadful thing, and he was starting up the affair with Lothian. One time he just disappeared at noon."

A mind troubled with low ratings plus the weight of the guilt of an extra-marital affair was not one likely to be able to concentrate on clowning. And as a result, the show suffered and NBC yanked it in the spring of 1970.

Red did enjoy one glorious moment of victory in 1970, however, and that was when he received an invitation from President Nixon to perform in the first of a series of "Evenings at the White House" in which this country's most famous entertainers did their thing before an audience of invited guests.

The East Room of the White House, in which President Nixon held his press conferences, was temporarily converted into a "theater in the half-round" to accommodate the strictly black-tie affair. The guests, over three hundred of them, included Vice-President and Mrs. Agnew, Cabinet members, Congressmen, friends, staff members, and a sprinkling of nonperforming, pro-Nixon entertainers—Connie Francis, the Orson Beans, the Lionel Hamptons, and the Gene Autrys.

President Nixon himself introduced a beaming Red Skelton to the audience: "Red's been on television for nineteen years and the Vice-President has never had an unkind word to say about him." He added, "Agnew says he's going to ask for equal time." Then speaking seriously about Red, the President said, "He's known and loved in all America as a great comedian. . . . The American people like him because he has heart."

Facing the audience, with the President and Mrs. Nixon in the center of the front row and portraits of George and Martha Washington on the wall in the background, Red performed a one-man show of his classic pantomimes and monologues: the new baby in the hospital; the politician who inadvertently delivers his son's ABC's as a speech; "Guzzler's Gin"; and a lady driving a car.

Red freely mixed pratfalls with wisecracks, tossed out a few of his favorite lines ("I'm nuts but as long as I keep 'em laughing they ain't gonna lock me up"); some old jokes; some new ones ("It's exciting being here—and to be the first one to do it—I just hope I'm not the Seventh Crisis"). For fifty minutes, Red had his audience, especially Richard Nixon, laughing long and heartily.

Toward end of his show, Red, as was his custom during one-man performances, turned deadly serious. At President

Nixon's request, Red recited his own special version of the Pledge of Allegiance, and closed with his classic, "The Old Man at the Parade," Red's mime of an old relic Civil War vet gaping at the youth passing by in a Fourth of July small-town parade. The latter—just about the most frequently requested in his repertoire—moved the politician-filled audience to tears, and when Red finished, such a hush fell over the East Room that you could hear a bribe drop.

25

Although the Skelton show was cancelled officially in the spring of 1971, it played in reruns on NBC through the following summer in order for NBC to recoup some of its losses.

By then Red had had his bellyful of network TV and was thinking of retirement. Why not? He could afford to spend the rest of his life just pruning bonsais, painting, and wishing oblivion on his worst enemies. He wasn't even bitter about his network cancellations any longer, and was suddenly waxing philosophical about the end of his broadcasting career to newspaper reporters who asked him why he was no longer on the tube.

To one reporter, Red quipped, "The reason CBS cancelled

me after seventeen years was because they were afraid if I stayed for twenty they'd have to give me a gold watch."

To another reporter he said, "Just the other night, I caught a rerun of one of my TV shows. I said to Little Red: 'I ended up just where I began, pitching medicine. On TV, it's been aspirin, Alka-Seltzer, and Geritol. For Doc Lewis's Medicine show, it was his elixir."

Red had indeed come full circle, from patent medicine shows to tent shows to riverboats to circuses to burlesque to walkathons to vaudeville to nightclubs to radio to movies to television to Vegas to the White House, for the second time, and this time performing for a Republican. What else was there left but complete retirement?

So in January of 1972, after playing an eleven-day "filler" between Barbra Streisand and Elvis Presley at the Hilton International in Las Vegas, Red, his hair now a kaleidoscope of red, white and gray, made his farewell-to-show-business speech before a packed house.

It was a warm and sentimental speech up to a point; then just when he was about ready to walk into the wings for possibly the last time of his career, he had an unexplained attack of paranoia. Suddenly turning bitter and maudlin, Red blamed his premature retirement on the shabby treatment accorded him by TV web executives who had been unappreciative of his contribution to the industry. Red concluded with, "My heart has been broken," and walked off the stage, seemingly a beaten and broken man, a shadow of his former self.

Unlike generals, old comedians don't fade away; this one wound up getting married again.

On October 9, 1973, Red married Lothian Toland in the First Unitarian Church in San Francisco. The bride wore a floor-length pink chiffon gown, and the bridegroom was in a dignified-looking business suit as the pair left the church. But his clothing was the only thing about Red that was dignified.

"This was a double ring ceremony," he joked to his audience of reporters and photographers waiting for him at the bottom of the church steps. "We had two rings—one for her finger, and one for my nose."

In reply to how it felt to be a bridegroom again at his age, Red quipped, "I woke up this morning and I didn't see my name in the obituary column, so I decided to go through with it. I got up and ran up and down the hall to get my heart started."

After their marriage, Red and Lothian lived in the house up in the mountains that the two of them had occupied before they were married. This place, in the town of Anza, was about twenty miles away from the Thompson Road house, which Georgia still occupied, and where Red still maintained his Japanese tea house office.

According to statements Red gave out, he and Georgia continued to have a friendly relationship, and he frequently dropped in to visit with her and give her advice.

Georgia was lonely, however, and ill. In 1972 she was treated at the Eisenhower Medical Center for some kind of a mysterious blood disease, and the following year she suffered a heart attack.

Between Georgia's various physical ailments and her drinking, it finally became necessary for her to have a full-time, live-in nurse at the Thompson Road house.

But a life without Red Skelton to fight with was apparently unbearable for the unhappy and lonely Georgia. Early in the evening of May 11, 1976, Georgia picked up her .38 caliber revolver from the nightstand beside her bed, walked out into the garden, and fired a bullet into her head.

This time Georgia didn't bungle the job.

In a statement to the police, Sally Young, her live-in nurse, said she missed Georgia a few minutes after dinner, noticed an open door from the bedroom to the garden and walking outside, discovered her mistress's body on the grass.

Georgia left no suicide note, but words would have been superfluous; she killed herself exactly eighteen years to the day after Richard had died of leukemia. She herself was fifty-four.

As soon as he heard about the shooting, a lachrymose Red drove the twenty miles to his former home, and personally took care of the funeral arrangements for Georgia.

Funeral services were private, with Georgia being buried in the same private crypt with her son Richard, at Forest Lawn Memorial Park, in Glendale, California.

Red remained in seclusion for an appropriate length of time, but by the end of 1976 began to show signs that he was ready to come out of retirement. Of course, Red had never completely retired, not even after his Las Vegas announcement. He had continued to pick up easy money at places like the Indiana State Fair; he also appeared once a year in a place called Sparks, Nevada—a small mining town that paid big money—where he was a tremendous favorite with the local dice-throwers. And he had even emceed part of the annual movie Oscar show in the spring of 1976. At this performance he proved he had lost none of his cunning when it came to making audiences—even the hard-boiled sophisticates of tinsel town—roll in the aisles in hysterics.

But he and his act seemed to be avoiding the major metropolitan centers, where he was likely to run into tough critics.

On New Year's Day, 1977, however, Red gave notice that he was not strictly for the stix. He appeared in the Pasadena Rose Parade riding on the front of a float, made of 10,000 roses, which was shaped to resemble Red's favorite TV character—Freddy the Freeloader.

"Freddy was unique," says Red, explaining his love for him. "He was ingenius. He made the best of everything. To him, anything was elegant—he used a sardine can for an ashtray, but handled it like it was platinum.

"Freddy would say to another bum, 'Come on over to my place, it's furnished Early American'—and invite the guy to sit on an orange crate—but he pretended it was Chippendale."

The crowds lining the boulevard at the 1977 Rose Parade apparently loved Freddy the Freeloader as much as Red did.

The reaction the two of them received from the fans that New Year's Day was so heartwarming that Red suddenly forgot his age, the few pains left over from years of continuous pratfalls, and the fact that he had officially sworn off performing for the big time as long ago as 1972.

A few days later there appeared an ad in the *New York Times* announcing:

Arthur Shafman presents
RED SKELTON
in concert
Carnegie Hall
March 12, 1977

It took considerable persuasion for promoter Shafman to talk Red into putting his whole reputation on the line in an appearance at Carnegie Hall in the Big Apple. But he finally convinced Red that he had nothing to worry about ("Look how you killed 'em at the Oscar show"), and Red eventually succumbed.

It turned out to be one of the most gratifying nights of Red's career.

He played to two packed houses at Carnegie—one at 8 P.M. and another at 11:00—and both shows were a smash reminiscent of his old Paramount–Lupe Velez days.

Even the *New York Times* reviewer couldn't help but be ebullient about the reappearance of Red Skelton, in a review in the *Times* on March 14, 1977.

It certainly took more than practice, but Red Skelton who has not performed in the flesh in New York in forty years or so, finally got to Carnegie Hall Saturday night, and did two shows.

In an age when everyone is constantly seeking rejuvenation, the audience at Carnegie, thank Heavens, found the same old Red Skelton it doted on. He is verging on sixty-four years of age—the third of Mr. Skelton's three ages of man, which are youth, middle-age, and gee, you look good—but he needs no rejuvenation. He is as hilariously rubbery as ever, nimble legs, facile hands, plastic-putty face, and expressive eyes.

Those who came to see him knew what they wanted, and Mr. Skelton delivered to taste, backed up by a seventeen-piece band. He has a warm stage presence, one that envelops and disarms you, more than perhaps it does on screen or television, and he is a consummate clown.

Mr. Skelton can convey, mostly in comedy, but also in pathos, the sense of being in a mass meeting, of looking at a flower dying in a storm, of watching a dude riding a horse, or of going with a man as he walks up the Eiffel Tower, and much more. He uses few props, basically a battered hat, and his own keen perception for essentials that separates a talented pantomimist from a novice playing charades. His voice routines go over equally well.

Mr. Skelton gave a clean family show. He lapses touchingly and unflinchingly into sentimentality. But most of the time he makes you forget whatever intellectual pretensions you may be harboring, and he makes you laugh. Laugh hard. Anyone who can do that these days (as they've been saying for the last century or so) should be invited to town more often. After an enthusiastic ovation, Mr. Skelton said, "If I had known it would be like this, I would have studied the violin." Exit laughing.

Although there is much of Red that longs for the camera, for the nationwide fame and applause that was a part of his being on every week for so many years, today he seems content to spend his sunset years playing Las Vegas and Sparks, Nevada, state fairs, conventions, college campuses—where he is a huge hit among the young adults the television moguls claimed would never tune him in—and making cigar commercials for very big money.

Occasionally, he will appear on a television special or one of the talk shows, but in the main he avoids any regular TV assignments.

When he's on the road, Red usually travels alone, but sometimes he is accompanied by Lothian, with whom he has at last found the peace and happiness that eluded him when he was married to Georgia. The couple have no children of their own, but Lothian is extremely fond of Red's eight-year-old granddaughter, Sabrina, and occasionally she brings her along on Red's travels to fairs and conventions and his "in-concert" appearances around the nation.

Although today his thinning red hair is mostly white, his rubbery face etched with lines, and his six-foot-two body slightly stooped, the years haven't changed Red Skelton much, nor tarnished his reputation as a comedian.

Red is more mellow now, and his onstage falls aren't quite so violent nor as frequent as they once were. But the yocks are as big as ever, and there is no question in the minds of most people that Red, although pushing seventy, is still one of the great clowns of the twentieth century.

Red would be the last person to deny it, of course, but today he isn't at all certain that that is how he'd like the world to think of him after he is gone.

In an interview on television recently, Red was asked how he would like to be remembered—as a great clown, movie actor, or television comedian?

Red mulled the question over for a moment, then chose none of the three. "I think I'd just like to be remembered as a nice guy," he replied modestly.

Bibliography

ALLEN, STEVE. *The Funny Men*. New York: Simon and Schuster, 1956.

BACON, JAMES. *Hollywood Is a Four Letter Town*. New York: Avon Books, 1976.

DAVIDSON, BILL. "I'm Nuts and I Know It." *Saturday Evening Post*, June 17, 1967.

JENNINGS, DEAN. "Sad and Lonely Clown." *Saturday Evening Post*, June 2, 1962.

ROSS, SID. "Red Skelton—His Plane Was in Trouble." *Parade*, September 23, 1951.

ROSTEN, LEO. "How to See RED—SKELTON That Is." *Look*, October 23, 1951 and November 6, 1951.

SHEARER, LLOYD. "Is He a Big Laugh!" *Collier's*, April 15, 1950.

———. "The New Red Skelton." *Parade*, January 6, 1963.

INDEX

INDEX

INDEX

INDEX

About the Author

Born in New York City, Arthur Marx spent his early years being toted around this country's "small time" vaudeville circuits by his parents, one of whom was a struggling comedian named Groucho Marx. When Arthur was eight years old, the Marx clan settled in Southern California. A five-year stint as a tournament tennis player and four years in the U.S. Coast Guard during World War II followed his education at the University of Southern California. Later he worked as an advertising copy writer, a gag man for Milton Berle, and a writer of Pete Smith Specialties for MGM. He wrote his first novel, *The Ordeal of Willie Brown*, a satire on the amateur tennis world, when he was working at MGM. He followed this with the best-seller, *Life with Groucho; Not as a Crocodile; Son of Groucho; Everybody Loves Somebody Sometime—Especially Himself* (the story of Dean Martin and Jerry Lewis); and *Goldwyn*. In addition Marx wrote with Bob Fisher the Broadway comedy hit, *The Impossible Years*, and the musical, *Minnie's Boys*.